SOVIET-MIDDLE EAST RELATIONS

CHARLES B McLANE

Volume One of

SOVIET-THIRD WORLD RELATIONS

Published by
Central Asian Research Centre
London
1973

Distributed by
Columbia University Press
New York

Published in 1973 by The Central Asian Research Centre,
1B Parkfield Street, London N1 0PR

ISBN 0 903424 06 1

Text set by Peter Coxson Typing Service
Printed by Expedite Multiprint Ltd
51 Tothill Street, Westminster
London SW1H 9LQ, England

CONTENTS

Tables

SOVIET-THIRD WORLD RELATIONS
FOREWORD TO THE SERIES

Soviet-Middle East Relations is the first volume in a three-volume series of regional surveys of Soviet relations with the countries of the Third World. The other volumes will be Soviet-Asian Relations and Soviet-African Relations.

This series is itself the companion to a comprehensive study of Soviet policies in Asia, the Middle East and Africa since Stalin, Russia and the Third World, which will be completed shortly. This undertaking is the sequel to a more narrowly focused study published by Princeton University Press in 1966, Soviet Strategies in Southeast Asia: An Exploration of Eastern Policy under Lenin and Stalin.

It seemed wise to make the material in this series available separately from the parent study. The latter, already a full-length investigation of Soviet Third World policies and of global considerations affecting Russian behaviour in Asia, the Middle East and Africa, would be greatly lengthened by the detail presented in the three volumes. Regional specialists, meanwhile, will find data relating to their areas of concentration more accessible if presented in a regional study instead of a single (and more costly) volume covering Soviet activity throughout the two continents.

It should be emphasized, however, that the material presented in this series is supportive rather than interpretative. I am aware that some readers will be disappointed not to find more analysis here, but it is the record of Soviet ties with Asia, Africa and the Middle East that I am interested in setting straight in these three volumes - the intensity of political and cultural exchange, the extent of Soviet aid, the amount of trade, arms transfers, and the general pattern of Soviet commentary on individual states. Russian motives in the Third World, as well as the strategies devised in pursuit of particular objectives, are dealt with more explicitly in the parent study.

The 66 Afro-Asian nations covered in this series are divided into three regions: the Middle East and North Africa (normally referred to as the Middle East); South and South-East Asia (referred to as Asia); and Africa south of the Sahara (referred to as Africa). Although the assignment of states to one or another region, especially the Middle East, may be contested, the criteria for selecting the 66 nations are the same in the three volumes: all are sovereign; all are underdeveloped; and none are Communist. The dozen or so dependencies in the three regions are accordingly omitted, as are the four Communist states in Asia (China, Mongolia, North Korea and North Vietnam) and developed nations like Japan, Israel and South Africa. This selection admittedly leaves gaps in any comprehensive geographic coverage of Soviet behaviour, especially in Asia, but allows a focus on what is commonly understood as the Third World exclusive of Latin America.

The chronological tables, which bear a heavy burden in the presentation of hard data concerning Moscow's relations with individual Third World states, deserve a word here. These tables were designed initially for my own use, to keep in handy perspective Moscow's intricate dealings with developing nations and major domestic developments in these nations that might affect the course of the relationship. It soon became apparent that the chronologies could be no less useful to readers, and they were accordingly refined and rounded out for inclusion in the final text. The data are drawn mainly from Russian sources, supplemented occasionally by Western sources where the former were obscure. Since the data deal for the most part with specific episodes, such as political and cultural exchange and aid agreements, there is little reason to doubt their accuracy; where there is doubt, an appropriate source is shown. Any reader, however, will want a more exacting estimate of the reliability and completeness of these tables. I give mine at an appropriate place below (see note on Chronologies, in the next section).

I owe a special debt of gratitude to the Central Asian Research Centre in London, where much of the preparation of the present project was undertaken during a sabbatical leave from Dartmouth College in 1969-70. The Centre's library is unique for students of Soviet policies in the Third World (a focus of the Centre that now surpasses its original focus on Soviet Central Asia). David Morison, Director of the Centre, and his staff were stimulating colleagues with whom to debate issues of Soviet behaviour, past and present. The Centre's publications, meanwhile, especially Mizan (the word means "balance" in Arabic), were an indispensable source of documentation and ideas on Russia's Third World policies; it is altogether fair to say that my project could not have been undertaken, at least in its present scope, were it not for the rigorous sifting through of Soviet commentary on the developing nations that is reflected in these publications.

Apart from this particular debt to the Central Asian Research Centre, there is the more general debt to scores of fellow students of Moscow's Third World policies whose studies, often more detailed than mine with regard to given countries, enabled me to carry my investigation forward; these studies are listed, along with relevant Russian and other materials, in the bibliographies at the end of each of the three volumes. I am also grateful to Daniel Stephen Papp, an Honours student at Dartmouth in the class of 1969, who helped me in the early preparation of the chronological tables. To Dartmouth College I am indebted not only for the sabbatical year in London but for grants to cover typing and other expenses. Previous visits to Moscow and South-East Asia in connexion with work on my earlier volume, made possible by grants from the Russian Research Center at Harvard and the South-East Asian Treaty Organization, also produced material and insights for the present study; a year at the University College of Sierra Leone in 1964-65 gave me an opportunity to become acquainted with developments in a number of West African states. It goes without saying, of course, that none of the individuals or institutions mentioned bears responsibility for any shortcomings in these volumes.

The present volume focuses on Soviet relations with 16 nations in the Middle East (or, properly, the Middle East and North Africa). Any tally of states in this complex region is likely to be disputed. Afghanistan and Sudan, for instance, are not included in this volume, although either might be considered Middle Eastern through its ties with Islam. Cyprus, usually counted a European nation, is included – on no sounder argument than my decision to include it. Those Persian Gulf states which were dependencies of the United Kingdom during the period reviewed are omitted.

Despite the divisions and axes in the Middle East, Soviet policies have had a sharper focus here than in other regions of the Third World. This is due in part to the closeness of the Middle East to the USSR. It is also due to the urgency of security considerations, which we shall

presently explore. And it is due to a more intense interaction within the Arab community than is to be discovered in comparable communities elsewhere in Asia and Africa. A shift of policy or a coup in Damascus, for instance, is more likely to have repercussions in Cairo than similar episodes in Rangoon or Accra have in Delhi or Lagos; Russian strategies in Arab countries, in consequence, have to be carefully orchestrated.

It is these considerations that have determined the regional rather than continental division in the present series: that is, Soviet relations with Asia, Africa and the Middle East, rather than simply with Asia and Africa. The same considerations also give particular point to the following investigation of Moscow's regional strategies in the Middle East (although these strategies are discussed more fully in the forthcoming parent volume).

NOTE ON CHRONOLOGIES

The tables which follow represent an effort to chart chronologically all significant milestones in Russia's political, economic and cultural relations with different countries in the Middle East. The data are taken from Soviet sources in the main, but other sources have been consulted. Activity or episodes which might affect Soviet relations with another great power, especially China (CPR), are also shown; these entries are underlined.

Column 1 (Political) includes major landmarks in diplomatic relations, such as recognition, treaties, and major government and party exchanges; exchanges of heads of state and premiers are shown in capital letters. Military exchanges and arms agreements are also included in Column 1 as well as courtesy calls by Soviet naval units.

Column 2 (Economic) shows major developments in economic relations, including the exchange of important trade and aid missions, agreements, protocols and contracts; agreements involving Soviet credits are shown in capital letters. The term "agreement" is normally used to denote an initial commitment, with or without credit, and "protocol" to indicate a supplementary or implementing instrument. Soviet usage, however, is not consistent in this matter. The date given is normally the date of signing, not ratification; the latter date is shown only where there was a significant lapse in time before ratification. The dispatch of Soviet technicians to assist in specific projects is not shown, though the departure of these teams is normally reported in the Russian press. Similarly, the arrival of Asian specialists for further training in the USSR is omitted. The completion date of Russian-aided projects, where reliably reported, is indicated.

Column 3 (Cultural) is limited to the most important exchanges concerned with cultural co-operation and trade union relations, as well as the principal agreements and reported protocols. The following are not included (unless they represent the only activity reported): exchanges of youth, women, athletic, and Friendship Society delegations; the exchanges of performing artists; visits by tourists and individuals (unless of ministerial or other high rank); the arrival and departure of working missions (such as Russian teachers, engineers and doctors) and of Afro-Asian students enrolled in educational or cultural courses

in the USSR. The reason for these omissions is twofold: to show this activity would greatly lengthen the tables for many countries; the reporting of cultural exchanges at lower levels is irregular and a fuller listing would still leave many gaps.

Readers using the chronological tables may wish an estimate of the reliability of the data in them. My own estimate is that in the political arena, state and ministerial exchanges shown in the tables may be taken to be nearly 100 per cent complete since these were normally reported in the Soviet press, if not at the time then subsequently; the same is true of major diplomatic agreements. Government exchanges at lower levels were less regularly reported and there are in consequence omissions in the tables – but not, in my view, a significant number. Communist party exchanges in both directions are complete for major conferences and congresses, when lists of the delegations attended are made public, but the periodic visits of Afro-Asian party delegations to Moscow between congresses and world conferences are less reliably reported – especially where the party in question is illegal. Military exchanges shown in the tables are probably incomplete before the 1960s, when reporting was irregular; since about 1962 important military exchanges appear to have been regularly noted in Soviet journals (though with little detail). Evidence of arms agreements comes almost entirely from Western sources and both the data and sums involved in the agreements shown should be treated with caution. Exchanges with China indicated in the chronologies cover only high state and ministerial delegations; evidence of exchanges at this level is reliable, but the tables do not pretend to reflect the full scope of Chinese activity.

In the economic sphere, all major credit and technical assistance agreements may be assumed accurate with these exceptions: the exact date of such agreements is often in doubt, due to uncertainty as to whether the date given represents the signing, ratification or coming into force of the agreement in question; the precise sum involved is sometimes in doubt due to different exchange rates and other considerations. (Where there is wide discrepancy in the sums reported in different sources, the discrepancy is discussed in the text preceding the table.) Protocols and contracts are reported less systematically in Soviet sources and there are in consequence omissions in the tables with regard to these supplementary instruments. The exchange of economic delegations may be considered nearly complete when of ministerial or equivalent rank, but with omissions at lower levels due to irregular reporting. Completion dates of projects are not fully shown in the tables because of the difficulty of verifying Soviet claims in this regard (sometimes anticipating by several years the actual opening of an enterprise).

In regard to cultural co-operation, the data shown in the chronologies, as indicated above, are more suggestive of Soviet activity than definitive; omissions are therefore the consequence of my selection of what to include or omit, rather than of gaps in reporting of cultural exchange in Soviet sources. Of the activity which I have attempted to cover fully, exchanges of major cultural delegations may be taken as complete, or nearly so. Trade union exchanges were undoubtedly more numerous than shown, since many such exchanges, especially in the 1960s, were reported only in trade union journals which I covered less systematically than others. There are similarly gaps in professional exchanges - that is, of lawyers, doctors, journalists, educators, and the like.

It is worth noting, finally, that the principal defect in the chronologies is omission, not padding; the tables may omit activity - even some activity of significance - but they do not show exchanges that never occurred or agreements that were never negotiated. The Russians, in short, were at least as active as the tables show them to have been and in most countries more so.

1. THE SOVIET UNION AND THE MIDDLE EAST:
A REGIONAL PERSPECTIVE

Soviet interest in the Middle East developed fitfully in the early 1950s, intensifying somewhat after Stalin's death in March 1953; a significant engagement did not emerge until 1955. The Russians' engagement must be related to American efforts to create a new pro-Western security system in the so-called Northern tier; this system came into existence with the signing of the Baghdad Pact in February 1955. (1) The American effort, in turn, arose from concern in Washington that Soviet aggression might occur in an area where a "power vacuum" had developed through the weakening of traditional French and British influence and from the conviction that the surest deterrent to Soviet aggression was a strong posture of defence in areas believed to be vulnerable to Soviet or Communist attack; the latter conviction, greatly fortified by American experience in Korea, was central to United States foreign policy in the mid-1950s.

It is doubtful whether history will give a clear verdict on the question of which nation acted and which reacted in the Middle East. In this writer's view (though nothing in what follows hangs on it) there is no convincing evidence that the Russians, at the time the United States took action to thwart them, were engaged in activities in the Middle East likely to compromise Western interests; one might indeed cite evidence to the contrary – for instance, Moscow's inaction during promising Leftist upheavals such as that in Persia in 1953. (2) Such evidence suggests that the Russians' engagement in the Middle East owed much to the Americans' obsession with policies of "containment".

The Russians responded to American defence efforts in the Middle East by overleaping the Northern tier (as they had done periodically in the past) (3) and concentrating their attention on the Arab world. Egypt, because of modernizing forces released in its 1952 revolution and because Cairo was the political centre of the Arab world, was the logical focus of Moscow's interest, and the Egyptians, for reasons of their own, were responsive; it was with Cairo that Moscow negotiated the famous arms agreement announced in September 1955, properly considered the first important landmark in Russian-Arab relations after Stalin. Arms agreements followed with Syria and Yemen in 1956. Embassies were exchanged with Libya and Tunisia; for a time it appeared the Russians would succeed in establishing relations even with the feudal but intensely pro-Arab kingdom of Saudi Arabia.

Whether without the Baghdad Pact there would have been this flowering of Soviet-Arab relations in 1955 and 1956 is uncertain. No one could argue, of course, that Russia's interest in the Arab world stemmed only from American defence activity in the Northern tier. A careful reading of Soviet moves in the Middle East after Stalin, and even during the year or so before he died, shows a quickening of Moscow's interest in the Arab nations, comparable to the quickening interest in South Asia; the retreat of Western nations from the Middle East, reflected in their reluctance to finance new ventures such as the Aswan High Dam, created a vacuum to be filled. The Arab world, in short, was certain to become a focus of Moscow's attention as Soviet interest shifted increasingly to the developing nations in the mid-1950s. The pace of Soviet activity, however, was something else again; this, it may be argued, was accelerated by American manoeuvres

in the Northern tier.

Soviet influence was well established in the Arab world when the Suez crisis developed in autumn 1956. Moscow had quite naturally supported Cairo's nationalization of the Canal in July and opposed all Western moves towards "internationalization", both in the United Nations and outside. (4) When the crisis came to a head in early November, the Russians were too preoccupied with the Hungarian revolution to risk a clash with the Western powers by offering significant support to the Arabs. However, once American opposition to the English-French-Israeli effort was clear, the Russians could safely intervene diplomatically, and they did so with a certain gusto. Russia was "firmly resolved to use force" if necessary, the British, French and Israeli governments were warned, to protect the rights of the Egyptians. Paris and London were reminded that they were vulnerable to Soviet nuclear attack, should it come to that; Tel Aviv was reminded that even the existence of the Israeli state was not a settled thing. Meanwhile, Moscow agreed to send "volunteers" in response to Nasser's request, though none were actually sent. (5)

Whether or not the Russians were the Arabs' defenders behind the cloak of American opposition to the Anglo-French-Israeli venture is less important than the way in which the Arabs viewed Moscow's role in the episode. Many apparently believed that Russia's prompt support of the Arab cause deterred the attackers and that it was Moscow's stern warning to them which brought about the cease-fire. Arab spokesmen made this abundantly clear in official statements of gratitude during the following weeks.

The prestige which the Russians gained during the Suez crisis was of great consequence in the development of Soviet-Arab relations during the next few years. The USSR was now unambiguously acknowledged by the great majority of Arabs as their protector against Western imperialism. Diplomatic relations were strengthened with all Arab states, except Saudi Arabia and Jordan. Political and cultural exchanges proliferated. Trade with Arab nations trebled during the three years following the Suez crisis. During the same period the Russians extended credits totalling more than half a billion dollars; arms deliveries totalled at least as much, and probably more (see Tables at the end of this volume).

In 1959 and 1960 Soviet doctrines relating to the Third World hardened under the impact of Peking's more militant formulations on the national liberation movement, formulations that made Moscow's appear too bland. (6) This new rigidity in Russian ideology inevitably affected Moscow's relations with Arab regimes resistant to Marxist ideas. Ties with the UAR were weakened for a time; the promising relationship with Iraq turned sour. Communist persecution by Arab governments was everywhere attacked, and Arab "socialism" was mocked. Even Ben Bella's comparatively radical regime in Algeria, which would have been welcomed in the mid-1950s, was not fully accepted until a year or more after it had come to power. The net effect of Soviet strategies during these years was to weaken in Arab eyes Russia's credibility as a disinterested power. Arab leaders became alarmed over a new threat to their independence; the more "inevitable" Moscow proclaimed Communism to be, the greater the uneasiness in Arab capitals. The era of Moscow's ideological reaffirmation accordingly marked the nadir in Soviet-Arab ties. Soviet publications, it is true, continued to affirm cordial relations, (7) but the record does not support this claim: trade levelled off and, in some cases, fell; official exchanges were curtailed; arms transfers were negligible; and economic aid declined. Only the Aswan High Dam, of Russia's many projects in the Arab world, appears to have been unaffected by the impasse in Soviet-Arab relations - presumably because Russian prestige was at stake in its early completion.

Soviet aims in the Middle East during these years are not entirely clear. The initial object - defusing the Baghdad Pact and denying to the West a monopoly of influence in the Arab states - had been in large measure accomplished; Western political authority was not likely to assert itself again as in the past. But more specific goals had not yet been formulated for the Middle East. Were the Russians interested in Arab unity, for instance, or in playing one Arab regime against another (say, Nasser's against Qasim's) in order to increase Soviet options? Were they interested in progressive reform, and ultimately in socialism? Was there a resurgent interest in Arab Communism, whose open suppression in 1959 had been a major reason for shifting policies in the Middle East? The Russians, to judge from press commentaries and scholarly articles, had not yet faced these questions. Meanwhile, the focus of Soviet attention had shifted to Africa by 1960. Policies in the Middle East were accordingly allowed to drift. The diplomatic alliance with the Arabs was, on balance, preserved and Soviet commentaries continued to support Arab causes. But Moscow's enthusiasm was lukewarm. The Russians no longer felt it necessary to treat their Arab allies with the tact and deference they had shown after 1955. Khrushchev perhaps also contributed to Soviet-Arab tension by showing his insensitivity at times to complex Arab rivalries - for instance, his intervention, in remarks to an Iraqi delegation in 1959, in the delicate issue of Egyptian-Iraqi relations after Qasim's coup (see under Iraq). It is not difficult to imagine proud and insecure Arab leaders deeply resentful of Khrushchev's offhand approach to Arab politics.

Russia's image in the Arab world was not so damaged, however, as to bar a revival of Soviet influence when formulations regarding the Third World became less militant in 1963 and Moscow's attention was again focused on the Middle East. Arab nationalists could not, after all, turn back to the Western powers; if relations with Moscow were sometimes uneasy, the Russians were still preferable as allies to the Americans, British or French. Soviet-Arab ties were accordingly strengthened from 1963 on.

The Palestinian issue was by this time central in Arab strategies, and the Russians enthusiastically endorsed the Arabs' objectives. This was made clear in commentaries on the conference of Arab leaders held in Cairo in January 1964 (the first Arab "summit"). (8) Khrushchev, during his crucial tour of the UAR in May, reiterated Soviet support of the Arabs' cause. (9) Khrushchev's successors continued this support after his removal in October. For all their moderation in other respects, they failed to promote a sense of restraint among Arab leaders on the Palestinian question, in consequence of which the Soviet Union became increasingly wedded to the Arab course during the years preceding the Six Day War. Arms transfers, which had been resumed in 1963, were stepped up. Israel was persistently described as the agency for foreign imperialism in the Middle East. No effort was made to dampen rising Arab passions directed against the Israelis. Indeed, during the weeks immediately before the war, there is not a little suspicion that the Russians themselves contributed to the crisis atmosphere by reporting Israeli troop concentrations on the Syrian border, which led to Cairo's counteractions at Aqaba; this in turn led to the Israelis' pre-emptive strike. (10)

It is unclear in hindsight why Khrushchev's more moderate, pragmatic successors did not show greater restraint in dealing with the Palestinian issue before the Six Day War. They apparently did not desire or expect a resumption of large-scale hostilities, but believed that if fighting nevertheless broke out, Arab military strength, thanks to Soviet arms, was sufficient to check the Israelis until a cease-fire could be arranged. The United States, deeply involved in Vietnam, was not likely to intervene actively on Israel's behalf whatever course the fighting took; world opinion, on balance, favoured the Arabs. Since therefore the risks seemed slight, the Russians were not constrained to urge caution on their Arab allies. Unstinting support of the Arabs' "just" cause against Israel, meanwhile, was the surest guarantee of continued Soviet influence among the Arab states. Another hypothesis is that the Russians were kept poorly informed of Arab strategies before the June war and so had no opportunity to advise caution until it was too late. Still another hypothesis, proceeding on a different assumption, is that, while communication with the Arab leaders was satisfactory, counsel on the Arab-Israeli issue was divided in Moscow; those in favour of an early showdown temporarily prevailing over moderates at a crucial juncture. (11)

However one interprets the Russians' motives before the June war, their miscalculations proved costly. Russia's principal allies in the Middle East suffered a humiliating defeat; an estimated 75 to 80 per cent of their arsenals was lost; and the Suez Canal was closed for an unforeseeable period. For the Russians themselves, however, the war was not a disaster, as many believed at the time, but merely a setback - and a brief one, at that. Soviet influence in the Arab world inevitably grew stronger after the June war as the defeated nations became more than ever dependent on the USSR for arms and other supplies. The net effect of the war, in short, was to give the Russians a greater leverage in the Arab world than had ever been exercised by the French, English or Americans in their day.

The Russians blended two strategies in the Middle East after the Six Day War: a strategy of uncompromising firmness towards the outcome of the war itself, designed to rebuild Arab morale and prevent Israel's military victory from becoming a political victory as well; and a strategy of moderation with regard to the means by which the status quo ante was to be achieved, designed to discourage fresh Arab ventures which could lead to new defeats. The Russians, in short, were determined that one-sided engagements such as those in 1956 and 1967 should not recur. The UAR became more than ever the central focus of these twin strategies. (12)

The essential first step in Soviet calculations was a prompt rebuilding of Arab armed strength. Even before the fighting ended, Moscow promised new aircraft and tanks to replace those lost, and within a fortnight the first of these were delivered. By the end of 1967 a significant portion of Arab losses was replaced with more up-to-date weaponry; by autumn 1968 an estimated $2.5 billion in arms had been shipped to Arab countries ; that is, nearly as much as had been delivered during the dozen years preceding the June war. (13)   Additional arms were provided periodically as the need arose, either to replace lost or obsolete equipment or to keep pace with Israeli purchases from the United States and elsewhere.

The Soviet military commitment did not end with the shipment of arms and dispatch of training personnel and advisers.   As the war of nerves and attrition along the Suez Canal steadily escalated, Russians gradually became involved in Egypt's defence in a combat capacity: by the spring of 1970 Russian pilots as well as gun crews had become operational in the Nile Valley; by midsummer they were operational along the western bank of the Canal itself.   It is estimated that by early 1971 as many as 20,000 Russians were engaged in combat operations of one type or another in Egypt.   The great majority of these served as crews for SAM-3 missile sites, but some 200 were pilots of the Russians' new MIG-21J; in an engagement between Russian and Israeli pilots reported at the end of July 1970, four of these MIGs were said to have been shot down. (14)

One should not assume that the Russians' extraordinary commitment in Egypt was the prelude, in their calculations, to a serious escalation of the Arab-Israeli conflict, as comparable American commitments in Vietnam before February 1965, for instance, proved to be the prelude to escalation there.   There was, to be sure, intensification of the fighting along the Suez Canal, especially on the part of the Israelis whose situation became more desperate as well-disciplined Russians replaced Arabs.   But neither escalation nor undue aggravation of the Israelis was part of Moscow's plan.   The parallel strategy to military readiness along the Suez Canal was caution and restraint with regard to any resumption of hostilities.   The official Soviet position on the Arab-Israeli dispute after the Six Day War was reflected in the United Nations resolution of 22 November, 1967, which stated that Israel must be made to surrender Arab lands seized in the war, but through sanctions and diplomacy, not force.   This was the "political solution" about which Soviet commentators wrote persistently from midsummer 1967 on and which Russian spokesmen urged on their Arab allies at the Khartoum summit conference in August and subsequently. (15)   The Russians adhered to this position through the various stages of the Arab-Israeli arms race and the various phases of negotiation looking to a cease-fire and eventually a settlement of the dispute.   The strengthening of Arab defences, the fortification of the western bank of the Canal and the deployment of Russian military personnel should be regarded as efforts to create parity of strength between Arabs and Israelis, which alone, the Russians felt, would allow a peaceful solution of the crisis.   It is undoubtedly significant that Brezhnev chose the moment when Russian-manned missile sites were at last securely emplaced along the western bank to make his most forceful call for peace in the Middle East.   "A settlement can now be approached from positions of realism and responsibility", he said in a televised speech in Alma Ata on 28 August, 1970.   "Those who have been trying in the past few years to impose their will on the Arab countries 'from positions of strength' have a chance to think better of it. . . .   It is our profound conviction that cessation of the conflict in the Middle East would meet the vital interests of Arab countries and Israel alike." (16)

Not all Arabs, needless to say, agreed with Moscow's essentially moderate posture in the Palestinian-Israeli question.   The Algerian leadership, for instance, was outspokenly critical of the Russian position, especially in the immediate aftermath of the June war; Soviet-Syrian relations were clouded over this issue for several years. It was the Palestinian guerrillas, however, who disagreed most profoundly with Soviet strategies and most seriously challenged them.   The fedayeen organizations, Al-Fatah in particular, (17) were adamant on the Israeli question: they rejected the UN resolution of 22 November, 1967; they urged persistent pressure on and reprisal against Israel through clandestine operations from Jordan and Lebanon; ultimately they sought the elimination of Israel itself.   Were the Russians to ignore the guerrillas, they would risk losing much good will in the Arab world, especially among young radicals who might serve Soviet purposes in the future and who for the present were vulnerable to more militant (and less responsible) Chinese propaganda on the Palestinian question.   On the other hand, too close an identity with Al-Fatah irregulars would undermine the prestige of Arab military establishments where Soviet influence was strongest.

The Russians accordingly practised a judicious ambivalence where the guerrillas were concerned.   In the months immediately following the June war, before Al-Fatah had gained significant strength, Moscow praised the goals and tactics of the Arab commandos; clandestine activity, under conditions of Israeli occupation of Arab lands, was "their lawful right". (18)   As Al-Fatah grew in prestige, however, making bolder and bolder raids on Israel while Egyptian forces (on Soviet advice) were engaged in a less dramatic war of nerves across the Suez Canal, the Russians changed their estimates of guerrilla activity: the objectives of Al-Fatah were still praised, but its operations were increasingly ignored and sometimes criticized.   As one Soviet correspondent expressed himself in April 1969, after an interview with Al-Fatah leaders, he left them with "mixed feelings of deep sympathy for the Palestinian resistance movement and certain doubts concerning its methods of fighting". (19)   The fact that Al-Fatah received its principal financial support from ultra-conservative regimes in Saudi Arabia and the Gulf sheikhdoms presumably did not make Russian observers more sanguine.   Meanwhile, behind the facade of bland press commentaries, Soviet diplomats put increasing pressure on Arab governments to curb the guerrillas and bring them under army discipline; if the transfer of arms to commandos was not halted, the Russians reportedly warned their Arab allies, Soviet deliveries would be suspended. (20)   But Moscow could no more restrain Al-Fatah than the tides. Yasir Arafat's role at the Rabat conference of Arab leaders in December 1969 and his success in blocking a unified approach to the Palestinian issue, as both Cairo and Moscow urged, was evidence of the reality of Al-Fatah's power in the Arab world. (21)   In February 1970 the Russians themselves saw fit to receive Arafat in Moscow, albeit unofficially (he came as a guest of the Afro-Asian Solidarity Organization) and without the compensation of personal interviews with any Soviet leaders.

This era marked the peak of Al-Fatah's fortunes. The effectiveness of commando raids against Israel had been declining for some years, especially when compared to the more sophisticated level of exchanges along the Suez Canal before the cease-fire of July 1970.   The dramatic hijacking and subsequent destruction of three international aircraft in Jordan in September again focused world attention on the fedayeen, but any immediate gain to their prestige from this exploit was more than offset by mounting concern in the Arab states over the liabilities of sheltering Palestinian extremists. The brief civil war in Jordan which followed the aircraft episode may have marked the beginning of the end of fedayeen power in Arab politics. The Soviet press observed a strict neutrality during the fighting, reserving its sharpest words for Americans and Israelis who allegedly threatened intervention; at least one Soviet commentator, however, blamed the struggle equally on Western-trained Jordanian officers in King Hussein's army and "crazy extremists among the fedayeen governed by the slogan: 'the worse it is, the better it is'". (22) If the guerrillas in reality suffered a critical setback in the civil war, as it appeared at the time, the Russians must have been silently grateful, for now the prospects of wider Arab support for the moderate Soviet-Egyptian approach to the Palestinian issue would be greatly enhanced.

Before one turns from the Russians' role in the Arab-Israeli conflict after the Six Day War, it is useful to consider whether the reopening of the Suez Canal played a part in their calculations. Russia was still a relatively modest user of the Canal before the June war; its traffic was merely 3.5 per cent of total shipping in 1966. But its rate of growth as a user since 1960 had been high. Moreover, Russia's rapidly developing trade with East Africa and South Asia, which had political as well as economic significance, depended heavily on the Canal.(23) It need not be doubted, then, that the Russians were inconvenienced by the Canal's closing. The crucial question is whether as time passed they wished it reopened - or wished it enough to shape their strategies in the Arab-Israeli dispute accordingly.

Western analysts are not in agreement in this matter. Some students of Soviet policy in the Middle East argued that the reopening of the Canal was central to Russia's world position, not only for trade but for naval strategy as well: only when the "flood-gates" of Suez were opened could the Russians develop an effective presence in the Indian Ocean. (24) Other specialists doubted the Russians' desire to see the Canal opened on the argument that the Western powers, especially the great oil carriers from the Persian Gulf, suffered infinitely more than the USSR from the continued closure; "cost effectiveness" was never a significant feature of Russian foreign policy and there was no reason to imagine the Russians would use it to argue for the opening of the Canal if there were better reasons for keeping the Canal closed. (25) Still another view was that neither the reopening nor continued closure of the Canal mattered so much to the Russians as their certain voice in policies affecting use of the Canal in the future. (26)

As for the Russians themselves, they publicly favoured the reopening of the Canal for the revenues it would bring to Egypt, not officially for any benefit to the USSR. "The mothballing of such an outstanding achievement of the human genius is criminal", Georgiy Mirskiy, a leading Soviet Arabist, argued in an article written expressly for Western readers. "From the legal point of view, no one has the right to close the sea waterway which unconditionally and undoubtedly belongs to the Egyptian state." (27) Still, official Soviet statements throughout 1970 did not accent the urgency of reopening the Suez Canal and one therefore concludes that the opening was not of itself central in Russian calculations. The Russians, meanwhile, were well enough entrenched on the Canal's western bank by the end of 1970 to feel assured of their "certain voice" in the future of the famous waterway.

*   *   *

The magnitude of Russia's commitment to the Arab cause in the latter half of the 1960s raises the question of peripheral or secondary objectives in the Middle East. Arab ascendancy over Israel was not a sufficient objective in itself for Russians; support for the Arabs, it may be said, was merely Russia's entrée into the Middle East. But to what purpose? Security against the Baghdad Pact, we have seen, was an early reason for Russia's pro-Arab policies. When security ceased to be a primary concern, Russia's continued activity in the Middle East may be explained by a determination to check any resurgence of Western influence; the USSR was henceforth to play the decisive role in Middle East affairs - not to any particular end, but against all contingencies. One can also detect in Soviet writing about the Middle East a persistent (though perhaps low priority) object of transforming traditional Arab societies into modern socialist states which would be responsive to Moscow's ideological leadership.

These objectives may be considered implicit in Russia's continuing presence in the Middle East. They occasion no surprise to students of Soviet strategies, and do not at this point need elaboration. (28) There are, however, several more explicit Soviet objectives which deserve attention. Among these are the development of Russia's naval strength in the Mediterranean, and access to Middle East oil. Both, it is true, relate more to global than to regional strategies, but since Moscow's activity in each case affected relations with individual Arab states, the activity may be considered as an aspect of Soviet policy in the Middle East.

Russia's naval build-up in the Mediterranean began in the mid-1960s, but developed especially after the Six Day War. By 1970 there were 35 to 50 vessels regularly in the Mediterranean, and at times as many as 75; the Russian squadron normally included eight or 10 submarines, 15 or more nuclear destroyers, and one or two helicopter carriers. (29) Ships refuelled at Port Said and Alexandria, where they often remained for extended visits, and called periodically at ports in Syria, Algeria and Morocco. When not in port, the fleet circulated freely about the Eastern Mediterranean.

The Russians' object, quite obviously, was to establish a Soviet naval presence in the Mediterranean for use in whatever circumstances might arise. Most observers doubted that a Soviet Mediterranean squadron could soon challenge the American Sixth Fleet. Both in fire power and in access to the Mediterranean the Americans appeared to hold a significant advantage, especially in conjunction with their West European allies. The Russians' presence might of course deter American intervention in a given political crisis - a crisis, for instance, like the one in Lebanon in 1958; but the Russian Navy, it was generally believed, could not stand up to combined American-West European forces in a direct confrontation. (30) Presumably the Russians had no thought of such a confrontation. Naval pre-eminence is not established in a day; a clear advantage might be won by a diplomatic tour de force or the sudden emplacement of a strategic missile system. It is in the nature of naval development, especially in areas where bases are insecure, that it proceed deliberately. In the case of the Russian build-up in the Mediterranean, as in the Persian Gulf and Indian Ocean, what was accomplished in the 1960s can perhaps best be regarded as the foundation for a naval authority of greater consequence in the 1980s.

To this end, the Russians cultivated their ties with Middle East nations, both radical states like the UAR and Algeria and traditional states like Morocco, in order to establish the necessary line of refuelling stations, repair docks and supply depots; for should the Dardanelles be closed to Soviet ships in time of crisis, the Russian squadron might have to remain for many months away from home ports. It should be noted, moreover, that the ships which constituted the Mediterranean squadron at the end of the 1960s were laid down many years before, at a time when naval strategists could not foresee the circumstances of their eventual use. Russia's activity in the Mediterranean, therefore, is best seen as part of a general development of naval strength throughout the world rather than as related to specific objectives in the Middle East. In due course Russia's naval presence might well affect Soviet strategies in the Arab world, but there is no convincing evidence that it did so during the 1960s.

*   *   *

Soviet oil policies in the Middle East, while part of wider diplomatic designs like naval development, are more directly linked to relations with individual states, if only because oilfields are less moveable than navies. In the latter half of the 1960s, beginning with the agreement of January 1966 with Iran on natural gas, Russian interest in Middle East gas and oil developed rapidly. By 1971 the Soviet Union had agreements with six nations for deliveries of oil, normally in exchange for Soviet aid, and was eyeing other suppliers. (31) Soviet purchases were still small compared to purchases by the Western powers, but the prospect of a far larger Russian role in the future, through a system of agreements with friendly states, was very real. Needless to say, concern in this matter was greatest in Western Europe, where about 80 per cent of oil imports normally came from the Middle East.

Since the Soviet Union, most authorities agree, was not likely to need oil for itself until the latter half of the 1970s at the earliest, and perhaps not even then, the reasons for Moscow's interest in Middle East oil must be sought elsewhere. It does not fall within the scope of this volume to consider Soviet motives in detail - a task undertaken by a growing number of specialists in this field (32) - but a brief catalogue of possible explanations may be useful at this juncture. One reason for Soviet activity may simply have been that the oil was cheap and close and therefore a sound investment; Russians, the Soviet government presumably felt, could play the part of middleman as well as anyone else. Meanwhile, it was advantageous to resell the cheaper Middle East oil to East European clients, whom the Russians were in any case determined to supply themselves, and save their own more costly exports for other markets. A more political motive perhaps was to wean Arab states from their dependency on European markets by providing an alternative market closer at hand. This would allow the Arab world greater freedom in its foreign policy, freedom, that is, to follow Moscow's guidance. It would also enable the more "progressive" nations in the Middle East to nationalize their oil industries, a step they were reluctant to take so long as their oil profits depended on Western markets and the development of their resources depended on foreign capital. Finally, Soviet control of the flow of Middle East oil to its greatest customer, Western Europe, would - if it were ever achieved - give Moscow a leverage in international politics more powerful than navies, aircraft and missiles. These

possible motives were not, of course, contradictory; nor were they in conflict with other Soviet objectives in the Middle East.

Moscow's oil diplomacy had not developed sufficiently by 1971 to permit a reasoned judgment of its impact on the marketing of oil generally, let alone on the profile of Middle East politics. Some observers argued that oil was already "one of the major reasons" for Soviet involvement in the Middle East. (33) Whether or not such a view could be supported, clearly Moscow's interest in oil (as well as natural gas) gave a new dimension to Soviet Middle East policies and established a special relationship between the Soviet Union and the oil-producing states. It appeared inevitable that the Russians would become even more involved in these activities during the 1970s when the British left the oil sheikhdoms on the Persian Gulf.

*   *   *

Mention should be made finally of revised Soviet policies in the Northern tier, the area where Western activity in the mid-1950s first stimulated the Russian thrust into the Middle East. In the first half of the 1960s Soviet strategies in Turkey, Iran and Pakistan changed dramatically. From having been the butt of hostile Soviet propaganda and for years recipients of threatening and often insulting official Notes, these countries suddenly became favoured neighbours - along with Afghanistan. (34) These four nations received, from 1963 to the end of 1969, approximately $1.2 billion in Soviet credits, or more than a third of all Soviet aid pledged to the developing nations during these years. Annual trade with the Northern tier during these years averaged about one fifth of Russia's total trade with the Third World (or one third if India and the UAR are excluded). More than a third of the state visits between Russia and the Afro-Asian countries during the same period were with the Northern tier. Subversion was clearly not the Russians' purpose, since local Communists were for the most part ignored and no "popular" alternative to the feudal, monarchical and capitalist systems in these four countries was seriously suggested. Moscow's object was, through friendliness, to immunize these nations against a Western orientation, as John Foster Dulles a decade earlier had sought to "neutralize" them through an anti-Soviet alliance.

Russia's policies in the Northern tier after 1963 were not alternative to policies towards the Arab nations, as they might once have been, when resources were too slender to permit offensives in both regions and when strategists felt Soviet interests were best served by playing Arab versus non-Arab. Now the Russians apparently felt well enough established in the Middle East to develop parallel policies: in the Northern tier, they followed a classic good-neighbour strategy, designed to assure Turks, Persians, Afghans and Pakistanis that they had nothing to fear from Russia; in the Arab world, Moscow supplemented traditional diplomacy with efforts to cultivate "progressive" partners who might one day remake the entire Middle East in the Soviet image.

References

(1) The Northern tier, a phrase used mainly by Western diplomatists, was a belt of nations said to separate Russia from the Arab world; it invariably included Iran and Turkey, and, depending upon circumstances, Afghanistan, Pakistan, or (though it was itself an Arab country) Iraq. The defence system, known generally as the Baghdad Pact,

came into existence through the following agreements: the Turkish-Pakistani security treaty of April 1954, the Turkish-Iraqi treaty of February 1955 (the "Baghdad Pact" proper), and Britain's and Iran's adherence to the latter, respectively, in September and October 1955. The United States never formally signed the Baghdad agreement but concluded bi-lateral treaties with Iran, Turkey and Pakistan in 1958. Following the Iraqi revolution of July 1958 and Baghdad's withdrawal from the alliance bearing its name, it came to be known as the Central Treaty Organization (CENTO).

(2) The Persian crisis concerned the survival of Mohammed Mossadegh's relatively Leftist National Front, which because of lack of Tudeh – and Soviet – support, fell to Rightist elements; see Manfred Halpern's account of this episode in Black and Thornton, Communism and Revolution, pp. 316-19.

(3) In 1948, for instance, following setbacks in Persia and Turkey, the Soviet Union had established close relations with Israel, apparently with the intention of neutralizing the Northern tier by gaining influence to the south.

(4) The Russians, for instance, boycotted the users' conference on the Suez Canal held in London in September on the grounds the Egyptians were not represented; they also vetoed a resolution in the United Nations in October which called for the opening of the Canal under international guarantees.

(5) Soviet statements during the crisis are given in D. T. Shepilov, Suetskiy vopros (1956), pp. 142-56, passim; for more detailed analysis of Soviet strategy during the Suez crisis, see Laqueur, The Soviet Union and the Middle East, pp. 236-41 and J.M. MacIntosh, Strategy and Tactics of Soviet Foreign Policy, Oxford, 1963, pp. 179-90.

(6) These shifts are discussed in some detail in chapter two of the parent study to this volume, Russia and the Third World.

(7) E.g. SSSR i arabskiye strany, 1917-1960gg and Sovetsko-arabskiye druzhestvennyye otnosheniya, both published in 1961; the two volumes included much material on relations since 1955 and implied that ties would become even closer in the future.

(8) The conference, called to deal with Israel's "exploitation" of the river Jordan, considered a number of other matters of common interest to the Arabs, including the formation of a joint Arab military command and the creation of the Palestinian Liberation Organization (PLO); for comments on the conference by leading Pravda and Izvestiya correspondents (V. Kudryavtsev, Ye. Primakov, K. Vishnevetskiy and others) see Mizan, February 1964, pp. 22-24.

(9) See excerpts from his official and unofficial statements and the final communiqué in Mizan, May 1964, pp. 62-65, passim.

(10) See, for instance, Laqueur, The Road to War, chapter three; also Robert E. Hunter in Adelphi Papers, No. 59 (September 1969), p. 10.

(11) These and other hypotheses concerning Soviet policy before the Six Day War have been explored by scores of students of Middle East politics. Among the more noteworthy commentaries (in addition to the two cited in the preceding footnote) are: Michael Howard and Robert E. Hunter in Adelphi Papers, No. 41 (September 1967); Nadav Safran, From War to War: The Arab-Israel Confrontation, 1948-1967, Pegasus, 1969, pp. 276-95; chapters by Geoffrey Kemp, Philip E. Mosely and others in Hurewitz, ed. Soviet-American Rivalry in the Middle East; Charles Yost, "The Arab-Israeli War: How it Began", Foreign Affairs, January 1968, pp. 304-20; and David Morison's articles in Mizan and elsewhere.

(12) What follows does not pretend to be a full analysis of Soviet strategies after the June war; such analyses are readily available elsewhere and another would be out of place here. Some discussion of Russian behaviour, however, is necessary in order to understand the course of Soviet relations with individual Middle Eastern states – which readers are reminded once again is the focus of the present volume.

(13) New York Times, 13 October, 1968.

(14) The Times, 31 July, 1970; the incident – the only one to have occurred so far as is known – is believed to have been deliberately provoked by the Israelis in retaliation for the earlier loss of two of their F-4s. For estimates of Soviet military personnel active in Egypt as well as a detailed review of military developments along the Suez Canal from the Six Day War to June 1971, see Lawrence L. Whetten's article in New Middle East, No. 33 (June 1971), pp. 15-25.

(15) The early statements after the war – e.g. Kosygin's statement at the United Nations on 19 June, the resolution of the CPSU Central Committee on 21 June, and a speech by Brezhnev at a military graduation in Moscow on 5 July (excerpts from which are translated in Laqueur, The Struggle for the Middle East, pp. 243-74, passim) – did not make explicit reference to a "political solution"; this phrase first appeared in Soviet commentaries in August, on the eve of the Khartoum conference; for a summary of such commentaries, see Mizan, September-October 1967, pp. 215-17.

(16) Pravda, 29 August, 1970.

(17) Al-Fatah, created before the Six Day War on the model of the Algerian National Liberation Front (FLN), came to dominate, after the war, the official Palestinian Liberation Organization (PLO); both were headed by Yasir Arafat. Al-Fatah was the most important of the guerrilla organizations, but by no means the only one. There were altogether, by 1970, a dozen or more, most of them members of the Command of the Armed Struggle for the Liberation of Palestine (PASC). For a helpful review of the leading guerrilla organizations, see J. Gaspard, "Palestine: Who's Who among the Guerrillas?", New Middle East, No. 18 (March 1970), pp. 12-16.

(18) For early comments on Al-Fatah after the June war, see Mizan, July-August 1968, pp. 143-44, and January-February 1969, pp. 8-17.

(19) Georgiy Dadiyants, in Sovetskaya Rossiya, 15 April, 1969; for other such commentary, see New Middle East, No. 15 (December 1969), pp. 17-18.

(20) E.g. Al-Hayat, 5 May, 1969, cited in New Middle East, No. 15 (December 1969), p. 16.

(21) Russian commentaries did not, of course, acknowledge the failure of Nasser's policies at Rabat. V. L. Kudryavtsev, for instance, Izvestiya's leading analyst on Middle East affairs, considered the conference "an important landmark on the path to Arab unity"; Izvestiya, 26 December, 1969.

(22) A. Vasil'yev, Pravda, 17 October, 1970.

(23) Trade with 15 developing nations south and east of Suez nearly tripled between 1960 and 1966 (from $278.0 to $805.7 million); for a detailed analysis of Soviet use of the Suez Canal before the June war, see Gary G. Sick, "The USSR and the Suez Canal Closure", Mizan, November 1970, pp. 91-98.

(24)   E.g. Robert A. Kilmarx in New Middle East, No. 27 (December 1970), p. 44.

(25)   See Neville Brown in New Middle East, No. 30 (March 1971), p. 21.

(26)   E.g. Lawrence L. Whetten in New Middle East, No. 33 (June 1971), p. 15.

(27)   "The Soviet View on the Future of the Suez Canal", New Middle East, No. 4 (January 1969), p. 18.

(28)   These broader objectives too are dealt with in more detail in my forthcoming study, Russia and the Third World.

(29)   Estimates inevitably vary, but they remained fairly consistent from 1968 to the end of 1970.   For commentary on Soviet naval activity in the Mediterranean, as well as periodic estimates of the size of the Mediterranean squadron, see the following: William I. Zartman, "The Mediterranean: Bridge or Barrier", Proceedings, U.S. Naval Institute, February 1967, pp. 63-71; Curt Gasteyger, "Moscow and the Mediterranean", Foreign Affairs, July 1968, pp. 676-87; D.C. Watt, "Soviet Presence in the Mediterranean", New Middle East, No. 1 (October 1968), pp. 14-19; Boris Guriel, "Two Hundred Years of Russian Interest in the Mediterranean", New Middle East, No. 2 (November 1968), pp. 35-41; "The Soviet Fleet in the Mediterranean", Bulletin, Institute for the Study of the USSR, February 1969, pp. 35-41; René Martens, "The Soviet Fleet in Arab Politics", New Middle East, No. 14 (November 1969), pp. 24-25; Ciro Zoppo, "Soviet Ships in the Mediterranean and the US-Soviet Confrontation in the Middle East", Orbis, Spring 1970, pp. 109-28; and Neville Brown, "Soviet Naval Expansion - the Global Scene Assessed", New Middle East, No. 30 (March 1971), pp. 17-21.

(30)   There were, however, some dissenting views on this point.   Robert A. Kilmarx, for instance, argued in December 1970 that the Russians had carefully nurtured an impression of naval inferiority in the Mediterranean in order to forestall any build-up of the American Sixth Fleet. But he believed that overall Soviet strength was at least equal to American, and possibly greater.   New Middle East, No. 27 (December 1970), p. 44.

(31)   The six were Iran, Iraq, the UAR, Southern Yemen, Algeria and Syria; negotiations were under way with Kuwait and with the new regime in Libya.

(32)   E.g. in the journal New Middle East, articles by D.C. Watt and Lincoln Landis (No. 3, December 1968, pp. 16-23); by Boris Rachkov, a Russian oil expert (No. 8, May 1969, pp. 36-37); and by Jean-Jacques Berreby (in a regular series which began in No. 12, September 1969). Also Robert E. Hunter, "The Soviet Dilemma in the Middle East.   Part II: Oil and the Persian Gulf", Adelphi Papers, No. 60 (October 1969); Laqueur, The Struggle for the Middle East, chapter 6; and Lincoln Landis, "Petroleum in Soviet Middle Eastern Strategy", Georgetown University doctoral thesis, 1969.   For an account of Soviet views on the usefulness of Middle East oil to the USSR and the Eastern bloc countries, see David Morison's article in Mizan, May-June 1968, pp. 79-85.

(33)   Jean-Jacques Berreby in New Middle East, No. 16 (January 1970), p. 11.

(34)   Iraq was not linked with other Northern tier states in Soviet strategies after 1958, though it had been earlier.

2. RELATIONS WITH ALGERIA

The Russians were handicapped in their early dealings
with the Algerian provisional government, formed in 1958,
by their relations with France. They could not, without
risking a rupture with Paris, deal openly with Algerian
nationalists engaged in a civil war against French authority.
Moscow accordingly withheld de facto recognition of the
provisional government until 1960 and accorded de jure
recognition only after the Evian agreements in 1962. The
Chinese, by contrast, felt no such constraint and so recognized the provisional government as soon as it was formed;
from 1958 to 1962 Peking reportedly provided aid to the
National Liberation Front (FLN) worth five to 10 million
dollars. (1)

The Soviet Union remained scrupulously neutral in
respect of internal struggles within the FLN before independence. Ferhat Abbas, the first Premier of the provisional government and a moderate, was well received in
Moscow in 1960; on the other hand, Ben Bella and his
more radical associates, jailed in Paris since their capture
in 1956, were frequently the topic of sympathetic commentary in the Soviet press.(2) This detachment concerning
rivalry within the FLN continued after independence, as
Ben Bella worked his way to the Algerian presidency.

The principal concern of the Russians after Algeria's
independence was not which faction would prevail in the
FLN but the relations of the provisional government with
Algerian Communists. The Parti Communiste Algérien
(PCA), though active for many years in the national liberation movement, had dissociated itself from the FLN in the
early stages of the civil war. In 1956 the Communists
sought belatedly to collaborate with the FLN – and Soviet
writers subsequently claimed a certain Communist success
in "uniting all patriotic forces" (3) – but there is little
evidence that significant collaboration ensued. By the
end of the 1950s Soviet observers tended to emphasize the
dominant role of Communists in the struggle with France
and to treat the FLN as merely one of the forces in the
national liberation movement. (4) Meanwhile, PCA
delegations came frequently to Moscow and their views
were given prominence in the Soviet press: Kommunist,
for instance, carried an article in 1960 by the PCA First
Secretary, Larbi Bouhali, in which he described the provisional government, however praiseworthy in some
respects, as "bourgeois-led" and inclined to anti-Communism. (5) The Russians' obvious preference for Algerian
Communists over the FLN during the last years of the civil
war created certain difficulties between Moscow and the
provisional government after independence.

In November 1962 the PCA was banned along with
all other parties except the ruling FLN. The Russians
reacted as they normally did in such situations. The Party
Central Committee adopted a resolution in early December
expressing "deep regret and alarm". (6) In January, and
again in April, Algerian Communist delegations were
received in Moscow to consider what course the PCA
should follow. What decision was reached is not known,
but the Soviet Union clearly was unwilling to let the
Communist issue cloud its relations with Algeria, as earlier
it had clouded relations with other Arab nations (the UAR,
for instance, in 1959 and Iraq in 1960). By 1963 the
Russians were beginning to abandon their militant posture
of the preceding years, when support of Communist parties
over nationalist leaderships had been normal. Algerian
Communism, moreover, was a particular liability – in an

Arab setting – because of its association with the French
Communist Party, long suspected of pro-Jewish sympathies.
Under these circumstances it was prudent for the Russians
to avoid giving too firm a commitment to the PCA, despite
its size and vigour. (7)

The new Algerian government, meanwhile, was
moving steadily Leftwards, carrying out Ben Bella's Tripoli
Programme of May 1962 and taking the first steps towards
nationalization of property left by the French. Could this
be a recurrence in North Africa of the Castro experience
in Cuba – that is, a gradual if unorthodox transition to
socialism without the benefit of Communist participation?
What, after all, was the purpose of "national democracy",
proclaimed as the ideal formula in developing nations since
the world Communist conference of 1960, if not the accom-
modation of routes to socialism in the Third World outside
the normal channels of Communist hegemony?

From the end of 1962 Soviet commentators began to
look at Algerian developments in the light of such considerations. An article in International Affairs in December,
for instance, gave a very favourable account of Ben Bella's
draft programme for the FLN prepared in June. (8) In
January 1963 a staff writer of Mirovaya ekonomika i
mezhdunarodnyye otnosheniya praised Algeria's non-alignment and other aspects of its foreign policy, regretting
only the ban on the PCA. (9) Later in the year even the
ban on Communists was ignored in most commentaries as
nationalization and economic reform held central focus.
In November two Soviet scholars suggested that, as a result
of "radical reforms" initiated in March, Algeria was in the
process of transition "from national liberation to socialism".
Ben Bella was quoted approvingly as having said, "All our
state activities have a single purpose – the acceleration of
Algeria's progress along the path leading to socialism." (10)

Developments in 1964 such as the land decrees in
March and the adoption of the new FLN programme in
April (which went considerably further towards socialism
than the Tripoli Programme two years earlier), strengthened
Soviet confidence in the Algerians' course. When Ben
Bella came to Moscow after the FLN Congress in April,
Khrushchev made a special point of addressing him as "com-
rade"; Ben Bella on this occasion was awarded the Lenin
Peace Prize, Russia's highest honour. The communiqué
at the close of Ben Bella's visit acknowledged the FLN to
be "the unifying centre in Algeria's struggle for socialist
reconstruction". (11) Subsequent commentaries were in
this vein. Though occasionally questioning the part played
by foreign capital in Algeria's development and the persistent role of Islam in FLN policies, Soviet Arabists continued throughout Ben Bella's rule to picture Algeria as one
of the most "progressive" Third World states – ranked with
Ghana and Guinea and for a time ahead of the UAR. (12)
The fact that these appraisals were not appreciably affected
by Khrushchev's fall in October 1964 indicates how important Algeria had become in Soviet Third World strategies.

The Algerian Communists under these circumstances
were easily forgotten. By mid-1964 the PCA had ceased
to exist except in name. Many of its members joined the
FLN; its principal organ, Alger Républicain, which had
continued to appear legally despite the ban on the PCA,
declared itself in the spring of 1964 an instrument of the
FLN. (13) Meanwhile, from 1964 on, FLN delegations
came regularly to Moscow to attend CPSU congresses, to
consult with Party leaders and, generally, to play the part

played by an orthodox Communist party.

The overthrow of Ben Bella by his Defence Minister, Colonel Houari Boumedienne, in June 1965 posed a delicate problem for the Russians. This was the first successful coup against a favoured Third World leader and had been carried out, moreover, not by a Rightist faction - which the Russians could easily have condemned as "imperialist agents" - but by a long-term associate of Ben Bella who shared his views; indeed, Boumedienne had led a high military delegation to Moscow only a few weeks before the coup. If the Russians had foreknowledge of the plot, however, they never revealed it. Moscow recognized the new regime promptly (some of Russia's African allies thought it indecently prompt) and waited to see how it would develop. The Communist issue again took on importance, as the colonels now in power in Algeria showed the Army's traditional hostility to Communism in a new round of arrests. Protests were duly made in Moscow, (14) but more and more perfunctorily as it became clear that the new regime intended to carry out both the foreign policy and domestic programme of its predecessor. The chiefs had changed, and in some measure the style, but not the content of the Algerian revolution. Boumedienne was accordingly received with conspicuous cordiality during his state visit to Moscow in December 1965; the communiqué at the close of his visit, which was longer and more detailed than most communiqués of this sort, underscored Soviet-Algerian accord on many international and domestic issues. (15)

During the next year and a half, until the Arab-Israeli war, relations remained on an even keel. The pace of high-level governmental and military exchanges was intensive, and economic co-operation increased (see below). There was occasional mild criticism of the pace of the revolution and of the treatment of Communist prisoners; (16) there was also an awkward episode during the 23rd Party Congress in March 1966 when the arrival in Moscow of a PCA delegation caused the affronted FLN delegates to withdraw. (17) However, such episodes were rare and did not seriously disturb the smooth course of Soviet-Algerian relations.

The Six Day War brought on the first significant impasse in the relationship. Russia's more moderate policies in the Arab-Israeli dispute after June 1967 inevitably clashed with Algeria's, as Boumedienne became for a time spokesman for the most militant segment of Arab opinion in this matter. In public statements following the conflict, Boumedienne openly doubted Russia's commitment to the Arabs' cause; the Algerian press questioned whether Moscow's policy of "peaceful coexistence" was consistent with pledges to fight imperialist aggression. (18) Tension between the two countries was defused by Boumedienne's visits to Moscow in June and July, but differences over strategy lingered. They were reflected in official Soviet and Algerian positions on the Middle East crisis during the following years.

One should not attach too much importance to differences between Moscow and Algiers in the Palestinian-Israeli issue. Of greater consequence in the relationship was the expansion of economic co-operation, the increase in arms transfers, the growing number of naval calls at Algerian ports, and the active pace of exchanges at all levels and in all areas (see below) Algeria's dependence on the USSR unquestionably increased during the years following the June war. Soviet criticism of Algerian developments, it is true, was occasionally blunter than before the war: A.S. Kaufman, for instance, noted in 1968 the

wide gap between "theory and reality" in Algerian socialism; (19) Pravda's veteran North African correspondent, Yu. Potemkin, found agrarian reform still inadequate in 1969, and in 1970 he argued that the FLN had lost its pre-independence unity. (20) Such criticism, however, was intended to be constructive. The general tenor of Soviet commentary on Algeria was sympathetic.

As time passed and as the Algerians became more and more preoccupied with domestic problems, the Arab confrontation with Israel in the Eastern Mediterranean appears to have grown more distant to them. Boumedienne's role as chief spokesman for Arab militancy accordingly declined. The Russians were undoubtedly happy to have it this way. A few Western observers continued to view Algiers as Moscow's "agent for subversion" in North Africa, even replacing Cairo in this respect, (21) but a more careful reading of Soviet behaviour in Algeria would accent different objectives: the relative isolation of the mercurial Algerians from the rest of the Arab world, in order to keep Arab passions at a minimum in the Palestinian question; the cultivation of a reliable ally in the Western Mediterranean with usable harbours; access to new oil reserves, as in a growing number of Middle Eastern states; and the nurturing of a "non-capitalist" economy that could serve as a model to other Third World nations.

*   *   *

Chinese-Algerian ties, despite Peking's early advantage in Algiers, presented no serious challenge to the Russians. When Ben Bella was in power the Chinese had some influence with the Algerians and high-level exchanges were relatively frequent; a $50 million credit was extended in 1963 and equipment was reportedly provided for a popular militia, designed to counter early Soviet arms transfers to the Algerian Army. (22) After Ben Bella's fall, however, Peking's influence declined. Apparently little of the 1963 credit was utilized and few exchanges were reported during the latter half of the 1960s. Doubtless Boumedienne's more militant posture in the Arab-Israeli conflict was closer to Peking's position than Moscow's, but Algeria's growing dependence on the USSR - especially in arms - was proof against any resurgence of Chinese influence. Boumedienne would have found it quite illogical to risk Moscow's friendship by courting good will too enthusiastically in Peking. This situation did not change significantly with the resumption of Chinese diplomatic activity after the Cultural Revolution.

Economic, Military and Cultural Relations

Soviet economic aid to Algeria, extended in two credits in 1963 and 1964 totalling approximately a quarter of a billion dollars, was concentrated on one major project - a steel works at Annabah (at an estimated cost of $125 million) - and approximately 80 smaller undertakings; among the latter were 25 dams, 10 repair shops, an irrigation system, technical institutes and training schools, and a number of oil and mineral surveys. In addition, the Russians provided 500 tractors and more than 100 combines. (23) Utilization of the aid appears to have been relatively high. Although few important projects were reported as completed by 1971, work had started on most of those provided for in the initial credit agreements. The number of Soviet engineers and technicians active in Algeria was said to be in the thousands. (24)

Trade grew steadily after 1962; exports to Algeria continued to predominate over imports, reflecting the shipment of Soviet supplies under the aid programme, but by the end of the decade exports and imports were more nearly in balance. An important seven-year trade agreement in 1968 projected a large increase in the total volume of trade and pledged Moscow's purchase of two-thirds of Algeria's annual wine production in exchange for agricultural machinery. From 1966 to 1969 a tenfold increase was reported in Soviet-Algerian trade and Algeria ranked fifth among Russia's Third World trading partners. (25)

Soviet-Algerian military relations were a critical aspect of the total relationship because of Algeria's growing dependence on Russia: by the end of the 1960s Russia was virtually the sole supplier of Algeria's modern arms. Up to the end of the June war of 1967 the estimated value of arms transfers was approximately $200 million; activity during the next few years suggests that this amount again may have been provided by the end of 1970.

The earliest shipments - apart from arms rumoured to have been sent to the FLN via Morocco and Tunisia before independence - followed the agreement of October 1963. These included an estimated 300 tanks and various types of aircraft, most of which was intended for use in the border war with Morocco. Deliveries probably declined after this conflict was resolved in March 1964 but continued at a rate sufficient to cause the Moroccans continuing concern. After the Six Day War the arms delivered to Algeria were more sophisticated, including modern MIG fighters, SAM-2 guideline missiles, new tanks, and 25 to 30 naval vessels. (26) There were an estimated 2,000 Soviet military advis-

ers in Algeria by 1968, and another 2,000 naval advisers were expected shortly at Mers-el-Kebir. (27) The frequency of Soviet naval calls in Algeria after 1967 accented Moscow's growing interest in fuelling rights and perhaps, in due course, bases for the Mediterranean squadron. Meanwhile, there were periodic rumours of Soviet bases in the Algerian Sahara, from which arms were reportedly flown southwards to Russia's allies in Black Africa (for instance, Nigeria after 1967); there were also reports of training camps for Arab and African guerrillas. (28) Whether or not such reports were credible, the Soviet Union surely had the capability by the end of the 1960s of using its influence in Algeria to a variety of ends.

Cultural relations between Algeria and the USSR appear to have been secondary to political, military and economic ties, at least insofar as exchanges of performing artistes, academicians, and the like are concerned. The principal areas of activity were education and medicine, and many Russian school teachers and doctors regularly went to Algeria, often for several years at a time, to take part in Soviet-sponsored courses. At the end of 1968 there were fewer than 200 Algerian students in Soviet institutions of higher education and less than 100 trainees, a drop from previous years and fewer than one might expect from a nation enjoying such cordial relations with the Soviet Union in other areas of activity; the number of Algerian students in the USSR increased somewhat during 1969. (29)

ALGERIA

Chronology

	Political	Economic	Cultural
Pre–1960			
Oct 1954	Civil war begins in Algeria		
Sept 1958	FLN forms provisional government; recognized by CPR (Dec)		
Jan 1959	CP delegation in USSR for XXI congress		
May 1959			TU delegation in USSR
Sept 1959	CP, FLN delegations in CPR for 10th anniversary		
1960			
Mar	– Khrushchev in France on state visit		
May		– Foreign minister Belkacem Krim in CPR for aid talks	
Sept	– FLN premier Ferhat Abbas in Moscow and Peking: USSR recognizes regime de facto		
Oct		– Gift of tractors, food to Algerian refugees in Tunisia	
Nov			– Artists in USSR
Dec	– CP delegation in Moscow for world conference – President de Gaulle in Algeria		
1961			Feb – Cultural agreement
May	– FLN–French negotiations open at Evian	– Finance minister in USSR for trade talks	
Aug		– Gift of wheat	
Oct	– CP secretary Bouhali in USSR for XXII congress		
1962			
Feb		– Additional aid to Algerian refugees	
Mar	– Evian agreements signed; USSR grants de jure recognition to provisional government		
May	– CP secretary in USSR – Tripoli programme adopted by FLN (nationalization plan)		
June		– Aid to orphans	
July	– Independence: diplomatic relations with CPR	– CPR gift of wheat, steel, medical supplies	
Aug		– Soviet gift of wheat, foods	
Oct	– Government delegation in Algeria		
Nov	– CPR military delegation in Algeria – All parties banned in Algeria, including Communists		

Political	Economic	Cultural

<u>1962</u> (cont.)

Dec - USSR, Algeria exchange embassies

Political	Economic	Cultural
<u>1963</u>		
Jan - CP delegation in USSR		Jan - Journalists in USSR
Mar - Government delegation in USSR		
Apr - CP delegation in USSR		
		May - TU delegation in USSR
June - Military delegation in Algeria	June - Agreement on mine clearing	
July - Government delegation in Algeria for anniversary	July - Economic delegation in Algeria for aid talks	
Sept - Government delegation in USSR		
Oct - <u>Algerian-Moroccan fighting on border</u> - Reported arms agreement (30)	Oct - CREDIT AGREEMENT for mining, training schools, dams, fertilizer and sugar plants ($100m) - CPR credit ($50m)	
Nov - CPSU delegation in Algeria	Nov - Trade delegation in Algeria: long-term agreement	Nov - Cultural agreement
Dec - Government, FLN delegation in USSR - <u>Chou En-lai in Algeria on 7-day visit</u>	Dec - Gift of aircraft to Ben Bella	Dec - Cultural delegation in USSR - Medical delegation in Algeria

---

Political	Economic	Cultural
<u>1964</u>		
	Jan - Aid to flood victims	Jan - Doctors in Algeria to work in hospitals - Cultural mission in USSR: protocol
	Feb - Air service opens	
Mar - <u>Cease-fire in border war with Morocco</u>		Mar - Cultural centre opens in Algiers
Apr - <u>FLN congress adopts more radical programme</u> - BEN BELLA IN USSR on 12-day state visit; awarded Lenin peace prize	Apr - Gift of tractors	Apr - TU delegation in USSR - Information officials in USSR
	May - CREDIT AGREEMENT for steel works ($126.5m); gift of oil institute	
	June - Economic delegation in Algeria: protocols on technical schools, steel and textile plants; protocol on 2 commercial planes	
Aug - Parliamentary delegation in USSR	Aug - Trade delegation in USSR - Contract for 28 dams - Gift of harvester	Aug - TU delegation in USSR
		Sept - Russian-built Africa institute opens
Oct - Party, government delegation in Algeria - Deputy defence minister Vershinin in Algeria		Oct - TU delegation in USSR for anniversary

ALGERIA

	Political		Economic		Cultural
1964 (cont.)					
Nov	- FLN, military delegations in USSR for anniversary - CPR military delegation in Algeria - Deputy foreign minister Malik in Algeria	Nov	- Oil institute opens		
		Dec	- Aid to earthquake victims - Technical institute opens		
1965					
		Jan	- Gift of naval research unit - Gift of medical equipment		
Feb	- Supreme court chairmen in Algeria	Feb	- Steel workers training centre completed	Feb	- Academician Solodovnikov heads delegation to Algiers for Afro-Asian conference - Journalists in USSR - TU delegation in Algeria
Mar	- Parliamentary delegation in Algeria - Chou En-lai in Algeria - 260 officers in USSR for military training	Mar	- Economic delegation in USSR for aid, trade talks: trade protocol for 1965	Mar	- Cultural delegation in USSR; protocol for 1965
Apr	- Defence minister Boumedienne in USSR: agreement on arms and training				
May	- FLN delegation in USSR - Military delegation in CPR				
June	- Ben Bella overthrown by Boumedienne; Afro-Asian conference cancelled - Revolutionary council envoy in USSR	June	- Vocational specialists in USSR: protocol on training		
		July	- French-Algerian oil agreement ($400m aid promised)		
Aug	- Government delegation in CPR				
Sept	- Foreign minister Chen Yi in Algeria	Sept	- CPR aid mission in Algeria		
Oct	- Government, military delegations in Algeria for anniversary				
		Nov	- Technical experts in Algeria to train specialists		
Dec	- BOUMEDIENNE IN USSR for 5-day visit	Dec	- Additional aid promised	Dec	- Journalists in USSR
1966					
		Jan	- Protocols on hospital and irrigation network		
Feb	- FLN delegation in USSR	Feb	- Planning aide in Algeria - Gift of medical supplies		
Mar	- Another FLN delegation in USSR for XXIII congress; leaves because of presence of PCA delegation	Mar	- Economic delegation in Algeria: trade protocol for 1966; protocol on oil equipment deliveries	Mar	- TU delegation in Algeria
Apr	- Naval squadron visits Algeria	Apr	- Mines nationalized in Algeria		
May	- Military delegation in Algeria: arms agreement			May	- Press chief in USSR
July	- Deputy foreign minister Malik in Algeria	July	- Power minister in USSR: protocol on steel works at Annabah, power stations,		

20

Political	Economic	Cultural
1966 (cont.)		
	July (cont.) – distillery; trade protocol	
	Aug – Planning official in Algeria	Aug – Health delegation in Algeria
Oct – Deputy foreign minister Semenov in Algeria – Government, military delegations in Algeria for anniversary	Oct – Planning chief in USSR	
	Nov – Aviation minister in USSR – Labour ministry delegation in USSR to study technical training	Nov – TU delegation in USSR
1967		
Jan – Navy patrol boats visit Algeria – FLN delegation in USSR	Jan – Planning officials in Algeria – Protocol on oil refinery – Trade protocol for 1967 – Aid for flood victims	
	Feb – Further protocols on steel works, distillery	Feb – Medical delegation in Algeria for public health seminar
	Mar – Trade minister in USSR	
	Apr – Economic aid chief Skachkov in Algeria	Apr – Cultural delegation in USSR: protocol for 1967
May – CPSU delegation in Algeria to observe conference on Arab socialism	May – Contract for oil drilling rigs	May – Journalists in Algeria: information exchange agreement – Red Cross delegation in USSR
June – BOUMEDIENNE IN USSR for 2 days during Middle East crisis – Defence official in USSR for talks – Algeria breaks relations with USA		
July – Deputy defence minister in Algeria – Boumedienne again in USSR for talks on Middle East crisis		
Aug – Naval squadron visits Algeria	Aug – Iron and steel delegation in USSR: protocol on equipment for Annabah works	
	Sept – Deputy trade minister in Algeria	
Oct – High party, government, military delegations in Algeria for 5th anniversary	Oct – Engineers in Algeria for talks on technical school	
Nov – Government delegation in USSR for anniversary	Nov – Gift of hospital	
		Dec – Education minister in USSR; protocol on teacher exchange
1968		
	Jan – Trade protocol for 1968	Jan – Geologists in Algeria: protocol on scientific co-operation
	Mar – Protocols on oil prospecting, iron ore extraction	

	Political		Economic		Cultural

1968 (cont.)

	Political		Economic		Cultural
				Apr	– Oil workers in Algeria
		May	– Additional industries nationalized in Algeria		
July	– Defence minister Grechko in Algeria	July	– Power minister in USSR: expanded trade, aid agreement for 1969-75		
				Aug	– War veterans minister in USSR
		Sept	– Trade delegation in Algeria for international fair		
Oct	– Komsomol delegation in Algeria – Military delegation in Algeria – Party, government delegation in Algeria for anniversary	Oct	– Engineers in Algeria for talks on steel plant	Oct	– TU delegation in USSR
		Nov	– Economic delegation in Algeria for talks on July agreement		
		Dec	– Protocol on mineral prospecting in 1969-75		

1969

	Political		Economic		Cultural
Jan	– Moscow city delegation in Algiers	Jan	– Contract for irrigation network – Oil minister in Algeria: agreement on research centre – Contract for glass works – Contract for industrial equipment	Jan	– Cultural protocol
		Feb	– Deputy premier Baybakov in Algeria for economic talks	Feb	– Medical delegation in Algeria for conference on TB
Mar	– Foreign minister in USSR – Algerian Socialist Vanguard party delegation in USSR for preparatory commission and world communist conference (June)	Mar	– Contracts for distillery – Geology minister in Algeria – Soviet-Algerian economic commission established – Economic delegation in Algeria: protocol on 1968 agreement		
Apr	– Naval vessels call at Annabah – Navy chief in USSR – Military delegation in USSR	Apr	– Trade protocol for 1969 – Contract on oil equipment	Apr	– Education minister in USSR: protocol on student exchange, 1969-70, and recognition of diplomas
		May	– Protocol on mining equipment – Metallurgy minister in Algeria		
		June	– Sales agreement on meteorological equipment	June	– TU delegation in USSR
		July	– Wine delegation in USSR for trade talks	July	– Protocol on student scholarships – Cultural minister Furtseva in Algeria
				Aug	– Radio, TV delegation in USSR
Sept	– Air marshal in Algeria – Revolutionary council delegation in CPR	Sept	– Labour ministry delegation in USSR for talks on professional training		

	Political		Economic		Cultural
1969 (cont.)					
Oct	– Government delegation in CPR for anniversary	Oct	– Aid for flood relief – Skachkov in Algeria for first meeting of joint economic commission: protocol on training technicians	Oct	– Cultural and news agreements
Nov	– Soviet and CPR delegations in Algeria for anniversary – Planning and finance minister in USSR for anniversary				
1970					
		Jan	– Trade delegation in USSR for talks on long-term agreement		
Mar	– Fleet admiral Gorshkov in Algeria	Mar	– Contracts for oil surveys by Soviet specialists	Mar	– Moscow university delegation in Algeria: agreement on exchange of teachers, students – Medical agreement with CPR
				Apr	– Azerbaydzhani oil experts lecture at Algerian institute
May	– Naval vessels call at Algiers	May	– Contracts for oil surveys, development	May	– Azerbaydzhani writers in Algeria
		June	– Contract for oil rigs in Sahara fields	June	– Veterans' delegation in USSR
		July	– Algeria nationalizes some foreign oil companies		
		Aug	– Trade minister in USSR for long-term talks: agreement to share shipping costs		
Oct	– Kosygin, Boumedienne meet in Cairo at Nasser's funeral	Oct	– Deputy ministers of geology and metallurgy in Algeria		
		Nov	– Foreign economic relations delegation in Algeria: agreement on Soviet specialists in various areas		
		Dec	– Protocol on dams at Oran, Grand Kabylie and Tlemcen		

References

(1)   See Goldman, Soviet Foreign Aid, p. 46.

(2)   E.g. New Times, No. 48 (29 November), 1961, p. 15, reporting a hunger strike by Ben Bella.

(3)   R.G. Landa, writing in Voprosy istorii, No. 5 (May), 1961, p. 81; other Soviet commentaries on Algeria during the civil war are reviewed in Mizan, October 1961, pp. 1-7.

(4)   E.g. N.F. Pospelova, Alzhir (Moscow), 1959, pp. 98-100.

(5)   Kommunist, No. 16 (November), 1960, p. 84.

(6)   Pravda, 4 December., 1962.

(7)   The PCA is reported to have had over 5,000 members at this juncture; if the estimate is accurate, the PCA was the largest Communist party in the Arab world at that time. See Arslan Hubaraci, Algeria: A Revolution that Failed (New York: Praeger, 1966), pp. 174-75.

(8)   I. Chelnokov, International Affairs, No. 12 (December), 1962, pp. 76-77.

(9)   Mirovaya ekonomika i mezhdunarodnyye otnosheniya, No. 1 (January), 1963, pp. 13-15.

(10)   V. Kaboshkin and Yu. Shcherovskiy, "Alzhir: ot natsional'no-osvoboditel'nosti do sotsializma", Kommunist, No. 16 (November), 1963, pp. 113 and 117.

(11)   Pravda, 7 May, 1964.

(12)   The following are a few of the more important commentaries on Algerian developments in the latter half of 1964: N.N. Prozhogin, "Vybor Alzhira-sotsializm", Kommunist, No. 10 (July), 1964, pp. 99-107; R.G. Landa, "Nekapitalisticheskiy put' razvitiya Alzhira", Narody Azii i Afriki, No. 5 (September-October), 1964, pp. 10-21; Yu. Potemkin, "Alzhirskaya revolyutsiya; sversheniya i perspektivy", Mirovaya ekonomika i mezhdunarodnyye otnosheniya, No. 10 (October), 1964, pp. 26-37.

(13)   See Richard Lowenthal, "Russia, the One-Party System and the Third World", Survey, No. 58 (January 1966), p. 51.

(14)   E.g. Pravda, 27 September and 13 November, 1965.

(15)   Pravda, 20 December, 1965.

(16)   E.g. TASS, 28 April, 1966 (a telegram from the Soviet Red Cross to the Algerian Minister of the Interior concerning a hunger strike by Communist prisoners); also Yu. Potemkin in Pravda, 19 August, 1966 (a somewhat negative judgment on the pace of agrarian reforms).

(17)   Following the Congress, the Russians apparently cautioned the PCA not to send further delegations to Moscow, at least officially; none are reported until the spring of 1969 when a delegation from the Socialist Vanguard Party, which had by then replaced the PCA, arrived to take part in the World Communist conference.

(18)   See Mizan, July-August 1967, p. 149, citing Algerian radio broadcasts on 10, 14 and 19 June, 1967.

(19)   Narody Azii i Afriki, No. 4 (July-August), 1968, p. 56.

(20)   Pravda, 1 November, 1969 and 4 July, 1970.

(21)   See, for instance, Est et Ouest, 1-15 June, 1969, p. 19.

(22)   Goldman, Soviet Foreign Aid, p. 149.

(23)   For a fuller discussion of Soviet projects, through both loans and gifts, see Goldman, op. cit., pp. 147-49, and The USSR and Developing Countries, pp. 59-61; a more recent review of aid to Algeria may be found, inter alia, in a Radio Moscow broadcast on 1 November, 1969.

(24)   Potemkin in Pravda, 1 November, 1969.

(25)   See TASS, 21 January, 1970 for the 1966-69 estimate; the rank is determined from comprehensive trade tables prepared for my forthcoming study, Russia and the Third World.

(26)   Christian Science Monitor, 3 April, 1970 (a summary of Soviet arms shipments by Joy Gerville-Reache). For other estimates of Soviet arms deliveries to Algeria at different times, see Goldman, op. cit., p. 148, and Joshua and Gibert, Arms for the Third World, pp. 14-16.

(27)   "Les Relations entre l'Algérie et l'Union soviétique", Est et Ouest, 1-15 June, 1969, p.17.

(28)   Ibid., p. 19.

(29)   U.S. Department of State, RSE-25, 7 May, 1969, p. 25 and RSES-35, 12 August, 1970, p. 21.

(30)   Joshua and Gibert op. cit., p. 15.

Russian journalists greeted with some scepticism the announcement in early 1959, following conferences on Cypriot independence in Zurich and London, that a republic would soon be proclaimed. How could a nation become "independent" when foreign bases remained intact and a prior commitment to join an aggressive military pact (NATO) had been extracted from the prospective "republic"? (1) Eighteen months later the Russians were more conciliatory. Cyprus was not to join NATO and stubborn resistance by Cypriot nationalists had led the British to make concessions. The formal launching of the republic in August 1960 was therefore noted with qualified approval and embassies were promptly exchanged. (2) During the next three years relations were friendly, though contacts were meagre.

The Cypriot Communists were undoubtedly a factor in Moscow's early attitude toward Cyprus. The party, called the Reform Party of the Working People (or AKEL), was one of the largest Communist organizations in the Third World and, apart from two in Israel, the only one legal in the Middle East. Predominantly Greek in membership, AKEL supported the Greek inclinations of the Makarios government and this view must have been pressed upon Soviet officials during frequent consultations between the two parties. (3) Meanwhile, Russia's strained relations with Turkey during the early 1960s meant that the Soviet government did not need to moderate its support of Archbishop Makarios because of concern for the Turkish minority in Cyprus. "Cyprus cannot be neutral", a Turkish Cypriot newspaper was quoted as having argued in 1961, following Makarios's pledges in Cairo that Cypriot bases would never be used for an attack on Arab countries; "all neutral states are weapons of Moscow". (4) Arguments such as this, needless to say, alienated the Russians still further from the Turkish minority and strengthened Soviet sympathies for the Makarios regime.

Russian support of the Nicosia government during the 1964 Cypriot crisis was accordingly predictable. Makarios's New Year's Day message to the Soviet government, announcing the abrogation of treaties with Great Britain, Greece, and Turkey, was commented on favourably. (5) Subsequent commentaries blamed disorders in Cyprus on "Turkish terrorists" and argued that Turkish terrorism was in turn stimulated by NATO powers which sought an excuse to occupy the island. Khrushchev, in identical Notes on 7 February to England, France, the United States, Turkey and Greece, charged that the sole object of the so-called peace plan put forward by the Western powers was the "actual occupation by NATO armed forces of the Republic of Cyprus, which is following a policy of non-alignment with military blocs"; the Cypriots, he said, were quite capable of governing themselves if passions were not "kept at a boiling point from outside". (6) The Soviet government, preferring a United Nations peace-keeping force to a NATO contingent in Cyprus, voted in the end for the Security Council resolution, but not without misgivings: before the vote, Pravda's UN correspondent expressed fears that the object of the Western powers "was to get the UN to 'confirm' their plans for the occupation and partition of the island". (7) The Russians abstained from voting on the clause which allowed the Secretary-General to set the size of the force and in the following months persisted in their argument that if left alone the Cypriots could work out their problems. (8) In July, as tension in Cyprus continued

to mount, Khrushchev reiterated the Soviet position: "The imperialists, inciting national conflicts between the Greek and Turkish communities, are seeking to fasten on Cyprus a new occupation"; he blamed Turkey especially for its "adventurous designs" in Cyprus and implicitly threatened reprisals if Turkey invaded the island. (9)

The Turkish air attacks on Cyprus on 8 August marked a climax in the Cypriot crisis. Pravda, in reporting the attacks, labelled them "undisguised aggression". (10) An official government statement a week later noted that Makarios had requested military assistance and put the Soviet position as follows: "If foreign armed invasion takes place against the territory of the Republic, the Soviet Union will give aid to the Cyprus Republic in the defence of its freedom and independence against foreign intervention and is now ready to begin talks on this question." (11) Although "armed invasion" did not follow the air attacks, as the Russians appear to have feared, negotiations for arms deliveries proceeded and an agreement was reached at the end of September. This provided for defensive weapons valued at an estimated $28 million, including artillery, tanks, torpedo boats, and SAM-2 missiles. (12)

The arms agreement was the high point in Soviet-Cypriot relations. The rapprochement with Turkey after Khrushchev's fall required a stricter neutrality in Cyprus and this was articulated following the Turkish Foreign Minister's visit to Moscow at the end of October 1964. The veteran Pravda correspondent N. Bragin, writing in November of his recent visit to the Turkish sectors of Cyprus, for the first time gave Soviet readers a relatively sympathetic view of the Turkish side of the Cypriot question. (13)

In January 1965 Gromyko explicitly approved the idea of a "federal form of government" in Cyprus if both the Greek and Turkish communities wished it; (14) in taking this position, he of course dissociated the Soviet Union from the Nicosia government in this matter, since Makarios – together with the Cypriot Communists – had long favoured enosis (that is, union with Greece). During the following years the Russians periodically reaffirmed their neutrality with respect to enosis, most conspicuously in the communiqués which terminated the frequent exchanges between high Soviet and Turkish officials.

Soviet-Cypriot relations were more subdued after 1964. There were few official exchanges. Trade, which had developed rapidly during the preceding years, levelled off. No aid was extended, apart from the arms specified in the 1964 agreement; deliveries under this agreement were apparently completed, but a request for additional arms in the autumn of 1966 was rejected. (15) Anti-Soviet sentiment, meanwhile, grew within the Greek community and flared up periodically in demonstrations – as on the occasion of Kosygin's state visit to Turkey in January 1967. (16) Disillusion also appeared among the Cypriot Communists. Pappaioannou, General Secretary of AKEL, dismissed charges of Soviet "betrayal" after Gromyko's statement in January 1965, but he was hard put during the following months to persuade his colleagues of Moscow's continuing good will. (17)

One should not conclude from this record, however, that Soviet-Cypriot relations deteriorated wholly. It was, of course, disillusioning to Greek Cypriots to see Moscow abandon its support, or implied support, of enosis, but the Russians did not go beyond neutrality in this issue; they did not desert Greek Cypriots to take up the cause of

Turkish Cypriots. When Cyprus itself was threatened, the Russians were quick to support the Nicosia government against its external enemies. Thus, during the disorders of November 1967, which Moscow blamed on the Greek junta in Athens seeking to overthrow the Makarios regime, an official Soviet statement made a point of warning Turkey as well as Greece that any "manoeuvring" against the Cypriot government would not be tolerated; "restraint and common sense" were required by all parties. (18) There was meanwhile some evidence that despite the absence of official exchanges and an aid programme, relations were gradually improving at the end of the 1960s. Unofficial exchanges, arranged through the Soviet-Cypriot Friendship Society in Moscow and its counterpart in Nicosia, multiplied during 1968 and 1969; a cultural centre in Nicosia, authorized in 1968, was completed the following year; more than 300 Cypriot students were studying in the USSR at the end of 1969 (a comparatively large number from a country the size of Cyprus), and Nicosia had agreed to recognize Soviet degrees in engineering. (19)

The 10th anniversary of Cyprus, in August 1970, was marked in the Soviet press by a large number of articles that praised Cypriot neutrality and that were sanguine with regard to Soviet-Cypriot relations. (20)

As far as the Cypriot Communists are concerned, they appear gradually to have overcome their disappointment in Russia's shift in policy after 1964 and to have re-established close ties with Moscow. Articles by AKEL leaders again appeared in Soviet publications and Pappaioannou, though his hostility towards "reactionary chauvinists in Ankara" was undiminished, (21) came periodically to Moscow to attend conferences and official celebrations - for instance, the world conference of Communist parties in June 1969 and the Lenin Jubilee in the following April.

*   *   *

Cyprus, it will be apparent from the foregoing brief account, was not a major focus of Soviet policies in the Middle East. The sympathy expressed for the Makarios government during the 1964 crisis was generated by two circumstances, neither of them fixed indicators of Soviet behaviour: a belief in Moscow that the prospects for the Cypriot Communists, who supported Makarios, were relatively promising; and persistent hostility towards Turkey. The interest in Cypriot Communism, undoubtedly stimulated during the era of ideological reaffirmation early in the 1960s, proved ephemeral - as Moscow's interest in such movements usually proved to be where Soviet goals and those of local Communists failed to coincide. Meanwhile, the shift in Soviet policy towards Turkey after Khrushchev's fall meant that any preference the Russians may have had for Makarios in Cyprus had to be abandoned. Soviet-Cypriot relations accordingly became more reserved, though remaining outwardly correct.

Chronology

	Political	Economic	Cultural

Pre-1960

Feb 1959 — Zurich, London conferences: independence offered, with British bases guaranteed

1960

Aug — Final agreement on independence; USSR, Cyprus agree to exchange embassies

Oct — AKEL (CP) secretary Pappaioannou in USSR for anniversary, world conference

1961

Apr — Collective farmers in Cyprus

Aug — Parliamentary delegation in USSR

Oct — Pappaioannou in USSR for XXII congress

Dec — Trade agreement

1962

Mar — CPSU delegation in Cyprus to attend AKEL congress

1963

Jan — Trade protocol

Apr — TU delegation in Cyprus

June — AKEL delegation in USSR

July — Agricultural group in USSR

Sept — Journalists in Cyprus
— Delegation in Nicosia for Afro-Asian conference

Dec — Makarios abrogates foreign treaties: Cyprus crisis begins

1964

Jan — Trade protocol

Feb — USSR opposes Western peace plan on Cyprus

Feb — Aeroflot delegation in Cyprus: air service agreement

Mar — Acting foreign minister heads delegation to USSR

June — Acting foreign minister, trade minister in USSR

July — Trade protocol

Aug — Turkey attacks Cyprus by air; Makarios asks for Soviet military aid

Aug — Gift of medical supplies for air attack victims

Sept — Acting foreign minister again in USSR: arms agreement

1965

Jan — AKEL delegation in USSR

	Political	Economic	Cultural
1965 (cont.)			
		Feb – Trade delegation in Cyprus: agreement for 1965–67	
			Apr – TU delegation in Cyprus
		Aug – Economic experts in Cyprus to advise Turkish Cypriots – Prefabricated houses delivered to Cyprus	Aug – Writers in Cyprus
1966			
	Jan – AKEL delegation in USSR for talks on Cypriot situation	Jan – Co-operative delegation in USSR for trade talks	
	Mar – AKEL delegation in Moscow for XXIII congress – CPSU delegation in Cyprus for AKEL congress – Government delegation in Cyprus		
1967			
			May – Orthodox church leaders in Cyprus
1968			
			Feb – Agreement on recognition of Soviet degrees
		Mar – Trade delegation in Cyprus: agreement for 1968–70	
			Aug – Journalists in Cyprus
1969			
			Feb – Agricultural workers in Cyprus – TU delegation in Cyprus for labour congress
	June – AKEL delegation in USSR for world conference		June – Agricultural, forestry workers in USSR
			Aug – TU delegation in USSR to study vocational training
1970			
	Mar – CPSU delegations in Cyprus for AKEL congress		Mar – Co-operative delegation in Cyprus
	Apr – Pappaioannou in Moscow for Lenin centenary		
	May – Youth delegation in USSR for Komsomol congress		

References

(1)   E.g. Pravda, 15 February, 1959 and Mirovaya ekonomika i mezhdunarodnyye otnosheniya, No. 5 (May), 1959, pp. 101-104.

(2)   See Pravda, 17 and 20 August, 1960.

(3)   The 10th AKEL Congress in 1962, which reviewed a wide range of topics, was given extensive coverage in Soviet publications: e.g. Pravda, 2, 3, and 7 March, 1962; also X s"yezd progressivnoy partii trudovogo naroda Kipra, 1963, 100pp.

(4)   Quoted by Yu. Kuznetsov in an article in Pravda, 29 June, 1961.

(5)   Pravda, 1 January, 1964.

(6)   Pravda, 8 February, 1964.

(7)   Pravda, 5 March, 1964.

(8)   See, for instance, Khrushchev's statement in Izvestiya, 5 May, 1964.

(9)   Izvestiya, 9 July, 1964.   Soviet commentaries on the Cypriot crisis, which were extensive throughout 1964, were reviewed regularly in Mizan.

(10)   Pravda, 9 August, 1964.

(11)   Pravda, 16 August, 1964; see also Khrushchev's remarks on Cyprus in a speech made in Frunze on the same day.

(12)   Joshua and Gibert, Arms for the Third World, p. 22, citing English news reports; the Russians are reported to have rejected Makarios's request for aircraft and submarines, not wishing to escalate tensions further.

(13)   Pravda, 18 November, 1964.

(14)   Pravda, 22 January, 1965.

(15)   See Joshua and Gibert, op. cit., p. 22; also an explicit TASS denial of rumours of additional Soviet military aid to Cyprus in Pravda, 11 July, 1967.

(16)   A Soviet protest on demonstrations at this time was carried in a Radio Moscow broadcast, 25 January, 1967.

(17)   See T.W. Adams and A.J. Cottrell, "Communism in Cyprus", Problems of Communism, May-June 1966, p. 28.

(18)   Pravda, 23 November, 1967.

(19)   U.S. Department of State, RSE-25, 7 May, 1969, pp. 82-83, and RSES-35, 12 August, 1970, p. 70.

(20)   E.g. A. D'yakov in Pravda, 18 August, 1970; V. Shmarov in Izvestiya, 19 August, 1970; and N. Bragin in Pravda, 1 October, 1970 (reviewed in Mizan, July-August 1970, Supplement A, p. 3 and September-October 1970, Supplement A, p. 6).

(21)   See Pappaioannou's greetings to the world conference in Pravda, 8 June, 1969; also his article in Pravda, 29 June, 1968.

4. RELATIONS WITH EGYPT

It is not easy to disentangle Soviet policies in Egypt from those in the Arab world as a whole. The major landmarks of Soviet-Egyptian relations - such as the arms agreement of 1955, the Suez crisis, the impasse following Nasser's anti-Communist campaign in 1959, and the Six Day War of 1967 - were also the landmarks of Russian-Arab relations; the Aswan Dam, though beneficial primarily to Egyptians, was a symbol of Russian aid to the Arab community at large. In what follows, then, we omit episodes dealt with in the introductory essay to this volume and focus on aspects of Russian policy in the UAR not yet discussed.

Moscow's early estimates of the regime in Cairo following the 1952 revolution were unsympathetic. The revolution, it was asserted, was the work of "reactionary officers linked with the USA"; its "savage repression" of workers and Communists was deplored. (1) This judgment, however, which persisted for several years, did not prevent the Russians from encouraging Cairo's resistance to Britain in negotiations over the Suez Canal in 1953 and 1954. A trade agreement was concluded with the Egyptians in March 1954, as a token of Moscow's good will; the Russians also vetoed, as a violation of Egypt's sovereignty, a Security Council resolution which would have forced the Egyptians to open the Canal to Israeli shipping. So long as the Egyptians resisted London, the Russians applauded. But when Cairo yielded, as in the Anglo-Egyptian agreement in July 1954, the Soviet press charged the Egyptians with shortsightedness and considered Nasser's regime "utterly dishonoured". (2)

The Russians did not develop a consistent attitude towards the Cairo regime until after the Baghdad Pact in early 1955. From this time on the Russians made Egypt the centrepiece of their Arab policies and relations between the two nations developed rapidly. Negotiations were carried on through the spring and summer leading to the famous arms agreement, announced in September. The arms deal was followed by the opening a few weeks later of a Soviet cultural centre in Cairo, the conclusion of a nuclear co-operation agreement in the following January, the establishment of a permanent Russian trade mission in Cairo in July and by intensified activity in all areas (see Chronology). The Egyptians, meanwhile, were fully responsive to Soviet initiative during this era. Their concern over the Baghdad Pact matched Moscow's, though for different reasons; their anxiety after the Israeli attack on Gaza in February 1955 made them more determined than ever to stamp out Western influence in the Middle East. They accordingly welcomed Russian interest in the Arab world and were willing beneficiaries of Soviet largesse. (3) These developments were the prelude to Russia's first direct involvement in Middle East affairs during the Suez crisis of 1956 (see Chapter 1).

Soviet-Egyptian relations continued to mature after the Suez crisis. Negotiations now proceeded in earnest on the construction of the Aswan High Dam, leading to the initial agreement of October 1958; in the meantime a $175 million loan, the largest Soviet credit so far extended in the Third World, had been negotiated in the preceding January. Additional arms were supplied to cover losses during the Suez war. Exchanges multiplied at all levels and in all areas. Nasser visited Moscow twice in 1958 - a state visit, his first, in April and a hastily arranged second visit during the Lebanon crisis in July. Soviet commentators, meanwhile, grew more enthusiastic than heretofore, considering Nasser's regime, as one writer put it, "the logical continuation of the national revolutionary struggle of the Egyptian people". (4) State capitalism in Egypt was regarded with favour, and measures such as the nationalization of foreign companies, designed to strengthen state capitalism, were approved. (5) The two years following the Suez crisis, in short, were a period of exceptional warmth in Soviet-Egyptian relations; the relationship with Egypt set the tone for Khrushchev's Third World policies generally during this era.

The cordiality, however, was not to remain unbroken. Developments during 1958 placed a strain on Russian-Egyptian relations. First, the merger of Syria with Egypt in February abruptly terminated Moscow's promising relationship with Damascus and left the Russians resentful of Nasser's pan-Arabist ambitions, though powerless for the moment to oppose them (see under Syria). Second, the Iraqi revolution in July brought to power in Baghdad a regime which at the outset was more in tune with Moscow ideologically and which therefore rivalled the Egyptian regime in Soviet attention; when Nasser attempted to absorb Iraq into the Cairo-dominated United Arab Republic, along with Syria, the Russians were understandably concerned (see under Iraq). Third, in December Nasser launched a bitter and open attack on Communists in the UAR. It was the latter development that appears to have triggered active Soviet opposition to Cairo. So long as Arab leaders suppressed Communists discreetly and made no major issue of their anti-Communist sentiments, the Russians were willing to ignore the banning of Communist parties in the Arab world; this was an unwritten - and probably unspoken - condition of the Soviet-Arab relationship. The Russians could not, however, remain decently silent when Arab Communists, many of them well known in Moscow and long-time supporters of Soviet causes, were being openly assaulted by Arab nationalists. Nasser's declaration of war on Arab Communism accordingly brought on an immediate and impassioned Soviet response. (6)

Khrushchev, addressing the 21st Party Congress in January, called Nasser's campaign "a reactionary business" and defended the patriotic record of Communists in the Arab world. (7) Nuritdin Mukhitdinov, a close associate of Khrushchev at this stage and recently returned from a visit to the Middle East, labelled Nasser's charges of Communist disloyalty "slanderous". (8) In March Khrushchev widened the attack on Nasser to include his pan-Arab ambitions as well as his anti-Communism: his views on Arab unity, Khrushchev said, were totally "erroneous". (9)

In April Khrushchev is said to have called Nasser "a passionate, hot-headed young man"; in his attempts to annex Iraq, in addition to Syria, he "had taken on himself more than his stature permitted". (10)

The dialogue was not always as sharp as reflected in these comments by Khrushchev, but a new coolness towards Cairo persisted in Soviet commentaries for several years. Egypt's slow progress, especially when compared to the early gains of the Iraqi revolution, drew criticism from Russian ideologues during an era when doctrine was being more rigorously affirmed. In May 1961 there was another brief outburst of ill will in the Russian press following the reported death of an imprisoned Syrian Communist "as a result of savage torture"; the report proved to be false, but before it was discovered to be so a wide-scale protest on the matter had been mounted in the USSR. Pravda's "Observer" used the episode to ridicule Egypt's so-called socialist society - "a society in which exploiters rule and people make speeches about democracy, while for their political beliefs progressive people languish in torture chambers". (11) Egyptian journalists denounced the Pravda article, needless to say, and for some weeks escalated the verbal dialogue even further. This, however, marked the climax of the war of words between Moscow and Cairo. Criticism of specific anti-Communist measures, of course, persisted, but the Soviet press after the "torture" episode became gradually more conciliatory toward Nasser's regime.

The impasse in Soviet-Egyptian relations during these years appears to have had minimal effect on major aid programmes. Khrushchev was careful to state, in his initial criticism of Nasser at the 21st Congress, that "differences in ideological views must not interfere with the development of friendly relations between our countries". Soviet commentators, meanwhile, asserted periodically that Russia was punctually fulfilling its aid obligations to Egypt, "leaving the settlement of ideological controversies to History". (12) In fact, preparations for the Aswan project went forward without interruption: work began in January 1960, with appropriate ceremonies, and a supplementary credit was negotiated later in the year. The nuclear reactor promised in 1956 was completed in 1961. The Soviet-Egyptian impasse, in short, did not mean Moscow's disengagement from prior commitments to Cairo or even a disinclination to undertake new ones, but a reappraisal of Egypt's special position in Soviet Third World policies. The Russians no longer accorded Egypt special status among Afro-Asian nations; they would no longer overlook shortcomings in Cairo merely because Egypt was pivotal in the Arab world.

The gradual improvement in Russian-Egyptian relations after mid-1961 was due to several new circumstances. For one, Syria's departure from the UAR in September 1961 removed a persistent cause of Soviet irritation since 1958. Second, by the end of 1961 Moscow had grown thoroughly disillusioned with Qasim's regime in Iraq; although Soviet-Iraqi relations were to remain outwardly cordial until Qasim's fall in 1963, they no longer constituted a barrier to better relations with Cairo. Meanwhile, the Russians themselves early in the 1960s were on the threshold of more pragmatic, eclectic approaches to Third World developments: what had seemed "reactionary" and retrogressive in Egyptian behaviour after 1958 no longer seemed so in 1962.

Another reason for improved relations between Moscow and Cairo was the Russians' fresh appraisal of Egyptian developments after Nasser's economic reforms of July 1961. The Soviet response, to be sure, was not immediately favourable. Pravda's correspondent in Cairo, Viktor Mayevskiy, reported on the decrees in August but explicitly rejected the government's claim that they were "socialist" measures. (13) V.L. Tyagunenko, writing six months later on economic conditions in the UAR, begrudged the reforms faint praise - as the one bright development in an economy that was otherwise in need of extensive overhauling. (14) One Soviet Arabist, however, Georgiy Mirskiy, was enthusiastic. In a popular article in January 1962, he wrote that "no other non-socialist country in Asia or Africa has ventured on such radical reforms". (15) In a more serious analysis in April, co-authored with

R.M. Avakov, Mirskiy argued that the "extremely radical reforms" of 1961 reflected serious changes in Egypt's political and social profile: "State power in the UAR is now used to restrict and weaken the influence of the wealthiest and strongest strata of society"; although the reforms themselves did not "transcend the framework of state capitalism", they demonstrated that the base of Nasser's regime was no longer "the base of bourgeois or, even less, feudal power". (16) Mirskiy returned to his defence of Egyptian progress towards socialism in subsequent commentaries. In an article on "creative Marxism" in early 1963, for instance, he called Cairo's leaders "revolutionary democrats who understand the necessity of turning the anti-colonialist revolution into an anti-capitalist one"; he explicitly linked the UAR with Ghana, Guinea and Mali - at this time Russia's most persistent models of "national democracy" in the Third World - as "states where the leading circles are speaking out for socialism". (17)

Mirskiy's optimistic appraisal of Egyptian developments, it should be noted, did not go unchallenged. Two former collaborators, R.M. Avakov (noted above) and L.V. Stepanov, in an article in May 1963 which appears to have been an opening attack on the sort of "revisionism" reflected in Mirskiy's writing, charged him with analysing the Egyptian reforms out of context. "Had Mirskiy not limited himself to one-sided evidence," they wrote, "had he instead attempted to follow the inter-relationship of all factors, negative as well as positive, he would doubtless have painted an ideologically more complex picture." As evidence of "negative factors", they cited the continued persecution of Leftists in the UAR and the failure of the Cairo regime to create an alliance with "progressive" forces in Egyptian society. (18) Mirskiy's views on the UAR, however, prevailed; although the "revisionist" ideas with which he was associated were in due course discredited, it was taken for granted from 1963 on that Egypt was one of the favoured "progressive" states.

Political and cultural ties, which had been somewhat curtailed during the impasse in Soviet-Egyptian relations, were intensified during the years following (see Chronology). They were climaxed by Khrushchev's long-awaited visit in May 1964, accompanied by his Foreign and Defence Ministers and a large entourage. The visit was perhaps the beginning of a personal disaster for Khrushchev - his behaviour in the UAR was given as one reason for his fall six months later - but at the time the visit dramatized not only the improvement in Soviet-Egyptian relations since the early 1960s but also the great importance Moscow again attached to the UAR as its principal ally in the Arab world, and indeed in the Third World as a whole. Addressing his Egyptian hosts as "comrades", Khrushchev complimented them for "embarking on the path of socialist construction"; he promised additional credits, apparently on his own initiative; there would be no difficulty about arms, he said, "when they are necessary". The official communiqué, though more restrained than Khrushchev's speeches as reported in the Egyptian press, showed agreement on an unusually wide range of international issues. (19) Back in Moscow, the First Secretary was no less exuberant. The UAR, he told Soviet listeners in a televised report on his visit, was seeking "to build a society on socialist principles". The persecution of Communists, he assured his audience, "has become a thing of the past"; Nasser's Arab Socialist Union (ASU) was becoming "an organ of the people". (20) Khrushchev, needless to say, had gone further than any other Russian official, journalist or scholar - including

Georgiy Mirskiy - in singing the UAR's praises.

Khrushchev's fall in October 1964 brought no significant change in Soviet policies in the UAR, though Cairo
thought initially that it might. A high Egyptian delegation attended the Russian anniversary celebrations in November to make inquiries; two high Soviet delegations went
to the UAR in the following weeks to give assurances.
Thereafter the pace of exchanges, the flow of aid and
transfer of arms proceeded normally, and even increased
(see below). If there was any change in the relationship,
it was in the style of diplomacy adopted by the new Russian
leaders. The approach was now more pragmatic; the
enthusiasm shown by Khrushchev during his 1964 visit was
tempered. Soviet commentators were more candid in
discussing concrete difficulties in the UAR, especially in
the economy: rising costs of living, production lags, trade
deficits and a growing foreign debt. (21) After the June
war, additional strains on the economy were noted as a
result of the loss of revenue from the Suez Canal.

The ancient question of "what kind of socialism"
continued to be discussed in Soviet publications. The
UAR posed a problem to the Russians in this respect. Although Egyptians professed to be socialists, even "scientific
socialists", and adopted measures which the Russians
normally approved, they possessed a weak sense of doctrine
and had no adequate party organization to reflect "prole-
tarian" leadership. Socialism in Egypt came from above,
through government decrees; it had no grass roots among
the common people. "Why", one writer asked in 1966, in
discussing the professed socialist ambitions of Egyptian
leaders, "do they not adopt the only scientific theory of
socialism, Marxism-Leninism?" (22) To hasten their doing
so, the Russians organized seminars (such as the Cairo
conference on African socialism in October 1966), established ideological institutes in the UAR, and invited ASU
delegations to Moscow for appropriate training. Meanwhile, the ASU was described as a "vanguard party" and
treated as a surrogate for the Communists, who dissolved
their organization in 1965. (23) In the end, however,
the Russians were obliged to acknowledge that Nasser
would not, like Fidel Castro, embrace Marxism-Leninism.
They accordingly fell back on the argument that if the
Egyptians were not proper Marxists they were at least
behaving as though they were. "It is a particular feature
of the situation in the UAR that those who head the Egyptian revolution, while not themselves Marxists, are putting
into practice measures which in many respects are similar
to the measures taken by Communists at a certain stage of
a socialist revolution." (24)

Soviet views on Egyptian socialism should be kept in
a proper perspective. The Russians surely welcomed
Cairo's moves towards the "non-capitalist course" (as Third
World socialism was normally called) and encouraged such
moves in any way possible, but Russia's alliance with the
UAR did not depend upon concrete progress in this direction. The central focus of Soviet policy in the UAR from
the mid-1960s on was not Egyptian socialism but Arab
confrontation with Israel. Cairo was the proper head-
quarters for this crusade and Soviet policies in the UAR are
therefore inextricably intertwined with strategies in the
Arab-Israeli dispute. Since these strategies are reviewed
elsewhere, what requires emphasis in the balance of the
present section is the enormous penetration of Soviet
influence into all aspects of Egyptian life that accompanied
Russia's commitment to the Arab cause.

Russia's involvement in Egypt intensified especially

after the Six Day War. It was evident first of all in the
Army, whose senior officers, the Russians felt, were mainly
responsible for the ignominious defeat in Sinai. It was not
merely their "complacency", Soviet analysts argued, that
made them negligent in "carrying out their official and
patriotic duty", but something more insidious: their hostility to the social and economic goals of the Egyptian
revolution. (25) The Russians accordingly applauded, and
perhaps stimulated, wide-scale purges in the Army following the June war. A few years later, when the purges had
been completed and Egypt's self-confidence restored,
Russian observers acknowledged the influence of the Soviet
Army's "political organs" in rebuilding Egyptian military
morale. (26) The 20,000 Russians assigned to Egypt by
1970 as military technicians and advisers undoubtedly kept
Egyptian morale from deteriorating (see below).

Economic and cultural co-operation, meanwhile,
kept pace with military collaboration. Joint Soviet-
Egyptian commissions were in more or less permanent session
and delegations moved continually between Moscow and
Cairo working out the details of Egypt's cultural and
economic plans. There was no significant area of activity
in the UAR in which Russians were not involved. Ali
Sabri, interviewed on Radio Moscow in December 1970 at
the end of one of his numerous visits to Russia, argued that
the collaboration thus far between the two countries was
merely a beginning; what was now required was "long-
range planning . . . for the UAR's economic development
is fundamentally built on strengthening co-operation with
the USSR". (27)

President Nasser, in the years following the Six Day
War, remained above criticism in Soviet eyes. Kudryavtsev, in a long report from Cairo following the June war,
praised Nasser's selflessness in resigning after the Egyptian
defeat and noted the popular demand that "he remain at
the head of his country in this crucial period". (28)
Belyayev and Primakov, two of Russia's most experienced
Middle Eastern correspondents, praised Nasser's "realistic
course" at the Khartoum conference of Arab leaders in
August; in consequence, Arab "extremism" was defeated.
(29) This deference to Nasser persisted in Soviet commentaries until his death. After his last visit to the USSR
in July 1970 (a visit that had been scheduled for three or
four days but was prolonged to nearly three weeks) Russian
observers made much of Nasser's "courageous initiative"
in seeking a peaceful solution in the Middle East; American
and even Soviet peace proposals were minimized beside
his. (30) Nasser, in Russian eyes, had become the apostle
of moderation in Arab politics and therefore uniquely
qualified to serve Moscow's purposes in the still escalating
crisis.

How then did Nasser's sudden death in September
1970 affect Soviet strategies? There can be no doubt that
the Russians were uneasy about the stability and even the
orientation of the new leadership, despite prompt assertions
that Sadat's election as Nasser's successor assured the
continuation of existing policies and "destroyed the web of
intrigue around the UAR". (31) Soviet commentators
similarly welcomed the announcement of the Federation of
Arab States (the UAR, Sudan and Libya) in November,
because it laid to rest Western rumours of "centrifugal
tendencies" in the Arab world following Nasser's death;
(32) they also approved Sadat's pledge in February 1971
to open the Suez Canal to the ships of all nations,
including Israel's, if Israeli troops withdrew from the east
bank. (33) Yet the Russians were not sanguine - and with

good reason. So long as Ali Sabri remained in the Egyptian leadership, Moscow had a loyal ally in Cairo and could count on being informed regularly of developments in the Egyptian capital. His dismissal, however, during the political crisis of May 1971, following Sadat's cordial reception of U.S. Secretary of State Rogers in Cairo in April, must have seemed to the Russians a serious threat to their influence in Egypt. Podgornyy's hastily arranged visit to Cairo immediately after the crisis and the signing of a long-term bi-lateral pact, a step nearly unprecedented in Russia's relations with Third World states, should be interpreted as a strenuous effort on Moscow's part to preserve the Soviet-Egyptian alliance at all costs. These latter events, however, fall outside the scope of the present study and are noted merely to emphasize the difficulties Russians were likely to face in Egypt in the post-Nasser era.

Egypt's central role in Russian strategies in the Middle East after the Six Day War deserves special emphasis. The "realistic course", for which Belyayev and Primakov complimented Nasser at the Khartoum conference, became the Russians' watch-word following the June war. This was true not merely in respect of the Palestinian issue and the confrontation with Israel but in respect of other developments as well. Through realism Moscow hoped to hold in check both Arab radicalism, as typified by the Palestinian commandos, and Arab conservatism, as typified by the oil sheikhdoms and other traditionalist forces in the area; the fact that Arab radicals and Arab conservatives came together in their fierce hostility towards Israel made the danger from extremists that much greater. Nasser's regime was the Russians' principal ally in the struggle against Arab extremism and it became increasingly so as the months and years passed. Inevitably the UAR was at times a heavy liability to Russia and the Egyptian aid projects a drain on Soviet resources. But there was no reasonable alternative, given Russian commitments in the Middle East. Unless Moscow was prepared to disengage from these commitments on a significant scale, the Cairo regime had to be kept strong enough to preserve a manageable balance between extremist Arab forces from all quarters. By 1970 this was not a matter of choice, but of necessity.

Seen in this perspective, Russia's massive military programme in the UAR after the June war and the deeper penetration into all aspects of Egyptian life are quite understandable. This activity did not constitute part of a revolutionary design, in the old-fashioned sense, but on the contrary was intended to promote moderation in the Arab world as Moscow interpreted it; moreover, it was the only practicable way of carrying out an engagement undertaken in a less turbulent era. The Russians' dilemma in the UAR was not unlike the Americans' in Vietnam – with the significant difference that at least through the spring of 1971 the Russians did not suffer the dire consequences of their engagement that the Americans did of theirs.

A word, finally, should be said of the impact of China's policies in the UAR on Russia's. On balance, the impact was slight. The Chinese appear never to have been congenial with the Egyptians, after the cordial talks between Chou En-lai and Nasser at Bandung which led to the establishment of diplomatic relations the following year. Chinese criticism of Nasser's anti-Communist crusade in 1959 was markedly sharper than Russian and left deeper scars – scars which Chou En-lai's visits in 1963 and 1965 did not entirely heal. Chinese aid

pledged to the UAR, to be sure, was second only to aid pledged to Pakistan, but much of it was unused. The largest credit – $80 million in January 1965 – was apparently intended to shake Cairo's support of Russia's participation in the forthcoming "Bandung" conference in Algiers; when Nasser proved unshakable, Peking's interest diminished. After the June war Peking's persistent support of the Palestinians and Cairo's growing reliance on Russia made any significant development of Sino-Egyptian relations out of the question. The USSR, in short, was at all times too firmly entrenched in the UAR to allow the Chinese an opportunity to exercise an influence on Nasser's policies which might have caused the Russians to alter theirs. (34)

Economic, Military and Cultural Relations

Estimates of Soviet credit extended to the UAR vary by nearly a quarter of a billion dollars, the discrepancies arising from uncertainty whether particular loans represented new commitments or a rescheduling of previous ones. The total shown in the Chronology (a relatively conservative estimate) is $842 million up to the end of 1969. (35)

The major project, to which approximately a third of Soviet funds were committed, was of course the Aswan High Dam – the most impressive foreign aid project undertaken anywhere in Africa and Asia and certainly the most publicized. Negotiations began in 1957, following the withdrawal in 1956 of a previous American offer (jointly with Great Britain and the World Bank). The initial credit of $100 million was extended at the end of 1958 – on the eve of a troubled period in Soviet-Egyptian relations (see above) – and work began in 1960; the first stage of the dam was opened during Khrushchev's visit to the UAR in 1964 and full operation began in January 1971. It is not within the competence of this study to analyse the economic value of the dam or to review the many engineering and other difficulties encountered during its construction, (36) but the significance of the project in Soviet-Egyptian relations should be noted. Aswan stood to the Egyptians, and through them to many of the peoples in Africa and Asia, as a symbol of what they most desired in economic development and modernization. Russia's association with the project, therefore, had the effect of dissipating traditional fears in Cairo concerning Communist aggression, persuading Egyptians that their policies and Moscow's were not incompatible, and reminding Nasser – especially when relations were strained – of Russia's continuing good will. The Aswan Dam, all things considered, must be judged one of the most successful of Soviet foreign aid ventures.

A detailed listing of other projects would go far beyond the scope of this study. We may merely note several of the more important undertakings which suggest the range of Soviet activity. In the industrial sector, a number of steel works were built, the most important of them at Helwan; power lines were constructed from Aswan to Cairo; oil refineries, dams, and additional power plants were constructed; a shipyard was built at Alexandria and the harbour improved. In addition, large quantities of industrial equipment were delivered at various stages and a vast programme of technical education was organized. By 1966 25 Soviet-supported training centres were said to be operating in the UAR, in which more than 13,000 Egyptians had already received certificates in 135 different specialities; (37) the numbers, needless to say, were greatly swelled in the latter part of the 1960s. The first nuclear reactor was completed in 1961.

In the agricultural and related sectors, the most important projects were in irrigation, land reclamation, cotton cultivation, and development of the fishing industry. The latter programme, initiated in 1964 and conducted under the supervision of the Soviet-UAR Fisheries Commission, involved research especially in the Red Sea and the Indian Ocean. There were also training programmes for Egyptian farmers and fishermen, both in the UAR and Russia.

The rate of utilization of the Soviet credits was high, especially during the 1960s. The 1958 credit was said to have been nearly exhausted by 1965, when the second major development credit (pledged by Khrushchev during his 1964 visit) came into operation; (38) the latter credit, to judge from the volume of economic activity between the two nations, would be used up well before the date initially planned (1971). Egyptian repayment of the loans was mainly in cotton, of which the crop was necessarily pledged for many years in advance as Cairo fell further and further behind in payments.

Soviet-Egyptian trade, already of some significance in 1955, grew steadily during the next 15 years. Egypt was Russia's principal trading partner in Asia and Africa at the end of the 1960s, accounting for 2.3 per cent of total Soviet trade from 1965 to the end of 1969. Russia, meanwhile, became the UAR's major partner after the Six Day War, accounting for about 20 per cent of Cairo's total trade. (39) Soviet exports were persistently higher than imports after 1960, reflecting the size of the Russian aid programme and Cairo's chronic inability to repay; after the June war exports exceeded imports by a margin of nearly two to one – and the ratio would have appeared higher still, of course, if military deliveries had been included.

Soviet military aid to the UAR preceded economic aid and remained at all times greater; by 1970 the total cost of military assistance was probably five or six times greater than credits extended for economic development.

The initial agreement of 1955 – the precise date of which is in some doubt as the result of research conducted by Professor Uri Ra'anan (40) – was periodically supplemented as the need arose. The arms lost in the Suez crisis of 1956, for instance, were promptly replaced and more up-to-date models were substituted for weapons which became obsolete. Deliveries were apparently suspended after 1958, but resumed in 1962. By June 1967 it is estimated that Russian arms deliveries to Egypt totalled $2 billion. This made Egypt recipient of the largest share of Soviet military aid and indeed of more Soviet arms than the rest of the Middle East and Africa combined. In Egypt's arsenal were an estimated 160 MIG-21 jets, in addition to several hundred planes of other types; anti-aircraft guns and SAM-2 guideline missiles, emplaced in the Sinai peninsula; light and medium tanks; various classes of naval craft in small, but adequate, number; and an ample supply of efficient Czech and Russian rifles. (41)

Approximately 80 per cent of this arsenal was lost in the Six Day War. Much of the equipment – especially aircraft – was replaced immediately; in due course all losses were covered, several times over in most cases and with the most advanced models. The cost of the new equipment delivered from June 1967 to October 1968 has been estimated at $2.5 billion and to mid-1971 at $3 billion. (42) By 1971 the Egyptians were reported to have the following arms of Russian design: an estimated 450 combat aircraft, including 50 improved MIG-21J interceptors and a small number of MIG-23s in addition to some 100 SU-7s and 50 jet bombers; more than 1,350 tanks; approximately 100 naval vessels of various types, including a dozen submarines; and both SAM-2 and SAM-3 missiles in batteries distributed along the west bank of the Suez Canal and in the Nile Valley. Of the 20,000 Russian military personnel said to be stationed in Egypt, about three-quarters were assigned to missile sites and many of the balance to supporting functions at air bases and elsewhere; an estimated 200 Soviet pilots were flying the new MIG interceptors in combat missions. (43)

Cultural relations between Russia and the UAR kept abreast of relations in other areas. They included activity not only in traditional areas such as education, trade union exchange, and entertainment but in more esoteric areas as well: Soviet space technicians, for instance, worked with Egyptians in 1969 in the construction of a satellite tracking station; Russian scientists joined Egyptians in photographing Mars; Egyptian physicists worked at nuclear research centres in the USSR. (44) By 1970, it could be said, Soviet-Egyptian ties were so extensive that wide cultural co-operation in all areas was taken for granted. There was accordingly nothing remarkable in the Russians' large and expensive programme – probably the largest and most expensive in the Third World; the programme would have been remarkable only if it had been less than it was.

Chronology

	Political		Economic		Cultural
Pre-1955					
1943	Agreement on diplomatic relations				
		Mar 1952	Barter agreement		
July 1952	King Faruq overthrown in military coup				
		Mar 1953	Banks agreement		
Mar 1954	Nasser takes power; USSR, Egypt exchange embassies	Mar 1954	First trade agreement		
July 1954	Anglo-Egyptian agreement on Suez canal				
1955					
Jan	– Military delegation reportedly in USSR (45)	Jan	– Aid to flood victims in Egypt		
Feb	– Israel attacks Gaza				
July	– Pravda editor Shepilov in Egypt for anniversary of revolution				
		Aug	– Trade agreement with CPR	Aug	– Soviet Muslims stop in Cairo en route to Mecca – Patriarch of Alexandria in USSR
Sept	– ARMS AGREEMENT with Czechoslovakia ($250m)	Sept	– Trade protocol	Sept	– Soviet cultural centre opens in Cairo
		Dec	– United States, England offer aid for Aswan dam		
1956					
		Feb	– Co-operative agreement on atomic energy		
Apr	– Egypt recognizes CPR				
				May	– Academic delegation in Egypt
June	– Foreign minister Shepilov in Egypt				
July	– Suez canal nationalized	July	– United States withdraws Aswan offer – Permanent Soviet trade mission in Cairo		
				Aug	– Education, TU leaders in USSR
Oct	– Suez crisis: England, France, Israel attack Egypt	Oct	– CPR credit for commodity purchases ($5m)		
Nov	– UN Emergency Force assumes control in Suez area – Additional arms credit reported (46)			Nov	– TU delegation in USSR
1957					
				Feb	– Atomic physicists in Egypt
May	– Government delegation in USSR			May	– TU delegation in USSR
				Aug	– Journalists in USSR

EGYPT

	Political	Economic	Cultural
1957 (cont.)			
Sept	- Government delegation in USSR	NOTE - Negotiations on Aswan Dam continue through year in Moscow and Cairo	Sept - Scientists in Egypt
Oct	- Defence minister in USSR: new arms agreement		Oct - Communications minister in Egypt
1958			
		Jan - Minister of industry in USSR: CREDIT AGREEMENT on industrial projects ($175m)	Jan - TU, co-operative delegations in USSR
Feb	- Egypt, Syria merge to form UAR		
Apr	- NASSER IN USSR for 17-day state visit	Apr - Protocol on factories, oil tanks, other projects under January credit	Apr - Cultural delegation in UAR
			May - Scientists' delegation in USSR
		June - Trade minister in USSR	June - Cultural delegation in USSR
July	- Nasser returns to Moscow during Lebanon crisis		July - Muslim delegation in USSR
		Aug - Agricultural minister in USSR	
		Sept - Air service agreement	Sept - TU delegation in USSR
Oct	- Vice-president Marshal Amir in USSR	Oct - AGREEMENT ON ASWAN DAM ($100m credit for first stage)	
			Nov - Lawyers in USSR
Dec	- CPSU secretary Mukhitdinov in UAR		Dec - Cultural delegation in USSR
	- Nasser launches anti-communist campaign in UAR		
1959			
Jan	- Khrushchev criticizes anti-communism in UAR at XXI CPSU congress	Jan - Business delegation in USSR	Jan - Muslim delegation in UAR
		Mar - Gift of mill, oil equipment	
		May - Public works minister heads delegation to USSR for talks on Aswan	May - TU delegation in USSR
		- Shipping agreement	
		July - Economic delegation in USSR	
		Aug - Contract for irrigation project	
Oct	- Government delegation in UAR to view dam site	Oct - Trade delegation in USSR	
	- CPR, UAR in dispute over anti-communist issue		
			Nov - Journalists in USSR
			- Cultural agreement for 1960
		Dec - Contract for factory equipment	

Political	Economic	Cultural
1960		
Jan – Government delegation in UAR for start of work on Aswan Dam		
	Feb – Protocols on pharmaceutical industry, oil prospecting – Deputy economic minister in USSR	
	Aug – Public works minister in USSR: SUPPLEMENTARY AGREEMENT ON ASWAN DAM ($225m for second stage) – Protocol on steel plant	
	Sept – Protocol on Alexandria shipyard	
Oct – Khrushchev, Nasser meet at UN	Oct – Economic minister in USSR: long-term trade agreement	
Nov – Marshal Amir heads government delegation to USSR: arms agreement	Nov – Protocols on various industrial projects	Nov – Russian patriarch heads religious delegation to UAR
		Dec – Cultural agreement for 1961-62
1961		
Apr – Parliamentary delegation in USSR		Apr – Communications minister in UAR
	July – Atomic reactor completed – Decrees on nationalization, agrarian reform in UAR	July – Journalists' delegation in UAR for anniversary
Sept – Syria leaves UAR		
Dec – Naval delegation in UAR		
1962		
	Jan – Power minister in UAR for Aswan anniversary – Protocols on various projects	
		Feb – Cultural protocol
Mar – Charter of national action adopted in UAR (political, economic reforms)	Mar – Contract for steel mills at Helwan	
June – Reported purchase of military planes (47)	June – Finance minister in USSR – 3-year trade agreement – Aswan minister in USSR to study Soviet dams	June – TU delegation in USSR
July – Khrushchev's daughter and son-in-law Adzhubey in UAR for 10th anniversary	July – New agreement on Aswan dam: earlier credits refinanced (48)	July – TU delegation in UAR for 10th anniversary
Oct – Military delegation in UAR	Oct – Protocol on oil refinery	
Dec – CPR delegation in UAR to give Chinese side of Sino-Soviet dispute		
1963		
	Jan – Power minister in UAR for Aswan anniversary: protocol on final stages of construction	

	Political	Economic	Cultural
1963 (cont.)			
Feb			– Education minister in USSR – Cultural protocol for 1963–64
Mar		– Training centres completed at Aswan, Alexandria	– Education delegation in UAR
Apr	– Premier Ali Sabri stops in USSR en route to CPR – Reported installation of Soviet missiles in UAR (49)		– Radio delegation in USSR
June	– Adzhubey, wife in UAR – Marshal Amir leads military delegation to USSR – Vice-president Nixon in UAR	– CREDIT AGREEMENT for power equipment (reported $44m) (50) – Aviation delegation in USSR: air service agreement	
July			– Railway TU leaders in UAR
Aug			– Social affairs minister leads delegation to UAR
Oct	– Adzhubey again in UAR	– Protocol on radio, TV plant	– Cinema delegation in UAR for Soviet film festival
Nov		– Industries minister in USSR for aid talks	
Dec	– Chou En-lai in UAR – Deputy foreign minister Lapin in UAR		– Health minister in UAR
1964			
Jan		– Government delegation in UAR for Aswan anniversary	– TU delegation in UAR
Feb		– Co-operative agreement on fishing – Coking, pharmaceutical plants completed	– Academic delegation in UAR
Mar	– RSFSR social affairs minister in UAR – CP prisoners released in UAR		
Apr		– Contract for chemical plant	
May	– KHRUSHCHEV IN UAR on 16-day visit for opening of Aswan dam (first stage)	– CREDIT AGREEMENT for second development plan ($277m)	
June		– Economic delegation in UAR	
Aug	– Deputy premier in USSR	– Aswan minister in USSR	
Sept	– PREMIER ALI SABRI IN USSR for 9-day visit	– Protocols on various projects under May 1964 credit	
Nov	– Marshal Amir heads military delegation to USSR for anniversary: arms agreement (51) – Deputy foreign minister Malik in UAR		
Dec	– Deputy premier Shelepin heads parliamentary delegation to UAR	– Deputy premier heads trade delegation to USSR: protocol	
1965			
Jan	– Military delegation in USSR	– CPR credit for industrial projects ($80m)	

	Political	Economic	Cultural
1965 (cont.)			
		Feb – Agricultural delegation in UAR	Feb – Cultural protocol
Mar	– Admiral Gorshkov heads military delegation to UAR		
Apr	– Government delegation in USSR for May Day – Ali Sabri in CPR		
June	– Chou En-lai in UAR en route to abortive Algiers conference	June – Deputy premier Novikov heads economic delegation to UAR	
July	– Military delegation in USSR: arms agreement	July – Reported grain credit to UAR ($21m) (52)	
Aug	– NASSER IN USSR for 5-day visit – Military delegation in USSR		
			Sept – TV exchange agreement
Dec	– Deputy defence minister Grechko in UAR	Dec – Trade minister Patolichev in UAR: 5-year trade agreement	
1966			
		Jan – Economic delegation in UAR: protocols on metallurgical complex, other projects	
Feb	– Navy chief in USSR – Deputy foreign minister Kuznetsov in UAR		Feb – Agreement on tracking space flights
Mar	– ASU delegation in Moscow for XXIII congress		
			Apr – Cultural delegation in UAR – Minister of professional education in UAR
May	– KOSYGIN IN UAR for 8-day visit, accompanied by Gromyko, Admiral Gorshkov	May – Additional protocols on second development plan projects	
June	– Deputy foreign minister in USSR	June – Trade delegation in UAR: contract for cotton deliveries to USSR	
Aug	– ASU delegation in USSR – Soviet naval squadron in UAR	Aug – Deputy minister for electrical industry in USSR	
Sept	– Deputy foreign minister Semenov in UAR – Provincial governors in USSR	Sept – Economic delegation in UAR for wage talks	
		Oct – Engineers in USSR for 6-month study of cotton growing, irrigation	
Nov	– Marshal Amir in USSR for military talks		Nov – Economist Liberman in UAR
			Dec – Cultural protocol for 1967–68
1967			
Jan	– Moscow city delegation in Cairo	Jan – Deputy premier Yefremov in UAR for Aswan anniversary	

	Political	Economic	Cultural
1967 (cont.)			
Jan		– Land reclamation minister in UAR for irrigation study	
Feb	– Mukhitdinov stops in Cairo en route home from Yemen	– Trade delegation in UAR	– Radio delegation in USSR – Cultural minister Furtseva in UAR
Mar	– Gromyko in UAR	– Economic delegation in UAR for aid talks – Fisheries minister in UAR	– TU delegation in USSR
Apr	– CPSU delegation in UAR – Parliamentary delegation in USSR		– TU delegation in UAR
May	– Defence minister in USSR		
June	– Arab-Israeli 6-day war: USSR supports Arabs in UN – PODGORNYY IN UAR for 3-day visit – Chief of staff Zakharov in UAR: arms agreement	– Reported CPR credit ($21m) (53)	
July	– Soviet naval vessels stop at Port Said, Alexandria for a month – Deputy foreign minister Malik in UAR – Chief of staff Riyad heads military delegation to USSR	– Gift of foodstuffs to UAR – Protocol on pumping station	
Aug		– Trade protocol	– Tourism minister in USSR: agreement on tourist exchange
Sept	– Delegation in Baku for international conference of Eastern peoples – Foreign minister Riyad in USSR	– Protocol on Aswan equipment	
Oct	– Deputy defence minister in UAR – Soviet vessels call at Alexandria, Port Said		
Nov	– Vice-president Ali Sabri heads party-government delegation to USSR for anniversary		
1968			
Jan	– Deputy premier Mazurov leads government delegation to UAR – Soviet bombers visit Cairo	– Foreign trade minister in USSR: protocol for 1968	– Higher education delegation in USSR – Atomic scientists in USSR for conference
Feb		– Agreement to resume work on Helwan steel complex	
Mar	– Defence minister Grechko in UAR	– "March 30 programme" published in UAR (economic reforms)	
Apr	– Foreign minister Riyad in USSR	– Agreement on tele-communications improvement in UAR	
May			– Education minister in USSR: cultural protocol for 1969-70
June			– New Soviet cultural centre opens in Cairo; also one in Alexandria

	Political	Economic	Cultural

1968 (cont.)

	Political	Economic	Cultural
July	NASSER IN USSR for 6-day state visit; returns to USSR for medical treatment	July – Agreement on ship building programme at Alexandria	
Aug	Reported arms agreement (54)	Aug – Irrigation minister in USSR	
			Sept – TU delegation in USSR – Satellite tracking station completed
		Oct – Civil aviation minister in UAR for air service talks	
		Nov – Deputy premier Yefremov in UAR for talks on Aswan project: protocols	
Dec	Gromyko in UAR	Dec – Deputy electrification minister appointed to advise in Cairo – Joint USSR-UAR fishing commission meets in Moscow	Dec – Deputy social affairs minister in USSR

1969

	Political	Economic	Cultural
Jan	– Moscow delegation in Cairo – Reported agreement on planes (55) – Delegation in Cairo for Arab solidarity conference	Jan – Protocol on fishing industry and training – Agreement on construction of ships for USSR at Alexandria	Jan – Shelepin heads TU delegation to Cairo for conference – Space experts in UAR to discuss tracking station
		Feb – Trade protocol for 1969-70	Feb – Cultural delegation in UAR: protocol for 1969 – Lawyers in UAR – Education delegation in USSR
			Mar – Writers, scientists in UAR – High TU officials in USSR
		Apr – Trade delegation in USSR: contract on wheat deliveries to UAR – Skachkov in UAR for opening of steel mills – Agricultural delegation in USSR to study irrigation, cotton growing	Apr – Teachers' delegation in USSR
May	Komsomol delegation in UAR	May – Protocol on oil prospecting	May – Youth minister in USSR – TU delegation in UAR
June	Gromyko in UAR	June – Gift of industrial safety equipment – Agricultural delegation in UAR	June – TU delegation in Central Asia – Food workers in USSR – Scientific mission in UAR
July	Interior minister in USSR	July – Minister of industry in USSR: protocol on phosphorus, aluminium works	July – Minister of higher education in USSR – Patriarch of Alexandria in USSR – Woodworkers in USSR
Aug	Parliamentary delegation in USSR	Aug – Trade minister in USSR	
Sept	ASU youth delegation in USSR		Sept – Radio delegation in USSR: protocol on broadcasting exchange
Oct	ASU official in USSR		Oct – Education minister in UAR: protocol on training of

EGYPT

	Political	Economic	Cultural
1969 (cont.)			
			Oct (cont.) industrial instructors, labour university at Aswan
Nov		– Contract for delivery of sheet metal to USSR from Helwan plant – Deputy premier Novikov in UAR for aid talks – Agricultural delegation in Moscow for collective farm conference	
Dec	– Vice-president Sadat heads high delegation to USSR for talks on Middle East crisis	– Economic delegation in USSR: trade protocol – Shipping delegation in Alexandria: protocol on 1959 agreement	
1970			
Jan	– Supreme Soviet delegation in UAR – Another Supreme Soviet delegation in Cairo for parliamentary conference		
Feb	– ASU delegation in USSR		
Mar	– Deputy foreign minister Vinogradov in UAR – Arms deliveries to UAR speeded up	– Communications minister in USSR: protocol	
Apr	– Black Sea fleet commander in Cairo – Ali Sabri in Moscow for Lenin centenary		
May	– Israel charges Soviet pilots operational in UAR – Armenian CP secretary in Cairo for conference on Cambodia – ASU youth delegation in Moscow for Komsomol congress	– Odessa trade delegation in Alexandria – Airlines director in USSR to buy commercial aircraft	– Radio officials in Moscow for Lenin centenary – Lenin peace prize to Egyptian writer – Cultural minister in USSR
June	– NASSER IN USSR for 19-day visit and extended talks on Middle East crisis	– Skachkov stops in UAR en route home from Sudan	
July	– Suez governor in Leningrad – Komsomol delegation in UAR: protocol on co-operation with ASU youth movement – Ali Sabri again in Moscow	– Minister of industry in Moscow to open Egyptian exhibition – Land reclamation minister in UAR for gift of mechanized farm	
Aug	– Air force commander in UAR following loss of Soviet combat pilots – 90-day cease-fire begins along Suez Canal (7 August)		
Sept	– Nasser dies; Kosygin heads delegation to Cairo for funeral; CPR delegation also present	– Red Sea fishing survey completed by Soviet scientists	– Muslim delegation in Central Asia: agreement on scholarships for Soviet Muslims
Oct	– Sadat elected Nasser's successor – Deputy premier Polyanskiy stops in Cairo en route to Somalia		– Education delegations in USSR
Nov			– Cultural officials in Georgia

Political	Economic	Cultural

1970 (cont.)

Dec - Ponomarev heads CPSU delegation to Cairo for talks with ASU
- Ali Sabri heads high delegation to USSR

Dec - Deputy oil minister in UAR
- Deputy power minister in UAR for talks on completion of Aswan dam
- UAR fisheries delegation in Moscow for meeting of joint commission

ferences

(1)   Bol'shaya sovetskaya entsiklopediya, Vol. 15 (1952); see Mizan, February 1959, p. 4.
(2)   TASS, 25 and 28 November, 1954; for fuller discussion of Soviet policies during this period, see Laqueur, The Soviet Union and the Middle East, pp. 195-97.
(3)   For a more detailed analysis of Nasser's motives in encouraging Soviet activity in the Middle East, see Laqueur, op. cit., pp. 213-16.
(4)   V.B. Lutskiy, writing in Sovetskoye Vostokovedeniye, No. 2 (March-April), 1957.
(5)   E.g. L.N. Vatolina, writing in Sovremennyy Vostok, No. 6 (June), 1958 (reviewed in Mizan, February 1959, p. 7).
(6)   The impact of Nasser's anti-Communist campaign on a general shift in Soviet Third World policies is discussed in more detail in my forthcoming study, Russia and the Third World.
(7)   Pravda, 28 January, 1959.
(8)   Pravda, 31 January, 1959.
(9)   Izvestiya, 17 March, 1959 (translated in Mizan, April 1959, Appendix, pp. 2-3); see also an editorial in Pravda, 30 March, 1959.
(10)   Laqueur, The Struggle for the Middle East, p. 65, citing Western sources; the Soviet press does not show such strong personal condemnation of Nasser.
(11)   Pravda, 31 May, 1961.
(12)   E.g. Izvestiya, 8 January, 1960.
(13)   Pravda, 24 August, 1961.
(14)   Mirovaya ekonomika i mezhdunarodnyye otnosheniya, No. 3 (March), 1962 (cited in Mizan, April 1962, pp. 4-5).
(15)   New Times, No. 4 (24 January), 1962, p. 12.
(16)   Mirovaya ekonomika i mezhdunarodnyye otnosheniya No. 4 (April), 1962, p. 79 (translated in Thornton, The Third World in Soviet Perspective, pp. 297-98).
(17)   Mirovaya ekonomika i mezhdunarodnyye otnosheniya No. 2 (February), 1963, p. 65.
(18)   Mirovaya ekonomika i mezhdunarodnyye otnosheniya No. 5 (May), 1963, p. 51.
(19)   The text of the communiqué as well as a detailed summary of Khrushchev's statements during the UAR trip, including both Egyptian and official Russian texts where they differ, may be found in Mizan, May 1964, pp. 57-68.
(20)   Pravda, 28 May, 1964.
(21)   E.g. Ye. Primakov in Pravda, 25 November, 1965.
(22)   K.I. Grishechkin, in a chapter in L.V. Goncharov, Ekonomiki Afriki, 1965 (cited in Mizan, March-April 1966, p. 68).
(23)   See Mirskiy in New Times, No. 48 (1 December), 1965, p. 5.
(24)   I.I. Garshin, in a chapter in Ye. M. Zhukov, Sovremennyye teorii sotsializma "natsional'nogo tipa", 1967, p. 148. For a fuller discussion of Soviet views on Egyptian socialism, see Mizan, March-April 1966, pp. 67-72 and January-February 1968, pp. 38-43.
(25)   See New Times, No. 26(19 July), 1967, p. 7; also Za rubezhom, No. 27 (18 July), 1967, pp. 7-8.
(26)   E.g. Sergey Barudin in Pravda, 30 May, 1970.
(27)   Pravda, 27 December, 1970; details of Soviet-Egyptian co-operation are given below.
(28)   Izvestiya, 14 July, 1967.
(29)   Za rubezhom, No. 39 (20 September), 1967, p. 15.
(30)   E.g. Yu. Glukhov in Pravda, 30 July, 1970.
(31)   Pravda, 17 October, 1970.

(32)   Glukhov in Pravda, 29 November, 1970.
(33)   V. Matveyev in Izvestiya, 20 February, 1971.
(34)   For more detailed discussion of Chinese-Egyptian relations, see Harold C. Hinton, Communist China in World Politics, Houghton Mifflin, 1966, pp. 178-88 passim.
(35)   Other estimates to the end of 1965 (the date of the last announced credit) are as follows:

The USSR and Developing Countries (1965), p. 63	$1,012,000,000
Soviet Union - Friend of the Arab Peoples (1966), p. 31	$1,012,000,000
U.S. Department of State, RECS-5, 9 May, 1970, p. 3.	$1,011,000,000
Stokke, Soviet and East European Trade and Aid in Africa (1967), pp. 83-84	$934,000,000
Ob"yedinennaya Arabskaya Respublika: spravochnik (1968), p. 415	$842,000,000
Goldman, Soviet Foreign Aid (1967), p. 74	$842,000,000
Chertkov, SSSR i razvivayushchiyesya strany (1966), p. 52	$817,000,000
Matyukhin, Ob"yedinennaya Arabskaya Respublika (1966), p. 121	$772,000,000

(36)   For more detailed studies, see, inter alia, Goldman, op. cit., pp. 61-70; Stokke, op. cit., pp. 123-40, and Tansky, U.S. and U.S.S.R. Aid to Developing Countries, pp. 138-45.
(37)   Foreign Broadcast Information Service (FBIS), 14 May, 1966, monitoring a Russian radio programme.
(38)   Goldman, op cit., p. 74.
(39)   See The Middle East and North Africa, 1969-70, pp. 811-12.
(40)   Professor Ra'anan's argument, based on some circumstantial evidence but particularly on a 1965 Soviet source (International Affairs, No. 5, 1965, p. 61), is that the agreement was concluded in February, not September as generally believed; The USSR Arms the Third World, pp. 76ff. The circumstantial evidence, in my view, merits consideration, but the reference to a February date in the International Affairs article was probably inadvertent.
(41)   See Military Balance,1967-1968, pp. 39-42 and Joshua and Gibert, Arms for the Third World, p. 24.
(42)   A.Y. Yodfat, "Arms and Influence in Egypt - the Record of Soviet Military Assistance since June 1967", New Middle East, No. 10 (July 1969), pp. 27-32 and Lawrence L. Whetten, "June 1967 to June 1971", New Middle East, No. 33 (June 1971), p. 25.
(43)   See Military Balance 1970-1971, p. 45, and articles by William Beecher and Drew Middleton, respectively, in The Times, 14 May, 1970, and the New York Times, 3 October, 1970, p. 7.
(44)   See U.S. Department of State, RSES-35, 12 August, 1970, pp. 54-55.
(45)   Ra'anan, op. cit., pp. 83-84.
(46)   Joshua and Gibert, op.cit., p. 13, citing Western news sources.
(47)   Goldman, op. cit., p. 71.
(48)   Some Western sources show a supplementary credit of $170m at this time; see discussion of Soviet credits above.
(49)   Stephen P. Gibert, "Wars of Liberation and Soviet Military Aid Policy", Orbis, Fall 1966, p. 854.
(50)   Mizan, May 1964, p. 66, citing a statement by

President Nasser; also Goldman, op. cit., p. 74.

(51) Laqueur, The Struggle for the Middle East, p. 73.

(52) Goldman, op. cit., p. 80.

(53) U.S. Department of State, RSE-65, 5 September, 1969, p. 3.

(54) The Military Balance, 1969-1970, p. 60.

(55) Ibid.; the agreement was said to provide for delivery of 200 advanced MIG fighters.

Soviet relations with Iran must be seen in the context of policies towards the so-called Northern tier. The Northern tier has no essential cohesion, in race, religion, or other denomination. It exists more in the minds of students of world politics who find it convenient to postulate this echelon of states as a barrier, or bridge, between Russia and the Arab community.

The Northern tier had a certain reality in Russian eyes in the mid-1950s. Four of the five states then counted in the Northern tier - Turkey, Iraq, Pakistan and Iran - developed treaty obligations to each other as well as to the West, in an alliance system directed against the USSR. The Russians could not ignore this reality. While efforts were made to weaken the commitments of this or that nation to the alliance system (known originally as the Baghdad Pact and after 1958 as the Central Treaty Organization, or CENTO), the main thrust of Soviet policy for some years was to "overleap" or "bypass" the Northern tier by cultivating friendly relations with the Arab world south of it. How successful this strategy was is discussed elsewhere in this volume.

By the early 1960s a number of developments - the instability and inconstancy, by Soviet lights, of certain Arab states; a more pragmatic view of Middle East affairs in Moscow; a greater flexibility in the attitude of some states in the Northern tier - led the Russians to reconsider their strategies in this region. No tidily co-ordinated policy can be detected, but one by one the hostile states in the Northern tier were approached by Moscow and a wholly new relationship worked out. Having attempted without notable success to neutralize these states with threats, cajolery and ostracism, the Russians in the 1960s sought to neutralize the Northern tier with kindness.

Soviet policies in Iran from 1955 to 1970 best reflect these changing perceptions of the Northern tier and the strategies devised to protect Russia's interests.

*   *   *

During the latter half of the 1950s the Russians alternated between sharp criticism of Iran for adhering to the Baghdad Pact and stubborn efforts to lure her away. When Tehran's adherence to the pact was announced, Molotov (then Foreign Minister) protested that the action was "contrary to Iran's good neighbour relations with the Soviet Union and to certain of Iran's treaty obligations". (1) Molotov had specifically in mind the 1921 and 1927 Soviet-Iranian Treaties, which stipulated that neither state would enter into any military alliance directed against the other; Iran, of course, denied that the Baghdad Pact was directed against the USSR, but the Russians were not reassured and continued to criticize the Shah's government.

In 1956, on the other hand, during and after the Shah's visit to Russia, Moscow made a number of conciliatory gestures: aid was offered, Russia yielded its rights in the Iranian Oil Company, and an expanded trade protocol was negotiated. During the next two years there were a number of official exchanges between the two countries, and various diplomatic and economic agreements were concluded (see Chronology). Meanwhile the Soviet press was more restrained than it had been, though continuing to accent the liabilities of Tehran's membership in the Baghdad Pact. (2)

A turn for the worse in Soviet-Persian relations occurred in the autumn of 1958 when the United States, following Qasim's coup in Iraq, sought to shore up CENTO by concluding a bi-lateral military pact with Tehran. A Soviet Note to Iran at the end of October protested sharply against the proposed agreement "which intensifies still further the military, aggressive aspect of the Baghdad Pact . . . and exposes the southern frontier of the Soviet Union to immediate danger". Russia would be obliged "to reappraise the present state of Soviet-Iranian relations", including the scheduled visit to Tehran of President Voroshilov. (3) In January 1959 a Soviet delegation under Deputy Foreign Minister V.S. Semenov spent a fortnight in Tehran exploring the possibilities of a non-aggression pact between Russia and Iran, in lieu of the American agreement and in return for Soviet aid. The talks failed and Soviet comments on the failure were as bitter as any Moscow had directed against an Afro-Asian power since Soviet policies towards the Third World became more moderate in the mid-1950s. A statement by Semenov laid the blame squarely on Tehran: in going back on its own earlier draft of a non-aggression pact, the Shah's government had clearly played "a game of evil intentions designed to mislead public opinion". (4) Pravda's "Observer" remarked ominously that Tehran's rejection of a pact with the USSR meant a turning point in Soviet-Iranian relations. (5) Khrushchev carried the assault on Iran's policies to the Shah himself: "The Shah of Iran fears, above all, his own people, and by the signing of a bi-lateral military pact with the United States wants to ensure that American troops shall protect his throne." When the Shah objected to these discourteous remarks, Khrushchev made a point of repeating them. (6)

The conclusion of the American-Iranian defence pact in March closed the episode, insofar as any rapprochement between Moscow and Tehran was concerned. The Soviet Ambassador left Tehran for nine months, and for the next three and a half years relations were minimal. The Russian press continued to criticize Iran's foreign policy and to hold the Shah personally responsible for it. Pravda's "Observer" wrote in February 1960: "In his blind hatred of Communism and dreaming of leading an alliance of all reactionary forces in the Middle East against the national liberation movement . . . the Shah drags his country further down the road to the abyss." (7) Interest in domestic affairs revived during the 1961 elections when Mohammed Mossadegh briefly reappeared on the national scene at the head of a new National Front. (8) However, the return to conservative policies under the Amini government in 1962 cooled Soviet enthusiasm. The agrarian reform of January 1962, subsequently to be praised by Soviet writers, was ridiculed at the time. "This notorious 'reform'", a Soviet writer observed in June, "is intended to distract the popular masses from the struggle for their rights and, what is more important, to strengthen the rotten monarchical regime." (9) Moscow apparently made occasional overtures to Tehran to improve relations, (10) but little of this effort filtered down to the daily Soviet press which remained persistently hostile.

It should be noted that the uncompromising attitude of the Russian press towards Iran from 1959 to 1962 coincided with a period of heightened militancy in Soviet Third World policies generally. This gave a sharper edge to Soviet commentaries - certainly sharper than from 1955 to 1958 when Iran's alliance with the West was as close as during the three years following. Soviet militancy, then, no less than Iranian intransigence, contributed to the impasse in relations between the two nations after the American-Iranian pact of 1959. By the same token, Moscow's retreat from militancy and Tehran's from intransigence led to rapprochement in 1962. In an exchange of letters in September which marked an important shift in Russian-Persian relations, Iran assured the Soviet Union that "it will not give to any foreign state the right to have rocket bases of any type on the territory of Persia"; Russia, in return, assured Iran of its good will. (11) Khrushchev, addressing the Supreme Soviet in December, expressed satisfaction that "much of what had hampered the development of normal relations between the Soviet Union and Iran" had been eliminated; "we hope a good beginning will be carried further." (12)

The course of Soviet-Iranian relations ran smoothly after 1962. In fact, there was no more dramatic improvement in Soviet relations with any Afro-Asian nation during the 1960s than with Iran. Political ties multiplied as the years passed. By the end of the decade Iran was one of Russia's most active partners in economic co-operation and had even become a recipient of Soviet arms (see below). Soviet commentators meanwhile became more kindly disposed towards Iran. The 1962 reforms were belatedly approved as "a definite step forward" and a way of helping Iran "to break away from feudalism and foreign dependence". (13) It did not even matter, one Soviet specialist implied in 1966, that the reforms might lead "to a deepening of class differentiation in rural areas and to the formation of a relatively more influential and numerous stratum of kulaks"; this was all part of the process of "broadening the class base of the monarchy by attracting to its side moderate circles of the national bourgeoisie, liberal landowners and well-to-do peasants", a coalition capable of pursuing in Iran an honestly "national course in domestic and foreign policy". (14) In 1969 a Soviet journalist remarked that the appearance of private farms and corporations in Persia and the replacement of land-owners by capitalists should be looked upon as signs of progress, as the country lifted itself from the Middle Ages. (15) Russian observers, in short, were tolerant of virtually all domestic developments in Persia so long as Tehran grew no closer to the West in its foreign policy. Criticism of Iran's continuing ties to CENTO and of the 1959 defence alliance with the United States was meanwhile muted in the Soviet press after 1962; nor did the Russians openly fault the Iranians for their long estrangement with Cairo, which lasted from 1960 to 1968.

Moscow remained neutral, however, with regard to Tehran's claims to Bahrain in the Persian Gulf. Early in the 1950s, before Soviet interest in the Arab world had developed fully, the Russians had supported these claims against Saudi Arabia's. Nasser's persistent interest in keeping the entire Western shore of the gulf under Arab control, however, led to a shift in Moscow's position on Bahrain. For a time, early in the 1960s, Russia appeared to favour Arab claims, but by 1968, when diplomatic relations between Iran and Egypt were restored, Moscow was officially neutral in the matter. (16)

Soviet interest in the Persian Communists declined steadily after their abortive efforts in 1952. Their party, the Tudeh, had been illegal since 1949 and the Central Committee apparently met abroad. Moreover, the Tudeh remained sharply critical of the Shah and his reforms at a time when Soviet criticism had been suspended. To judge from published commentaries in the USSR, Russian attention to the Iranian Communists had all but disappeared by 1970, though Tudeh leaders still came to Moscow periodically for major conferences and celebrations (see Chronology).

The Soviet-Iranian relationship after 1962, it should be noted, was expressed predominantly in commercial and economic terms rather than political or ideological. The landmarks in the relationship were such episodes as the agreement on natural gas deliveries in 1966, the establishment of a joint economic commission in 1968, and the completion of the Soviet-Iranian pipeline in 1970. High political delegations were exchanged constantly, to be sure, but they were ceremonial for the most part or engaged in relatively minor negotiations, such as border adjustments. This does not mean, of course, that political considerations were unimportant in bringing the two nations together; indeed, on the Soviet side, political considerations appear to have been the main reason for Moscow's policies - that is, the neutralization of Iran by making Tehran less dependent on the United States and on CENTO. This, however, was the rationale for détente, not its substance. If reference was occasionally made to larger political consequences of the alliance - for instance, Podgornyy's remarking, on the occasion of the dedication of the pipeline, that Soviet-Persian friendship had a stabilizing effect on the unsettled politics of the Middle East(17) - this was merely a footnote to spiralling economic collaboration.

Economic, Military and Cultural Relations

Soviet-Iranian trade, to begin with the most persistent area of economic co-operation between the two nations, remained active during the 16 years under review. Iran was Russia's leading Afro-Asian partner in trade in the mid-1950s before the surge in trade with the Third World began; trade levels dropped only slightly during the years of greatest uneasiness in the relationship, from 1958 to 1962; from 1965 to 1969 there was a nearly sevenfold increase in Soviet-Iranian trade and Iran became Russia's third largest trading partner in Asia, Africa, and the Middle East (after the UAR and India). The bulk of the trade consisted of Iranian exports to Russia, which sometimes accounted for as much as 20 per cent of total Iranian exports; Soviet exports to Iran, on the other hand, rarely exceeded three per cent of Iranian imports. Russia ranked sixth among Iran's trading partners at the end of the 1960s (after West Germany, the United States, England, Italy and Japan), but it was anticipated that Soviet-Iranian trade would grow significantly in the 1970s; by 1974 Russia was expected to provide 12 per cent of Iranian imports. (18)

Economic aid to Iran, though promised during the Shah's visit to Moscow in 1956 and held forth as bait during the abortive 1959 talks (see above), was first spelt out in a credit agreement only in 1963, following Tehran's pledge not to allow foreign missile bases in the country. The initial credit of $39 million, mainly for a power station on the Aras River, was followed by two larger grants in 1966 and 1968; the 1966 credit of $290 million was the second largest ever extended by the USSR to a Third World nation in a single agreement (surpassed only by the 1959 loan to India for the Third Five-Year Plan). The 1966 and 1968 credits were for a steel plant at Isfahan, the Soviet-Iranian pipeline for natural gas and a variety of smaller projects. Total Soviet aid through the 1960s was considerably less than American aid had been - an estimated $1.9 billion from 1954 to 1967 (when American assistance ended on the argument that Iran no longer needed it) - but was nevertheless a powerful stimulant to the Iranian economy and, as noted above, an important factor in Soviet-Iranian relations.   From 1963 to the end of 1969 Russia provided more economic credit to Iran than to any other Third World nation except India, and over the 16-year period, 1954-1969, Iran ranked fourth among the recipients of Soviet aid (after India, the UAR and Afghanistan).

The Soviet Union first sold arms to Persia in 1967, during a period when Tehran was apparently dissatisfied with American military aid policies. (19)   Given the long-standing rivalry between the Iranians and Arabs, especially in the Persian Gulf, the Russians were careful to transfer to Iran only arms which could not be used aggressively against their Arab allies.   Thus Moscow refused to give surface-to-air missiles reportedly requested by Tehran and confined its deliveries to anti-aircraft guns, trucks and armoured vehicles. (20)   One should not exaggerate the importance of these deliveries to Iran's military capability.   The United States remained the principal supplier of arms to Iran: from 1956 to the end of 1967 the United States had supplied arms to Tehran valued at more than $625 million - as compared to Russia's $110 million - and it is probable that a long-term American-Iranian arms agreement in June 1968 pledged nearly as much again. (21)   Russian arms transfers to Iran must accordingly be regarded as a friendly gesture, a reminder that Tehran need not always rely on the United States, rather than as a serious effort to develop Persia's military posture.

Cultural co-operation between Russia and Iran, despite the formation of a Soviet-Iranian Cultural Relations Society in Moscow in 1963 and the initialling of a cultural agreement in 1966, developed much less rapidly than economic co-operation.   Comparatively few delegations were exchanged.   In 1967 Tehran relaxed its policy of not allowing Iranians to train in socialist countries, and an estimated 460 Persians took technical courses in the USSR during the next two years; 275 had completed these courses by the autumn of 1970. (22)

Chronology

	Political	Economic	Cultural
Pre-1956			
1921	Agreement on diplomatic relations (embassies exchanged in 1925)		
1927	Soviet-Iranian neutrality treaty		
July 1952	National front returns Mossadegh to power; supported by Tudeh		
		June 1953 Trade agreement	
Aug 1953	Mossadegh overthrown by military-royalist forces; Tudeh persecuted		
		June 1954 Trade agreement renewed	
Dec 1954	Frontier agreement		
Oct 1955	Iran adheres to Baghdad pact		
1956			
Jan	Parliamentary delegation in USSR		
		Apr – National bank director in USSR for aid talks	
June	SHAH IN USSR for 13-day visit	June – Promise of technical assistance	
		Aug – USSR cedes rights in Iranian oil company	
		Sept – Trade protocol for 1957	
			Dec – Journalists in USSR
1957			
Jan	Parliamentary delegation in Iran		
		Apr – Trade agreement for 1957-59 – Transit agreement (ratified Oct 1962)	
May	New frontier agreement (ratified Oct 1962)		
		July – Aid to earthquake victims	
		Aug – Agreement on joint development of Araks, Atrek rivers: irrigation and power stations planned	
1958			
		Jan – Railway agreement	
		Mar – Protocol on power, irrigation projects	
May	Government delegation in USSR		
July	United States proposes defence pact with Iran		
Sept	Parliamentary delegation in USSR		

IRAN

	Political	Economic	Cultural
1959			
Jan	– Tudeh delegation in USSR for XXI congress – Foreign office delegation in Iran for talks on non-aggression treaty in return for aid: talks fail		
Mar	– Iranian-US defence pact		
1960			
		Feb – Granary promised	
Dec	– Tudeh delegation in Moscow for world conference		
1961			
Oct	– Tudeh delegation in Moscow for XXII congress		
1962			
		Jan – Agrarian reform law passed in Iran	
Apr	– Shah in United States		
		May – Aid for flood victims – Aid promised for locust control	
		June – Trade protocol for 1962	
		July – Gift of tractors	
		Aug – Aid for earthquake victims	
Sept	– Iran pledges no foreign missile bases		
Oct	– Government delegation in USSR for ratification of transit, frontier agreements		
Dec	– Deputy foreign minister in Iran		
1963			
			Mar – Cultural delegation in USSR
		July – CREDIT AGREEMENT for power station, granaries, dredgers ($39m)	
			Oct – Cultural delegation in Iran
Nov	– BREZHNEV IN IRAN for 9-day visit	Nov – Transit protocol	
		Dec – Contract for oil survey	Dec – Orientalists in Iran to visit universities
1964			
June	– Royal princess in USSR	June – Economic minister in USSR: long-term trade, air agreements	
			Sept – Cultural delegation in USSR
1965			
June	– SHAH IN USSR for 12-day visit	June – CREDIT AGREEMENT for steel mill, tool plant, pipe line ($290m)	

Political	Economic	Cultural
1965 (cont.)	Oct – Transit protocol	
	Dec – Agricultural minister in USSR	
1966	Jan – Economic delegation in USSR: protocol on 1965 credit; agreement on natural gas deliveries to USSR	Jan – Doctors in Iran
Mar – Tudeh delegation in USSR for XXIII congress – Deputy foreign minister Kuznetsov in Iran		
		May – Academic delegation in USSR
June – Princess in USSR	June – Economic delegation in Iran: protocols on dam, roads, industrial projects	
Aug – Parliamentary delegation in USSR		Aug – Cultural agreement
	Oct – Trade delegation in USSR – Protocol on power station	
	Nov – Protocol on port expansion	
		Dec – Princess, cultural minister lead delegation to USSR
1967 Feb – Arms agreement ($110m credit)	Feb – Trade minister Patolichev in Iran: 5-year trade agreement	
	Mar – National bank director in USSR	
Apr – Government delegation in Iran	Apr – Gosplan chief in Iran: agreement on ore prospecting	
	June – Oil experts in USSR to discuss pipeline construction	
July – PREMIER HOVEYDA IN USSR for 9-day visit	July – Supplementary protocol on 1965 credit	
	Aug – Protocol on sugar deliveries to Iran	Aug – Journalists in USSR
Sept – Delegation in Baku for conference		Sept – Railway workers in USSR
Oct – Government delegation in USSR for anniversary	Oct – Supplementary protocol on dam, power station and Isfahan steel mill	
Dec – Chief of staff heads military delegation to USSR	Dec – Electrical experts in Iran	
1968 Jan – Parliamentary delegation in Iran		
	Mar – Economic delegation in Iran for start of work on steel plant	

	Political		Economic		Cultural

1968 (cont.)

	Political		Economic		Cultural
		Mar (cont.)	– Work begins on port expansion at Pahlavi and Nowshahr		
Apr	– KOSYGIN IN IRAN for 5-day visit	Apr	– Soviet industrial exhibition opens in Tehran		
May	– Marshal Zakharov leads military delegation to Iran				
June	– New arms agreement with USA	June	– Contract on pipeline construction and compressors – Soviet-Iranian economic commission established		
		July	– Deputy water and power minister in USSR for talks: agreement on electrical power from Azerbaydzhan		
		Aug	– Experts in USSR for talks on power station – Trade delegation in USSR for sugar purchases – Work starts on pipeline – First grain silos completed		
Sept	– SHAH IN USSR for 12-day visit	Sept	– Industrial delegation in USSR for aid talks: CREDIT AGREEMENT reported ($178m) (23) – Steel delegation in USSR for talks on Isfahan project – Agricultural delegation in USSR to discuss locust control		
				Oct	– Botanists in Iran – Cultural delegation in Iran
Dec	– Provincial governor in USSR	Dec	– Business delegation in USSR – Transport delegation in USSR: agreement on rail service – Trade agreement with Armenia, Azerbaydzhan		

1969

	Political		Economic		Cultural
Jan	– Deputy premier Novikov in Iran				
Feb	– Navy vessels visit Iran				
Mar	– Frontier protocol				
		Apr	– More silos completed – Transport delegation in Iran for further talks		
		May	– Agricultural minister in USSR to study rice and cotton production – Economic minister in USSR for trade, aid talks: protocol on long-range survey – Industrial exhibition opens in Moscow		
June	– Tudeh delegation in USSR for world conference	June	– Communications minister in USSR		

Political	Economic	Cultural
1969 (cont.)		
	July – Agreement on additional silos	July – TU leaders in USSR
		Aug – Cultural delegation in USSR – University delegation in Baku
	Oct – Protocol on freight turnover – Contract for fishing aid	
	Nov – Economic delegation in Iran for aid talks	
Dec – Hoveyda stops in Moscow en route home from Western Europe	Dec – Trade protocol	Dec – Workers' delegation in USSR
1970		
	Jan – Contract for cold storage plant in Tehran	
Mar – PODGORNYY IN IRAN for 7-day visit	Mar – Contract for new facilities at Isfahan steel works – Trade minister Patolichev in Iran: agreement for 1971-75	Mar – Science delegation in USSR: agreement on joint research
Apr – Radmanesh leads Tudeh delegation to USSR for Lenin jubilee	Apr – Shipping delegation in Tehran for talks on loading speed-up – Fish hatchery completed	
May – Government delegation in USSR for talks on border along artificial lakes: protocol prepared	May – Protocol on improved transport, cargo services between USSR and Iran	
	July – Economic minister in USSR to sign 1971-75 trade agreement; joint transport company established	July – Iranian prince in USSR to discuss sports
Aug – Parliamentary delegation in USSR	Aug – Agreement on natural gas sales to USSR	
	Sept – Foreign aid chief Skachkov in Iran: protocol on gas exports, steel works, power plants, farms, water use and other projects; CREDIT AGREEMENT for training centre ($9.9m)	
Oct – Kosygin, Hoveyda meet at Nasser's funeral	Oct – Podgornyy again in Iran for opening of gas pipeline	Oct – Conference of Soviet, Iranian doctors in Tehran
Nov – Majlis members in Armenia for anniversary – Queen in USSR on semi-official visit	Nov – Navigation delegation in Baku: protocol	
Dec – Border commission delegates in Tehran for signing of agreement – Moscow city delegation in Tehran	Dec – Soviet-built hydrofoil starts service in Persian Gulf	Dec – Cultural protocol for 1970-71

References

(1)   Pravda, 13 October, 1955.
(2)   See Mizan, February 1959, pp. 9-12.
(3)   Pravda, 1 November, 1958 (the note is translated in Mizan, January 1959, Appendix A).   The Russians believed at this time that the American-Persian agreement had already been concluded, which was not the case.
(4)   Pravda, 13 February, 1959 (translated in Mizan, March 1959, Appendix A).
(5)   Pravda, 14 February, 1959.
(6)   See Khrushchev's election speeches of 17 and 24 February, 1959; excerpts in Mizan, March 1959, Appendix B, pp. 1-6.
(7)   Pravda, 14 February, 1960.
(8)   See, for instance, Izvestiya, 27 July, 1961 and G. Mirskiy in Kommunist, No. 11, 1961 (cited in Mizan, December 1961, p. 15).   Mossadegh had received strong Soviet backing when he headed a National Front government with Tudeh support in 1952-53 and was still considered by Moscow to be the only "progressive" figure in Iranian politics.
(9)   G. Konstantinov, in Aziya i Afrika segodnya, No. 6 (June), 1962, p. 58.
(10)   For a discussion of Soviet approaches to Tehran in 1960 and 1961, see William B. Ballis, "Soviet-Iranian Relations during the Decade 1953-64", Bulletin, Institute for the Study of the USSR, November 1965, p. 18; see also Laqueur, The Struggle for the Middle East, p. 29.
(11)   Pravda, 16 September, 1962.
(12)   Pravda, 13 December, 1962.
(13)   V. Medvedev in New Times, No. 7 (20 February), 1963, pp. 22-23.
(14)   M.I. Volodarskiy, in Narody Azii i Afriki, No. 3 (May-June), 1966, p. 154.
(15)   T. Kolesnichenko, Pravda, 29 November, 1969.
(16)   For a discussion of changing Soviet views on Bahrain, see Mizan, March-April 1968, pp. 52-53.
(17)   Pravda, 29 October, 1970.
(18)   See A.Z. Arabadzhan, "O sovetsko-iranskom ekonomicheskom sotrudnichestve", Narody Azii i Afriki, No. 2 (March-April), 1968, p. 20; for Iranian trade figures between 1964 and 1968, see The Middle East and North Africa, 1969-70, pp. 264-65.
(19)   Iran was troubled by the suspension of American economic credits at this time but was more disturbed by Washington's suspension of arms sales to its ally Pakistan during the Kashmir dispute of 1965; should the United States do the same to Iran in some future crisis, Tehran might find itself without adequate defences because of reliance on American weaponry.   See Joshua and Gibert, Arms for the Third World, p. 21.
(20)   See Laqueur, op. cit., p. 40.
(21)   For the estimate of American military aid, see Joshua and Gibert, op. cit., p. 130 citing U.S. Department of Defense sources; for the Shah's efforts in 1968 to negotiate an additional $600 million see Laqueur, op. cit., p. 40.
(22)   Radio Moscow, 21 November, 1970; see also U.S. Department of State, RSE-25, 7 May, 1969, pp. 85-86.
(23)   U.S. Department of State, RSE-65, 5 September, 1969, p. 3.

Soviet relations with Iraq, after the revolution of 14 July, 1958, must be seen against the background of traditional Egyptian-Iraqi rivalry for leadership of the Arab world. This rivalry was especially acute after 1955 because of deep ideological differences between Nasser's revolutionary regime in Cairo and the conservative, Western-oriented regime of Nuri as-Sa'id in Baghdad. It was largely in consequence of this rivalry that Nasser, after Iraq's adherence to the Baghdad alliance in 1955, turned to Moscow: Nasser might have been prepared to lead an Arab coalition in collaboration with the West, but since this opportunity never seriously arose, he took the alternative course - Arab hegemony in collaboration with the socialist bloc.

The Iraqi revolution abruptly changed the profile of politics in the Middle East. The Baghdad Pact, a powerful threat to Russia's interests along her southern flank, was now crippled, or appeared to be so, with the loss of Iraq. Khrushchev expressed the prevailing sentiment in Moscow a week after the coup: "No one expected the Baghdad Pact would so soon cease to exist." (1) Such a reading of Qasim's revolution, needless to say, greatly stimulated Soviet activity in Iraq. Meanwhile, Nasser's hopes for a greater Arab republic were much encouraged by the prospects of Iraq joining it, and he immediately set out to ensure that this merger should take place. Much subsequent complexity in Middle East politics arose from Nasser's efforts in this regard and Qasim's resistance to them, for Qasim, observing the virtual disappearance of Syria after its merger with Egypt in January 1958, had no wish to see his revolution suffer the same fate. Qasim turned to Iraqi Communists for help in his struggle against pan-Arabists in Baghdad and found them to be willing and effective allies. It was indeed their success in blocking Nasser's plan for merger that led, at the end of 1958, to Nasser's bitter assault on Communists in the UAR - a development which led in turn to estrangement between Moscow and Cairo (see discussion under Egypt). (2)

Moscow's position on the merger question was unambiguous: traditionally opposed to pan-Arabism on ideological grounds and after the formation of the UAR on political grounds as well (since Soviet influence in Syria, which had been strong before merger, was now negligible), the Russians gave no support whatsoever to Nasser's project to bring Iraq into the Arab republic. They did more: they actively encouraged Qasim's defiance. Khrushchev, for instance, in greeting an Iraqi economic delegation in March 1959, cautioned his guests against a "premature union" with Egypt and said that how this matter developed "is not a matter of indifference to us". (3) It can be taken for granted, meanwhile, that Moscow strongly encouraged the Iraqi Communists in their support of Qasim on this issue - one of the few occasions when Arab Communist strategies and Moscow's coincided.

Soviet-Iraqi relations, it is clear from the foregoing, were launched on a cordial note after the 14 July revolution. Trade developed rapidly; from an insignificant trading partner of the USSR in 1958, Iraq ranked second only to the UAR in the Middle East during the Qasim years (1959-62). The credit extended in February 1959 ($137,500,000) was the second largest Third World credit extended by Russia until that time (after one to the UAR a year earlier). A steady pace of official exchanges was maintained for several years, climaxed by Mikoyan's visit

to Baghdad in April 1960. Meanwhile, official and unofficial commentaries on Iraq were enthusiastic. Khrushchev, in his greeting to the Iraqi delegation in March 1959 (cited above), complimented the regime on its economic and social reforms. "A more advanced system is being established in the Iraqi Republic", Khrushchev said, "than in neighbouring countries of the Arab East." This preference for Iraq over other Arab states was reflected in the writing of Soviet journalists and scholars until the end of 1960. (4)

Despite the early cordiality between Moscow and the Qasim regime, the relationship turned sour long before Qasim was overthrown. Economic co-operation continued (see below) and the Russians conscientiously sought to avoid diplomatic strains with Baghdad - for instance, over Kuwait (see under Kuwait) - but all warmth was gradually drained from the relationship after 1960.

One major reason for the impasse was Qasim's growing estrangement from the Iraqi Communists. During 1960, feeling no further need of their support and jealous of their growing power, Qasim turned against the CPI. In February, for instance, a splinter Communist faction was licensed instead of the official party; (5) later in the year the CPI daily newspaper was suspended and its editor imprisoned on charges of violating an act passed during the previous regime. (6) At first the Soviet press merely reported these events without comment, but by the end of 1960 and increasingly in 1961 Russian observers and Russian-controlled organizations such as the World Federation of Trade Unions (WFTU) and the Afro-Asian Solidarity Committee openly protested against anti-Communist measures in Iraq. (7) Reporting to the 22nd Party Congress in Moscow in October, the CPI secretary, Salim Adil, said that up to that time 112 Iraqi Communists had been sentenced to death and 770 imprisoned for various offences. (8) The pogrom continued during the remainder of Qasim's rule.

It is unlikely that Qasim's anti-Communist crusade of itself caused the deterioration in Soviet-Iraqi relations. Anti-Communism, after all, was endemic throughout the Arab world; if the Russians were to make an issue every time an Arab Communist was persecuted, they would soon have no allies left in the Middle East. Meanwhile, the suppression of Iraqi Communists, diplomats in Moscow must have felt, was a small price to pay for Baghdad's withdrawal from CENTO - other things being equal.

The question then is whether "other things" were equal by the early 1960s, from Moscow's viewpoint. Certainly the Iraqi revolution had lost its momentum and Qasim himself had become increasingly isolated as he abandoned former allies from both the Left and Right. From 1961 on it was not so much a question of whether his regime would last, but when it would be overthrown. (9) Why, then, should the Russians continue to identify themselves with a lost cause? In the meantime the impasse in Soviet-Egyptian relations had been surmounted and Syria's withdrawal from the UAR in September 1961 had reduced the menace of pan-Arabism. It was natural under the circumstances for the Russians to revive earlier associations in the Arab World, with Egyptians and Syrians in particular, and allow relations with Qasim's regime gradually to deteriorate.

There was another factor in the decline of Soviet-Iraqi relations after 1961: the Kurdish question. Russia had for many years adopted a protective attitude toward the Kurds, a non-Arab people numbering about six million and dispersed in adjacent portions of Iran, Turkey, Syria, Iraq and the USSR. The Kurdish leader, Mullah Mustapha of Barzan (known as Barzani), had spent 10 years in Russia following his defeat by combined Persian-Iraqi forces in the 1940s, and when he was allowed to return, after the 1958 revolution, he kept close ties with the USSR. In the summer of 1961 a Kurdish rising began in Iraq, aimed at gaining greater self-rule. The Russians could not, of course, give open support to the Kurds without offending Qasim, but Soviet commentators freely criticized Baghdad for its handling of the revolt and persistently defended the Kurds' right of autonomy. A major reason for Qasim's downfall, it was subsequently argued by Soviet observers, was his rejection of the Kurds' "just demands". (10) The sympathetic attention given to the Kurds during the last year and a half of Qasim's rule must then be seen as a further cause of estrangement between Moscow and Baghdad. (11)

In February 1963 Qasim was overthrown by Right Ba'thists (12) who established a regime in Baghdad many times worse, from the Russian viewpoint, than its predecessor. Iraqi Communists, who were seen by the Ba'thists, somewhat ironically, as the evil genius of Qasim's rule, were suppressed more fiercely than before; during the nine months the Ba'thists were in power, the CPI leadership was virtually obliterated. The Ba'thist programme, under the slogan "Arab Unity without Communists", was an attempt, Pravda's editors pointed out, "to turn back the historical development of the country". (13) The Central Committee of the CPSU officially condemned "mass reprisals and bloody terror" in Iraq, and in March a massive demonstration - the first of its kind - was organized against the Iraqi Embassy in Moscow. (14) Meanwhile, the unrelenting pursuit of the Kurdish war by Ba'thists prompted increased sympathy for the Kurds by Soviet commentators, now relieved of the need to deal circumspectly with the Kurdish question because of the earlier pretence of friendly relations between Moscow and Baghdad. A TASS dispatch in June charged the Ba'thists with "treachery of the Hitlerite type" for pretending to negotiate with the Kurds while building up forces for a final assault on the Kurdish regions; the Ba'thist "national guard" organized to suppress the Kurds was said to be "formed on the pattern of Fascist SS bands". (15) Soviet interest in the Kurdish question was "not a casual one", Pravda's "Observer" wrote, "inasmuch as the Kurdish region is situated in direct proximity to the Soviet border and is one which the imperialists look upon as a base for acts of aggression against the socialist states". (16) Whether this consideration or traditional sympathy for the Kurds was dominant in Russia's attitude on the Kurdish question, this issue now became the central focus of Soviet policy in Iraq.

When Soviet commentators tired of the Kurdish and anti-Communist issues, they turned to Ba'thist worship of "big capital" and oil. Iraqi Ba'thists, V. Petrov wrote in Izvestiya in August, are "an amalgam of bourgeois-feudal, pseudo-nationalist and Right-wing agents of the oil monopolies". (17) Since Baghdad's judgments of the USSR were as critical as Moscow's of Iraq, relations between the two countries came virtually to a halt during the period of Ba'thist rule, though diplomatic ties were never formally suspended.

Moscow's attitude towards Iraq changed dramatically after the overthrow of the Ba'thists in November 1963 by a military junta led by General Abd as-Salam Arif. The settlement of the Kurdish problem in February 1964 (though the settlement proved inconclusive) received much favourable comment in Moscow. Khrushchev congratulated General (now President) Arif on the occasion, saying that the Iraqi people now had "a real possibility of mobilizing all sound and progressive forces of the nation"; (18) Pravda's correspondent V. Mayevskiy considered the settlement "part of the democratization of the country". (19) Anti-Communist pogroms meanwhile ceased, partly, to be sure, because there were few Communists left to persecute after Qasim and the Right Ba'thists, but also because the new regime sought better relations with Moscow. In June 1964 the first important Iraqi delegation to visit the Soviet Union in nearly two years spent three weeks in Moscow negotiating new arms deliveries and a resumption of Russian aid. In August Pravda's "Observer" complimented the Arif government for the progress it had made in many areas - in particular, the elimination of the Ba'thist "national guard", the cease-fire in Kurdistan, improved relations with Cairo, and, most recently, the nationalization decrees; the latter, "Observer" wrote, were "a logical continuation of the progressive line which has been going forward since the coup d'état of 18 November, 1963". (20) There were, to be sure, certain reservations in Moscow's generally favourable appraisal of Iraqi developments under Arif: the economic reforms were said to be weak in rural areas; individual cabinet members persisted in anti-Communist measures; and the fighting which resumed in the Kurdish regions in early 1966 was blamed as much on "chauvinist circles" in Baghdad who sought to "solve" the Kurdish question through force as on "extremist elements" among the Kurds. (21) However, a firm basis for improved relations existed, and since both Moscow and Baghdad desired the improvement, there was steady intercourse between the two nations during the two and a half years of Abd as-Salam Arif's presidency (see Chronology).

Relations continued on an even keel under the government of Abd ar-Rahman Arif, who succeeded to the presidency following his brother's death in April 1966. The Kurdish issue, to be sure, cast a persistent shadow over the Soviet-Iraqi relationship. Despite another cease-fire in June and a personal visit to Kurdistan by President Arif himself in the autumn, Soviet observers remained apprehensive. In November an Izvestiya correspondent called attention again to "chauvinists" in Baghdad who wanted a decisive military victory over the Kurds; (22) a Pravda correspondent who was allowed to visit the Kurdish regime at the end of 1966 - the first to do so in three years - reported considerable uneasiness there. (23) The problem of the Kurds, however, was merely an irritant to Soviet-Iraqi relations; it did not hinder their progress. Meanwhile, the issue receded somewhat into the background in Soviet commentaries after the Arab-Israeli conflict of June 1967, which brought the Russians into more intimate association with all Arab regimes. The hastily arranged exchange of visits by Podgornyy and Arif in July marked the beginning of a still more intensive phase in Soviet-Iraqi relations. It is apparent from Soviet commentaries after the fall of the second Arif government in 1968 that Moscow did not regard this government as favourably as its predecessor, or for that matter as favourably as other regimes in the Middle East, both Arab and non-Arab. (24) Iraq, however, was a reliable ally for Soviet purposes in the Middle East, and Moscow maintained as cordial relations with the second Arif regime as with the first.

The return to power of Right Ba'thists in July 1968 brought less change in Soviet-Iraqi relations than both sides perhaps anticipated, recalling the dismal relationship between the earlier Ba'thist government and Moscow in 1963. Soviet observers from the start adopted a conciliatory (if slightly patronizing) attitude towards the new regime. Barely a fortnight after the coup, P. Demchenko wrote in Pravda that with the Kurdish war ended, with new blood in the Ba'th party, and with Ba'thist leaders having had five years to study their errors of 1963, the Al-Bakr government stood an excellent chance of success. (25) In this mood, political and military exchanges proceeded and economic activity increased. In 1969 a new credit was offered, the first in nearly a decade (see below).

Certain old difficulties, and a few new ones, troubled Soviet-Iraqi relations periodically. The Russians did not, for instance, lose sight of the Kurdish problem and continued to defend the Kurds' right to self-rule, though they no longer spoke of a Kurdish "national liberation" movement as they had as late as 1967. (26) Their sympathies were clearly on the side of the Kurds in a new phase of the long-drawn-out civil war during 1968 and 1969. The termination, or presumed termination, of the nine-year struggle in March 1970 and the proclamation of "Kurdish national autonomy" were therefore greeted with much enthusiasm in the USSR. Podgornyy sent congratulations to President Al-Bakr and noted that the settlement of the Kurdish issue opened up new prospects for economic and social change in Iraq; (27) the influential commentator Kudryavtsev, who was in Baghdad at the time of the settlement, wrote on his return to Moscow that now the much discussed "national front" of the Ba'th, the Syrian Communist Party, and the Democratic Party of Kurdistan could become a reality. (28) Ties between Baghdad and Moscow intensified following the Kurdish treaty, and Soviet commentaries on developments in Iraq became noticeably more cordial. (29)

Another irritant to Soviet-Iraqi relations was Baghdad's improved relationship with Peking as the Cultural Revolution released its grip on Chinese foreign policy. In May 1969 the Iraqi Chief of Staff made a sudden visit to Peking, after a decade of strained relations, presumably to express Baghdad's displeasure with some aspect of Russia's Middle East policies, possibly connected with arms deliveries. A series of further exchanges during the next 18 months, leading to several aid and trade agreements, was climaxed by the appointment of new ambassadors, replacing the chargés d'affaires, at the end of 1970. China's economic activity in Iraq could not, of course, soon overtake Russia's, but it is probable that Peking influenced Iraq's attitude towards the Palestinian guerrillas and towards a settlement of the Arab-Israeli dispute. In July 1970 Iraq rejected Nasser's cease-fire proposals, an attitude on Iraq's part that Pravda described as "negative" and "incomprehensible". (30) Baghdad's position was apparently reviewed at some length a few days later during the visit of a high government delegation to Moscow, but the Iraqis did not change their minds. (31)

Iraqi Communists, meanwhile, ceased to preoccupy the Russians except peripherally. Moscow took periodic note of reported arrests and maltreatment of Communists but did not press this issue. The Russians presumably were pleased that a Communist was included in the Al-Bakr government after a cabinet reshuffle in December 1969, though the Soviet press made no mention of it since the new cabinet member did not carry his party label. (32)

Greetings were sent to the Second CPI Congress in September 1970 and full endorsement was given to the party's "national front" policy; no Russian, however, attended the congress so far as is known. As elsewhere in the Middle East where Russia's relations with established regimes were proceeding satisfactorily, the role of local Communists was marginal in Moscow's calculations.

Economic, Military and Cultural Relations

The Soviet Union extended credits of approximately $180 million to Iraq during the Qasim era. (33) They were to cover a variety of projects, including more than half of the 32 enterprises listed in the 1961-66 Five-Year Plan. Among the projects were: a steel works in Baghdad, fertilizer and sulphur plants, a cotton mill, a pharmaceutical plant, a textile factory, various food-processing plants, and the 570-kilometre Baghdad-Basra railway. Work had reportedly started on a number of these projects by the end of the Qasim era, but only a few minor undertakings had been completed.

Work on all projects was apparently suspended during the nine-month Right Ba'thist regime in 1963 but was gradually resumed during the first Arif government. The railway was completed in the spring of 1964, and in March 1965 a new protocol was negotiated reactivating several of the original projects and initiating new ones; among the latter were a dam and power station on the Euphrates River, the cost of which has been estimated at $140 million; (34) several vocational training centres; a tractor-assembly plant; and preliminary surveys for oil extraction. The development of the oil industry became increasingly important in Soviet-Iraqi economic relations during the last half of the 1960s. In December 1967 a major agreement was reached on oil surveys and equipment, an early sign of Russia's intensive interest in Middle Eastern reserves. (35) In 1969, the surveys having been completed in several regions, Russia and Iraq negotiated new agreements and contracts which covered pipelines, storage tanks and separation plants, as well as additional credits of $121 million. (36) By the autumn of 1969, according to Iraqi sources, the Russians had completed 34 projects in Iraq and were working on 48 others. (37)

Military aid to Iraq paralleled economic aid - that is, extensive commitments during the early years of the Qasim era, total suspension in 1963, and a gradual resumption of shipments during the latter half of the 1960s. By the early 1960s Iraq had probably received as much as $200 million in Soviet arms, which would place her at that time behind only Egypt and Indonesia among Third World recipients of Russian military aid. The transfers included modern fighters and bombers, in addition to tanks, rockets, artillery and various other relatively sophisticated equipment. It is estimated that 1,300 Soviet military personnel were in Iraq during these years, training Iraqi soldiers and pilots. (38)

General Abd ar-Rahman Arif was able to arrange for a resumption of arms deliveries in June 1964, after the first cease-fire in the Kurdish war. Thereafter the transfer of Soviet weapons to Iraq continued at a steady rate; the flow was apparently not interrupted by the resumption of fighting in the Kurdish regions in 1966. By the end of 1967 Iraq had received more than half a billion dollars in Soviet military aid, including replacements for her small losses in the June war with Israel, and the number of Russian advisers was growing. (39) The pace of military exchanges between the two countries after 1967 suggests that this co-operation did not slacken. Following Marshal Grechko's visit to Baghdad in March 1968, it was reported that Iraq cancelled its order for French Mirages - presumably on the promise of additional fighters from the USSR. (40) Meanwhile, Soviet naval vessels from 1968 on periodically called at Iraqi ports, emphasizing Russia's interest in the Persian Gulf.

Soviet-Iraqi trade developed very rapidly during the Qasim era, as Baghdad cut its commitments to traditional trading partners in the West. By 1961 more than 20 per cent of Iraq's trade was with the socialist bloc; (41) during the years 1959-62 Iraq was second only to the UAR among Russia's trading partners in the Middle East and sixth in all of Africa and Asia. After 1963 trade remained fairly constant and showed a large preponderance of Soviet exports over imports - often 10 times larger (see Table D); this reflected Soviet shipments under the various aid programmes before Iraqi repayments began.

Cultural relations between Iraq and the USSR over the years did not show great variety, despite two general cultural agreements and periodic protocols (see Chronology). Even during the Qasim years, exchanges were fewer than with other Third World nations Moscow counted as its allies. A 1969 volume on exchanges sponsored by the Russian Academy of Sciences makes no mention of Iraq, (42) though several scientific delegations were in reality exchanged in connexion with the construction of a nuclear reactor. An Iraqi-Soviet Friendship Society existed in Baghdad until early 1966 when it was ruled illegal by the courts; it was re-established at the end of 1968.

The principal cultural activity was in the area of education. Many educational delegations were exchanged over the years, and, more particularly, large numbers of Iraqi students were educated in the USSR. Up to the end of 1962 an estimated 2,755 Iraqi students had gone to the Soviet bloc for their education - many more than from any other Third World country and indeed more than a quarter of all students from Africa, Asia, and the Middle East. (43) The numbers declined after Qasim's fall, but mounted later in the 1960s; at the end of 1968 there were 850 Iraqi students enrolled in academic courses in the USSR, again more than from any other Third World nation. (44)

*   *   *

The conclusion one reaches from the foregoing record is that despite the uneven course of Soviet-Iraqi relations and persistent misgivings in Moscow over certain of

Baghdad's domestic policies, Iraq remained important in Moscow's calculations. Iraq by 1970 ranked eighth among Russia's Third World trading partners in Asia, Africa and the Middle East, fifth among recipients of Soviet aid, and fourth or fifth among recipients of Russian arms; Iraq possessed one of five Russian-built nuclear reactors in the Third World; Iraq had sent more students to the USSR than any other Third World state. (45) Clearly the Russians had a sizeable commitment in a state which they made no pretence of considering "progressive", at least after the failure of Qasim's revolution in the early 1960s. Why? One reason was surely that the Soviet Union wished to prevent another Iraqi defection from the Arab community as in 1955, when Nuri as-Sa'id led Iraq into the Baghdad alliance with the Northern tier; Russia's friendship with Egypt was a liability in Soviet-Iraqi relations, given the ancient rivalry between Baghdad and Cairo, and Moscow sought to remove the liability through good will and largesse. Another reason relates to Russia's special relationship with the Kurds: the sense of responsibility which Moscow had for the Kurds' well-being required an accommodating policy in Baghdad, for an embittered Iraqi regime could exacerbate and deepen this complex problem. These reasons for Soviet strategies in Iraq may be considered preventive, that is, designed to prevent actions by Baghdad that might be damaging to Russian interests elsewhere. There were also positive objectives in Iraq itself. The Russians, for instance, were intensely interested in Iraqi oil, as the nearest and perhaps cheapest oil in the Arabian peninsula available to them if arrangements could be made to pipe it across Iran. They were also interested in Iraqi ports on the Persian Gulf, the most accessible to Soviet ships so long as Saudi Arabia and Kuwait remained hostile to the USSR and Iran an uncertain ally. Finally, the Russians appear to have perceived Iraq increasingly as a possible link between the two great communities of the Middle East, the Arabs of the Arabian peninsula and North Africa and the non-Arabs of the Northern tier; as Russia's relations improved with both of these communities, the bridge between them took on added importance.

The Soviet Union, then, did not lack motives for its activity in Iraq, even without regimes in Baghdad that could be counted as "progressive". The heavy commitment in technical assistance, aid and arms promised to pay significant dividends in many areas.

Chronology

	Political		Economic		Cultural
Pre-1958					
1944	Diplomatic relations established				
Feb 1955	Baghdad pact; Iraq breaks relations with USSR				
				Nov 1957	Muslim delegation in USSR
1958					
July	– Qasim overthrows Hashemites; diplomatic relations resumed with USSR and opened with CPR				
		Oct	– Trade agreement		
Nov	– Baghdad municipal delegation in Moscow – Reported arms agreement (46)				
				Dec	– Muslim education delegation in USSR
1959					
Jan	– CP delegation in USSR for XXI congress			Jan	– Education delegation in Iraq
		Feb	– Economic delegation in USSR: CREDIT AGREEMENT for irrigation, agricultural and industrial projects ($137.5m)		
May	– Government delegation in USSR	May	– Protocol on February credit	May	– Cultural agreement
July	– Government delegation in Iraq for anniversary – Uprising at Kirkuk; Communists blamed	July	– Protocol on port and shipyard		
		Aug	– Agricultural minister in USSR – Agreement on nuclear reactor		
				Sept	– Education minister in USSR
Nov	– Government delegation in USSR for anniversary	Nov	– Protocol on Baghdad-Basra railway		
		Dec	– Economic delegation in Iraq: protocol on technical training centres		
1960					
		Jan	– Iron works promised	Jan	– TU delegation in USSR
		Feb	– Electric bulb factory promised		
Apr	– Mikoyan in Iraq	Apr	– Contracts for sulphur prospecting and navigation		
		May	– Commerce minister in USSR – CREDIT AGREEMENT for widening railway ($45m)		

IRAQ

	Political	Economic	Cultural
1960 (cont.)			
		Aug – Public works minister in USSR	
	Sept – Chief of staff leads military delegation to USSR	Sept – Protocol on granaries	Sept – Education minister in USSR
		– Telephone exchange agreement	
	Nov – Kurd leader Barzani in USSR		
	Dec – CP delegation in Moscow for world conference	Dec – Business delegation in USSR for trade talks	
1961			
		Feb – Protocol on railway construction	
		Apr – Contracts for electrical equipment and agricultural machine plants	
	July – Government delegation in Iraq for anniversary – Kurdish rising begins	July – Radio station completed	
	Sept – Military delegation in USSR		
	Oct – CP secretary in USSR for XXII congress		
			Nov – Education minister in USSR
1962			
		Jan – Protocol on steel plant – Agreement on wagon deliveries to Iraq	Feb – Cultural protocol
	July – CPR military delegation in Iraq	July – Protocols on railways and tractor stations – CPR oil delegation in Iraq	
		Aug – Telephone exchange completed	
	Sept – Military delegation in USSR		
		Dec – Air service agreement	
1963 Feb	– Qasim overthrown by Right Ba'thists; USSR and CPR recognize new regime; CP suppressed		
		May – Aid to flood victims	
	Nov – Right Ba'thists replaced by regime under Abd as-Salam Arif		
1964 Feb	– Cease-fire in Kurdish war		
	May – Arif meets Khrushchev in Cairo – Reported arms agreement (47)	May – Baghdad–Basra railway completed	
	June – Military delegation under Gen. Abd ar-Rahman Arif in USSR		
			Sept – New cultural agreement
1965 Jan	– CP delegation in USSR		

60

Political	Economic	Cultural
1965 (cont.)		
	Feb – New industrial plants, training centres promised	
	Mar – Economic delegation in USSR: revised protocols on Euphrates power plant and other projects	
		Aug – Cultural protocol
	Sept – Protocol on 3 vocational training centres	
	Oct – Trade protocol	
	Nov – Granary completed	
	Dec – Agricultural minister in USSR	
1966		
Jan – Kurdish fighting resumes	Jan – Aviation minister in USSR	
	Feb – Aviation delegation in Iraq	
Mar – CP delegation in USSR for XXIII congress		
Apr – Military delegation under Gen. Arif in USSR – President Arif dies; succeeded by brother Gen. Abd ar-Rahman Arif; Supreme Soviet delegation in Iraq for funeral		
	May – Further protocol on industrial training centres	
June – New cease-fire in Kurdish war – Government delegation in Iraq		June – Cultural protocol for 1966
July – PREMIER BAZZAZ IN USSR for 7-day state visit		
Aug – Bazzaz replaced by Naji Talib – Reported arms agreement (48)	Aug – Gift of cholera vaccine	
Sept – Deputy foreign minister Semenov in Iraq		
	Dec – Deputy minister of industry in Iraq: protocol on oil drilling equipment	
1967		
	Feb – Protocol on agricultural equipment – Nuclear delegation in Iraq: reactor promised	
Apr – Foreign minister in USSR		
		May – Scientific delegation in Iraq
July – PODGORNYY IN IRAQ for 2-day visit during Middle East crisis – PRESIDENT ARIF IN USSR for talks on crisis – Defence minister in USSR	July – Gift of food	

	Political	Economic	Cultural
1967 (cont.)			
			Sept – Journalists in USSR
	Oct – Military delegation in Iraq	Oct – Trade protocol	Oct – Cultural protocol
	Nov – Government delegation in USSR for anniversary	Nov – Economic aid chief Skachkov in Iraq: protocol on oil development	
			Dec – Journalists in Iraq – TU delegation in USSR
1968			
		Jan – Nuclear reactor completed	
	Mar – Defence minister Grechko in Iraq	Mar – Trade protocol on harvester sales	
		Apr – Economic delegation to Iraq for textile study	Spring – Nuclear scientists in USSR
	May – Soviet naval vessels call at Iraqi ports	May – Ministers of agriculture, industry in USSR for aid, trade talks	
			? – Agreement on teleprinter link
	July – Right Ba'thist coup; Hassan al-Bakr becomes president – Defence minister in USSR		
	Sept – Chief of Staff in USSR	Sept – Contracts for agricultural, dredging equipment	
		Oct – USSR takes part in Baghdad trade fair	Oct – TU leader in USSR
		Nov – Protocols on fisheries and canning plant	Nov – Photo exhibition opens in Baghdad
			Dec – Cultural minister in USSR: protocol
1969			
		Jan – Agricultural minister in USSR: fishing agreement	
			Feb – Education minister in Iraq
	Mar – Foreign minister in USSR	Mar – Agrarian reform minister in USSR – Industrial exhibition opens in Baghdad	
		Apr – Protocol on various industrial projects	
	May – Defence minister At-Tikriti in USSR – Chief of Staff in CPR	May – Protocol on cotton mill – Deputy Premier in USSR	May – TU leaders in USSR for May Day – Co-operative official in Iraq for peasant congress – Nuclear delegate in Iraq for opening of centre
	June – Naval vessels call at Persian Gulf ports – CP delegation in USSR for world conference	June – CREDIT AGREEMENT on oil extraction and refining ($121m)	June – TU exchange agreement
		July – Protocol on oil prospecting	July – Cultural protocol for 1969–70 – TU delegation in Iraq – Protocol on nuclear co-operation

Political	Economic	Cultural
1969 (cont.)		
	Aug – Contract on importation of vehicles – Fisheries minister in Iraq: protocol	Aug – Cultural minister in USSR
		Sept – TU delegation in USSR
Nov – Military delegation in USSR	Nov – Civil air agreement with CPR – Aeroflot delegation in Iraq – Agrarian reform minister in Moscow for collective farm conference	Nov – TU leader in USSR for anniversary – Exhibition on October revolution opens in Baghdad
	Dec – Contracts for oil development, pipelines – Contract for merchant vessels – Contract for shipyard	
1970		
Feb – CP leaders in Moscow for Lenin centenary conference	Feb – Delegation in Iraq to study power station sites on Euphrates and Tigris	
Mar – Youth minister in USSR – Peace treaty in Kurdish war – Military delegation in Iraq	Mar – Economic delegation in Iraq: agreement on permanent joint commission; expanded trade agreement	Mar – Oil workers in USSR
Apr – CP, Ba'th, Kurdish delegations in Moscow for Lenin centenary		Apr – Labour minister in Moscow for world peace conference
May – Komsomol delegation in Iraq – Youth delegation in USSR for Komsomol congress	May – Contracts on silos, oil drills, equipment for seismological units	May – Railway workers in USSR
	June – Contracts on oil exploration in Rumaylah fields	June – Soviet-Iraqi news programme inaugurated – Atomic scientists in USSR
	July – Gas experts in Moscow for international conference – Sales agreement on Soviet machinery, agricultural equipment, vehicles	July – Teachers' delegation in USSR
Aug – At-Tikriti heads government-Ba'th delegation to USSR	Aug – Air service protocol – Economic minister in USSR: protocols on increased trade, technical assistance – Agricultural minister in USSR – Further contracts on 1969 oil agreement	
Sept – Defence minister Shibab in USSR on holiday	Sept – Fisheries agreement – Trade delegation in Iraq for talks on agricultural machine repair shops	

Political	Economic	Cultural

<u>1970</u> (cont.)

Oct – Baghdad mayor in Moscow

Oct – Economic delegation in USSR for crude oil talks
– Protocol on Rumaylah oilfield

Nov – Contract on vocational training centre.

Oct – TU leader in Moscow for WFTU meeting

Dec – Education minister in USSR
– Uzbek cultural delegation in Iraq

References

(1)   Pravda, 23 July, 1958.

(2)   These developments, which were of course far more complex than can be detailed here, are dealt with by a number of authorities, e.g: Majid Khadduri, Republican Iraq: A Study in Iraqi Politics Since the Revolution of 1958 (London: Oxford University Press, 1969), especially Chapters V and VI; Laqueur, The Struggle for the Middle East, pp. 94-104; Manfred Halpern, in Black and Thornton, Communism and Revolution, pp. 304-11.

(3)   Izvestiya, 17 March, 1959 (text in Mizan, April 1959, Appendix, pp. 1-6).

(4)   Many of these commentaries are summarized in Mizan during 1959 and 1960; see Bibliography.

(5)   See coverage of Soviet articles reporting this episode in Mizan, March 1960, pp. 7-8.

(6)   Pravda, 4 October, 1960.

(7)   A number of these semi-official protests are reviewed in Mizan, March 1961, pp. 2-6.

(8)   Pravda, 25 October, 1961; see also Laqueur, op. cit., p. 95.

(9)   On this point, see Black and Thornton, op. cit., p. 310.

(10)   Pravda, 26 February, 1963; see also Amin Salimov, "Iraqi Coup: Cause and Effect", International Affairs, No. 9 (September), 1963, pp. 38-45.

(11)   For the breadth and volume of Soviet attention to the Kurdish issue during these years, see the extensive listings in Bibliografiya po Kurdovedeniyu, 1963.

(12)   The Iraqi Ba'thists, an offshoot of the Syrian Ba'th movement, organized themselves as a political party in 1952. Since their principal goal was Arab union, they supported merger with Egypt after the 1958 revolution and so were in opposition to Qasim's regime. The Right Ba'thists were an extremist faction of the party, distinguished mainly by their militant anti-Communism.

(13)   Pravda, 26 February, 1963.

(14)   Black and Thornton, op. cit., p. 311.

(15)   Pravda, 16 June, 1963.

(16)   Pravda, 20 June, 1963.

(17)   Izvestiya, 8 August, 1963.

(18)   Pravda, 15 February, 1964.

(19)   Pravda, 5 April, 1964.

(20)   Pravda, 13 August, 1964 (reviewed in Mizan, September 1964, pp. 14-16).

(21)   Pravda, 7 February, 1966; see also the review of Communist developments in Iraq by I.N. Garshin, in V.V. Levin, Bor'ba narodov protiv kolonializma, 1965 (summarized in Mizan, October 1965, pp. 14-15).

(22)   Izvestiya, 3 November, 1966.

(23)   Ye. Primakov, Pravda, 15 and 18 January, 1967.

(24)   Ye. Primakov, for instance, argued that the regime was brought down by "corruption, inertia and a disastrous rift between slogans and deeds"; Pravda, 12 August, 1968. G.I. Mirskiy wrote that Arif's government fell "because it had no solid social base and no definite ideological orientation"; New Times, No. 33 (21 August), 1968, p. 13.

(25)   Izvestiya, 3 August, 1968.

(26)   M.A. Kamal', Natsional'no-osvoboditel'noye dvizheniye v Irakskom Kurdistane, Baku, 1967.

(27)   Radio Moscow, 17 March, 1970.

(28)   Izvestiya, 26 May, 1970.

(29)   E.g. A. Vasil'yev in Pravda, 17 July, 1970, marking the 12th anniversary of the Iraqi revolution.

(30)   Pravda, 1 August, 1970.

(31)   The joint communiqué in any case gave no indication of it, noting only an "exchange of opinions" on the situation in the Middle East; Pravda, 13 August, 1970.

(32)   See A. Yodfat, "The USSR and the Arab Communist Parties", New Middle East, No. 32 (May 1971), p. 30.

(33)   This is the figure most frequently given in Soviet sources: e.g. Vneshnyaya torgovlya, No. 12, 1962 (summarized in Mizan, January 1963, pp. 26-28); Sovremennyy Irak, p. 117; and Chertkov, SSSR i razvivayushchiyesya strany, p. 50. Several Russian sources show $243 million: e.g. Soviet Union - Friend of the Arab Peoples, p. 41 and The USSR and Developing Countries, p. 61. Marshall Goldman's estimate of $323 million through 1962 assumes a new credit in 1965 for the Euphrates River project; Soviet Foreign Aid, p. 150. Soviet sources, however, specifically state that the Euphrates project was to be covered by earlier loans; see Soviet Union - Friend of the Arab Peoples, p. 41.

(34)   Goldman, op. cit., p. 150.

(35)   O. Gerasimov, Irakskaya neft', 1969, p. 161; this volume includes the 1967 exchanges as well as an analysis of Iraq's dealings with foreign oil companies.

(36)   According to the US Department of State compilation of Soviet aid, one credit of $67 million was for the exploration of oilfields at Rumaylah and Ratawi, another of $54 million for refineries in the Al-Halfayah region; RECS-5, 9 July, 1970, p. 5.

(37)   Radio Baghdad, 9 September, 1969.

(38)   Details of Soviet-Iraqi military co-operation during the Qasim years may be found, inter alia, in Joshua and Gibert, Arms for The Third World, p. 13; Goldman, op. cit., p. 150; and "Soviet Military Aid Program as a Reflection of Soviet Objectives", 24 June, 1965 (a Georgetown Research Project, summarized in Stephen P. Gibert, "Wars of Liberation and Soviet Military Aid Policy", Orbis, Fall 1966, pp. 839-58).

(39)   Joshua and Gibert, op. cit., pp. 23 and 26-27.

(40)   A.Y. Yodfat, "Unpredictable Iraq Poses a Russian Problem", New Middle East, October 1969, p. 18.

(41)   Laqueur, op. cit., p. 97.

(42)   Korneyev, Nauchnyye svyazi Akademii nauk SSSR so stranami Azii i Afriki (1969); most other Arab countries are given extensive treatment, pp. 177-230.

(43)   U.S. Department of State, RSB-46, 29 March, 1963, p. 4; it is estimated that about 70 per cent of Third World students in the Soviet bloc study in the USSR.

(44)   U.S. Department of State, RSE-25, 7 May, 1969, p. 75.

(45)   These rankings are taken from a comparison of Soviet relations with all developing nations in Asia, Africa and the Middle East in my forthcoming study, Russia and the Third World.

(46)   Joshua and Gibert, op. cit., p. 13, citing Western news reports.

(47)   Ibid., p. 17, citing British news sources.

(48)   The Military Balance 1967-1968, p. 53; Joshua and Gibert, op. cit., p. 16, report an agreement in April 1966.

Until 1963 Jordan stood second only to Saudi Arabia as the Arab state most mistrusted in Moscow. There had been a brief moment in 1956, following the dismissal of Glubb Pasha (1) and Amman's assertion of a neutralist foreign policy, when it appeared that diplomatic relations between Russia and Jordan might be established. The moment passed, however, and another opportunity did not arise until the early 1960s, after Moscow had re-established close relations with Cairo, temporarily abandoned Iraq, and adopted a more tolerant posture towards Middle East developments. During these years Soviet commentaries on Jordan were uniformly hostile, attacking King Hussein's "reign of terror" and questioning the legitimacy of the nation itself – a kingdom created by Winston Churchill "in the interval between cigar and brandy". (2) Criticism was especially sharp after the revolution in Yemen in 1962 and Hussein's decision to help the Imam regain his throne. (3)

The improvement in Soviet-Jordanian relations in the mid-1960s was due to changes of attitude in Amman as much as in Moscow. Concerned about Right Ba'thist pressures on his government in 1963, after the coups in Iraq and Syria, King Hussein turned increasingly to Cairo, and this led inevitably to improved relations with the USSR. The new Jordanian posture was particularly apparent, as Soviet writers were quick to point out, during the Arab summit conference in Cairo in January 1964 when Hussein pledged collaboration with "progressive" Arab regimes. (4) Embassies were accordingly exchanged between Moscow and Amman in July 1964.

Relations developed slowly during the next three years. Soviet commentaries on Jordan, however, grew less severe. King Hussein's anti-imperialist policies were of course commended most of all, but domestic progress too was noted. "The first gusts of the winds of change" were said to be blowing over Jordan; "the positive beginnings" would be carried further. (5) Soviet irritation with Jordan occasionally reappeared – for instance, during Communist arrests in 1966 and during a brief impasse in Jordanian-Egyptian relations early in 1967 (6) – but on balance the commentaries were restrained.

The Arab-Israeli conflict of June 1967 stimulated closer ties between Moscow and Amman. King Hussein's visit to Moscow in October, the first important exchange between the two governments, gave Russians and Jordanians an opportunity to review all aspects of the relationship. A Soviet offer of arms was rejected, on this occasion as subsequently, but King Hussein was not unappreciative of the offer and used it to prod the United States into lifting its ban on arms sales to Jordan imposed during the June war. (7) The cultural and scientific agreement negotiated during Hussein's state visit was ratified the following year (in November) and initiated an exchange programme which grew rapidly during the next few years; at the end of 1969 more than 100 Jordanian students were enrolled in Soviet universities under the cultural exchange programme. (8) In January 1969 the first trade and technical assistance agreements were negotiated in Moscow, the latter accompanied by a promise of credits.

The growing antagonism after the Six Day War between Palestinian commandos operating from Jordan and King Hussein's government posed a delicate problem for the Russians. Moscow's ambivalent attitude towards the fedayeen was difficult to sustain under any circumstances but was doubly so when the fedayeen clashed directly with an Arab regime Russia was seeking to befriend. Were the Russians to criticize King Hussein's suppression of the fedayeen as too severe, they risked alienating a moderate Arab regime whose support both they and the Egyptians needed in their policies in the Arab-Israeli conflict; on the other hand, open criticism of the commandos would arouse popular antipathy throughout the Arab world. The Russians accordingly adopted a neutral position during the frequent outbreaks between the Palestinians and the Jordanian forces, blaming American and Israeli provocation above all and only occasionally hinting at the "irresponsible and reckless" actions of Palestinian extremists. (9) When full-scale civil war between the Palestinians and Jordanians broke out in September 1970, the Russians persisted in their neutrality but took an active part in urging an early truce. The consequences of civil war in Jordan would be "disastrous", an Izvestiya correspondent wrote soon after fighting began, "both for the Jordanian people and for other Arab nations". (10) Official Soviet statements on the crisis, noting ominous movements by the American Sixth Fleet, warned the United States not to attempt intervention under cover of "saving American lives" (including the lives of hostages still held by Palestinian commandos following the hijacking of three commercial planes earlier in September); the Russians meanwhile called on Syria and Iraq to co-operate in every way with Egypt to hasten a cease-fire. (11) The Russians, needless to say, hailed the cease-fire agreement concluded by King Hussein and Yasir Arafat in Cairo on 27 September – an agreement that took on more force than anyone imagined at the time because of Nasser's sudden death two days later and the shock this caused throughout the Arab world; a more detailed agreement between Hussein and Arafat was initialled in Amman in mid-October.

It was apparent from Moscow's attitude towards Jordan during the turbulent events of September 1970 that the Russians were determined to keep the good will of this still conservative Arab kingdom and strengthen its ties with Cairo. Jordan could not for some years be certified as one of the "progressive" Arab states, but the Russians hope at least to lessen its estrangement from those that were.

* * *

The attitude of the Soviet Union towards the Jordanian Communist Party over the years reflected Moscow's relations with the Amman government. In the years before 1963 Soviet commentators gave weight to the views of Jordanian Communists, often carried their speeches in official publications, and praised their resistance to "the anti-national, pro-imperialist regime of King Hussein". (12) After the establishment of diplomatic relations, less attention was given to the views of Communist spokesmen in Jordan, despite the fact that their views of King Hussein moderated as Moscow's moderated. The Russians had no further need for the small and ineffective Jordanian party. To be sure, Soviet observers noted and approved political amnesties involving Jordanian Communists (as in April 1965), and protested when Communists were arrested (as in the spring of 1966), but the fortunes of the CPJ were not of great consequence to Moscow. Communist parties were often a greater liability than asset in the Arab world, and the Russians relied on them only when no other course was open. If the Russians made much of Fuad Nassar in Moscow, as one of the veteran and most respected Arab Communists, it was because they had so little use for him in Amman.

Chronology

	Political	Economic	Cultural
Pre-1963			
Mar 1946	Anglo-Jordanian treaty: independence		
Mar 1957	Jordan abrogates treaty with England, seeks relations with USSR; Hussein assumes full powers, reverses policy		
Dec 1960	CP secretary Nassar in USSR for world conference		
Oct 1961	Nassar in USSR for XXII congress		
1963			
Aug	– Court minister in USSR: agreement on diplomatic relations		
			Oct – Armenian patriarch in Jordan
1964			
Jan	– Jordan agrees at Cairo conference to co-operate with Arab states		
June	– Nassar leads CP delegation to Moscow		
			Sept – First cultural group in Jordan
1965			
1966			
			Jan – Muslim delegation in Jordan
Mar	– Nassar in USSR for XXIII congress – Deputy foreign minister Kuznetsov in Jordan	Mar – USSR wins contract for dam project	
Apr	– CP arrests in Jordan		
1967			
May	– Jordan–UAR defence pact		
Oct	– KING HUSSEIN IN USSR for 3-day visit – Government delegation in Jordan – Government delegation in USSR for anniversary		Oct – Cultural, scientific agreement
1968			
Jan	– Chief of staff in USSR	Jan – Economic delegation in Jordan for aid talks	
Mar	– Arms agreement with USA		
			July – TU delegation in Jordan
		Oct – Iron works delegation in USSR: agreement on equipment purchases	
Dec	– Nassar in USSR		

JORDAN

	Political	Economic	Cultural
1969			
Jan		– Economic minister in USSR: first trade, technical assistance agreements; credits promised	
Feb			– TU delegation in Jordan
Apr	– Hussein in USA		– TU delegation in USSR
May	– Parliamentary delegation in USSR		
June	– Nassar heads CP delegation to Moscow for world conference		
July	– Parliamentary delegation in USSR		– Cultural protocol for 1969 – Minister of Islamic affairs in USSR – TU delegation in USSR
Oct			– Red Cross delegation in USSR – News delegation in Jordan to discuss co-operation – Editors in USSR
Nov	– Supreme soviet delegation in Jordan		– Soviet film festival in Amman
Dec		– Economic minister in USSR – Civil air delegation in Jordan for talks	
1970			
Feb		– Aviation delegation in Jordan: air services agreement	
Mar			– Muslim delegation in Jordan
Apr	– Nassar in Moscow for Lenin centenary		– Uzbek education minister in Jordan
May	– Youth delegation in Moscow for Komsomol congress		– Cultural agreement: scholarships for Jordanian students
June		– Transport minister in USSR to sign air services agreement	
Aug			– Hospital workers in Azerbaydzhan
Sept	– Palestinian commandos hijack Western commercial planes in Jordan; civil war between Palestinians and Jordanian forces		
Oct			– Jordanian TU federation joins WFTU – Medical unit in Jordan to aid victims in civil war

References

(1)   General John B. Glubb, a British officer, had headed Jordan's armed forces since independence; his dismissal, in the wake of efforts to bring Jordan into the Baghdad Pact, was an important landmark in the development of an independent Jordanian foreign policy.

(2)   N. Khokhlov, in Izvestiya, 28 March, 1959.

(3)   E.g. I. Belyayev, in Pravda, 14 October, 1962 and 23 April, 1963; also B. Solovyov, in International Affairs, No. 6 (June), 1963, p. 80.

(4)   See, for instance, the account of an interview with Hussein during the Cairo conference in Izvestiya, 18 January, 1964; also K. Smirnov in Izvestiya, 24 May, 1964, noting "positive advances" in Jordan since the Cairo meeting.

(5)   E.g. Ye.A. Lebedev, in Aziya i Afrika segodnya, No. 12 (December), 1964, p. 21; Pravda, 18 April, 1965. Other commentaries favourable to the Jordanians during this period are reviewed in Mizan, April 1965, pp. 8-9.

(6)   E.g. M. Kremnev, in New Times, No. 10 (8 March), 1967, p. 17.

(7)   On this point, see Aryeh Yodfat's article in Mizan, March–April 1969, pp. 77 and 79, citing Jordanian sources.

(8)   U.S. Department of State, RSES-35, 12 August, 1970, p. 67.

(9)   E.g. Ye. Primakov in Pravda, 12 June, 1970.

(10)   V. Matveyev, Izvestiya, 19 September, 1970.

(11)   See the official TASS statement on the crisis in Pravda, 20 September, 1970 and a statement by the Ministry of Foreign Affairs in Pravda, 24 September, 1970.

(12)   L.N. Chernov in Narody Azii i Afriki, No. 5 (September–October), 1961, p. 26; see also the views of the CPJ First Secretary, Fuad Nassar, in Pravda, 3 January, 1959 and Sovremennyy Vostok, No. 2 (February), 1961 (reviewed in Mizan, April 1961, pp. 1-4).

8. RELATIONS WITH KUWAIT

Kuwait is the only one of the Persian Gulf sheikhdoms with which the Soviet Union maintained diplomatic relations before 1970 and which Moscow recognized as sovereign. The recognition came slowly. Soviet commentators during the 1950s considered this British protectorate "virtually a colony", its people suffering under the "uncontrolled despotism" of a sheikh who received personally 50 per cent of the profits of the British-owned Kuwait Oil Company.(1) The Soviet Union reacted cautiously to the crisis of 1961, brought on by Qasim's claim - at the moment of Kuwait's independence - that Kuwait was "an indivisible part of Iraq"; his claim and reported Iraqi troop movements on the border prompted the return of British forces in early July. Russia was reluctant, in attempting to preserve the delicate balance of its relations with Arab states, to choose between Qasim's urgent claim and Nasser's equally urgent rejection of it. Accordingly, Soviet commentaries were confined to protesting against the "absolutely unjustified" landing of English troops - an issue, it was hoped, on which all Arabs could agree. (2)

In the midst of this crisis Kuwait's newly-won independence was generally ignored in Moscow. V.A. Zorin, Russia's representative at the United Nations, said in July that "under conditions of full control by the British authorities over the administration of Kuwait, it cannot constitute a sovereign state". (3) In August a Soviet writer charged Sheikh Abdulla with having "betrayed his people by opening the doors to foreign invaders", (4) although by the time he wrote Arab League forces had replaced British. This generally negative attitude towards Kuwait, especially towards Kuwait's independence, persisted as long as Qasim remained in power in Iraq and continued to urge his claims. "The experience of Kuwait in gaining formal independence", it was argued in October 1962, "shows that self-government alone is not enough. State sovereignty is largely illusory as long as the oil companies retain control of the entire economy of the sheikhdoms." (5)

After Qasim's fall the Russians for the first time explicitly repudiated his claim to Kuwait (6) and in March 1963 responded favourably to the sheikh's request for diplomatic relations. A Soviet ambassador was appointed in June. Diplomatic activity was minimal, however, until the end of 1964 - very possibly because of Khrushchev's supercilious attitude towards the sheikhdom. During his visit to Egypt in May 1964 he expressed his view bluntly and crudely: "There is such a state as Kuwait, Kuwait", he said, speaking informally to Egyptian trade unionists. "There is some little ruler sitting there, an Arab of course, a Muslim. He is given bribes. He lives the life of the rich, but he is trading in the riches of his people. He never had any conscience and he won't ever have any. Will you come to terms with him on unification? It is easier to eat three puds of salt than to reach agreement with him, although you are both Arabs and Muslims." (7) Such an attitude, needless to say, effectively blocked any development of a Soviet-Kuwaiti relationship.

After Khrushchev's fall the Soviet government took some measures to improve relations. The Kuwaiti Finance Minister, for instance, was invited to Moscow in November 1964, and a Soviet economic delegation concluded a technical assistance agreement with Kuwait the following February (see Chronology). There was of course no question of Soviet aid to Kuwait, since the sheikhdom was one of the richest nations in the Middle East. Trade, however, consisting almost entirely of Soviet exports, quadrupled from 1964 to 1968; the exports included seiners and ships of various types. Cultural relations, despite an agreement in 1967 and a protocol the next year, remained nominal. At the end of 1969 10 Kuwaiti students were reported to be studying in the USSR. (8)

Soviet policies in Kuwait, however, were not necessarily expressed in cultural and economic ties or political exchanges. Nor were they reflected in Soviet commentaries, which were infrequent. The object of Russian strategies where Kuwait was concerned was the strengthening of the sheikhdom's ties with the Arab world, especially with the UAR over Saudi Arabia. In this the Russians had no need to be disappointed, for Kuwait contributed liberally to Egypt and Jordan after the Six Day War and persistently supported Nasser's Palestine policies; Pravda, for instance, applauded Kuwait's "positive attitude" toward Nasser's peace "initiative" in July 1970. (9)

Chronology

	Political	Economic	Cultural
Pre-1963			
June 1961	Independence; crisis over Iraqi claims to Kuwait; British troops return		
1963			
Mar	– Agreement on diplomatic relations		
1964			Oct – Artists in Kuwait (first cultural exchange)
		Nov – Finance minister in USSR for aid talks	
1965		Feb – Economic delegation in Kuwait: technical assistance agreement	Feb – Doctors in Kuwait to teach medicine
1966		Aug – Trade minister in USSR: first trade agreement	
		Sept – Public works minister in USSR	
		Oct – Contract for delivery of cargo ships to Kuwait	
1967		Feb – Fishing delegation in Kuwait: contract for delivery of seiners to Kuwait	
			Mar – Cultural agreement
		May – Deputy trade minister in Kuwait	
		July – Oil minister in USSR	
		Aug – Fisheries minister in Kuwait	
1968			Sept – Cultural minister in USSR: exchange agreement for 1968-69
		Oct – Contract for delivery of additional cargo ships to Kuwait	
1969			May – Soviet tourists in Kuwait
			Oct – Education minister in Kuwait
		Dec – Ships completed for Kuwait	
1970		Oct – Oil delegation in USSR for talks on co-operation	

References

(1) A. Leonidov, in <u>Sovremennyy Vostok</u>, No. 10 (October), 1958 (reviewed in <u>Mizan</u>, January 1959, p. 7).

(2) <u>Izvestiya</u>, 30 June, 1961.

(3) <u>Izvestiya</u>, 7 July, 1961.

(4) <u>Aziya i Afrika segodnya</u>, No. 8 (August), 1961 (reviewed in <u>Mizan</u>, July-August 1961, p. 7).

(5) Y. Andreyanov, in <u>International Affairs</u>, No. 10 (October), 1962, p. 79.

(6) Qasim's pretension to Kuwait was given as one reason for his fall; see <u>Pravda</u>, 26 February, 1963.

(7) See <u>Mizan</u>, May 1964, p. 62; Khrushchev's remarks were toned down in official Russian and Egyptian versions of the speech.

(8) U.S. Department of State, RSES-35, 12 August, 1970, p. 68.

(9) <u>Pravda</u>, 1 August, 1970.

Soviet policies in Lebanon from 1955 to 1970 fit into no easy niche in Soviet Middle Eastern policies generally. Part Muslim, part Christian, Lebanon was neither a typical Arab state nor a state like Turkey or Iran, firmly linked to the West through military pacts.

The chronology below shows that Soviet-Lebanese ties remained fairly constant during the years reviewed, but they were never close. There were no exchanges involving heads of state or premiers and fewer than a dozen governmental exchanges of consequence. Economic relations were limited mainly to co-operation rather than aid and credits, since Lebanon was a wholly self-sufficient and even prosperous nation by most criteria. Trade grew slightly over the 16-year period, but Lebanon did not become one of Russia's important trading partners, or vice versa. (1) Cultural relations were more active, in large part because Beirut was the site of many international conferences attracting Soviet academicians. (2) In 1967 there were 380 Lebanese students in the USSR, though the number fell during the next two years; the USSR offered 40 study grants to Lebanese students in the academic year 1969-70. (3)

The Russians found few opportunities to improve relations with Lebanon, as they did at one time or another with all other Middle Eastern states except Saudi Arabia, because of Beirut's persistent orientation to the West. After the crisis of 1958 (the outbreak of civil war in May and the landing of American marines in July), a Soviet-Lebanese rapprochement seemed likely for a time. A comparatively liberal government under Rashid Karame, whom Soviet writers had praised when he was in opposition, repudiated the Eisenhower Doctrine and took steps to restrict foreign oil companies in Lebanon – measures which were of course approved in the Russian press. (4) However, no rapprochement occurred and with the fall of the Karame government in 1960 the chances of better relations between Moscow and Beirut receded. Successive governments in Beirut reaffirmed Lebanon's ties with the West (while professing neutrality), guaranteed foreign investments against nationalization, proclaimed their antipathy to Communism, and remained generally aloof from Arab alignments. Soviet commentaries, meanwhile, became more and more perfunctory: the occasional proclamations of neutrality were duly approved; any evidence of improved relations between Beirut and Cairo was applauded; periodic calls at Beirut by the American Sixth Fleet, the most persistent theme in Soviet commentaries, were formally condemned.

The absence of more sustained relations between Russia and Lebanon gave special importance to Moscow's relations with Lebanese Communists. Delegations from the illegal LCP made frequent visits to Moscow (undoubtedly more than were officially reported – see Chronology) and kept Soviet leaders informed of developments in Beirut; for instance, it may well have been Nicola Shawi's assurances about the Karame government of 1958-60 which led to the Russians' favourable judgment of it, in particular for not succumbing to the wave of anti-Communist hysteria then rampant in most Arab countries. (5) When later governments in Beirut began their own anti-Communist campaigns, Soviet journalists protested vigorously – perhaps

more so than in the case of such persecution elsewhere – and stoutly defended the "patriotic" role of the LCP. (6) Meanwhile, the unequivocal support given to Moscow by Lebanese Communists in the dispute with Peking assured them of Moscow's continuing good will. (7) It is difficult, of course, to measure with much precision the relative influence in Moscow of this or that Communist party, but it may be said of the Lebanese party that it perhaps served as more than a mere transmission belt of routine information and instruction; Shawi and his colleagues were in a sense surrogates for official Lebanese representatives who appeared too infrequently in Moscow to provide Russians with the intelligence they required. If one purpose of Soviet activities in Beirut was to maintain a convenient listening post in the Middle East, it may well have been Lebanese Communists who did the listening. (8)

The Six Day War led to a slight improvement in Russian relations with Lebanon. Beirut's prompt endorsement of the Arab cause and the dismissal of the American and British Ambassadors (though only for three months) won the Russians' respect and stimulated economic talks in the autumn; it is quite possible that arms were offered to Lebanon at this time (as they were to Jordan) though none, of course, were accepted. Although the Lebanese held to their pro-Arab position in the following years, the activity of Palestinian commandos operating in the southern border regions became of increasing concern to Beirut; guerrilla bases in Lebanese villages were often the target of fierce Israeli reprisals, with heavy losses to the Lebanese. The Russians, uneasy as they were about the Palestinian guerrillas, were doubtless sympathetic to Beirut's efforts to control the fedayeen, but it was impolitic to say so; moreover, it was unnecessary, Soviet diplomats probably felt, since Russia's stake in Lebanon was insignificant. The Russians, accordingly, took the part of the Palestinians when severe fighting broke out between the fedayeen and Lebanese armed forces in the autumn of 1969. The crisis was due, it was argued, to American-Israeli success in stirring up "native reactionary forces" (the Lebanese Army) against "national patriotic forces" (the fedayeen). (9) This interpretation, it may be noted, was in marked contrast to the Soviet view of similar clashes between Jordanian armed forces and the fedayeen a year later, when "extremists" among the latter were held partly to blame (see under Jordan).

Soviet-Lebanese relations thus remained in an uncertain state. Some episodes – like the inexplicable effort of two Russian nationals in September 1969 to buy a Lebanese Mirage fighter (10) momentarily soured the relationship. Others sweetened it – for instance, the legalizing of the LCP on the eve of the Presidential elections in 1970, which was seen as a sign that "progressive and patriotic forces are gaining an increasingly strong position" (a view that contrasted sharply with Vladimir Kudryavtsev's judgment three years earlier that Lebanon was "the Middle East appendage to Western business"). (11) Lebanon's steadfast support of the Arab cause against Israel, meanwhile, continued to provide the basis for a stronger rapprochement with Russia, but it was a rapprochement that up to the end of 1970 had still not matured.

Chronology

	Political	Economic	Cultural
Pre-1955			
1944	Diplomatic relations established with legations		
		Apr 1954 Trade agreement	
1955			
			Nov – Cultural delegation in Lebanon
1956			
		Feb – Economic mission in Lebanon	
June –	Foreign minister Shepilov in Lebanon: legations raised to embassies		
			July – Beirut metropolitan in USSR
			Sept – Cultural delegation in USSR
1957			
		Apr – Commercial delegation in USSR	
			? – Soviet cultural centre opens in Beirut
			Sept – Academicians in Beirut for international conference
			Oct – Medical delegation in USSR
1958			
May –	Civil war in Lebanon		
July –	US marines land at government request after Iraqi revolution		
1959			
Jan –	CP secretary Shawi in USSR for XXI congress	Jan – Trade protocol	
			Aug – Antioch patriarch in USSR
1960			
			Mar – Scientists in Lebanon
Dec –	CP delegation in USSR for world conference		
1961			
		Jan – Trade protocol for 1961-63	
Oct –	Shawi in USSR for XXII congress		
1962			
			? – Scientific vessels call at Beirut
			May – Cultural delegation in Lebanon

	Political	Economic	Cultural
1963			Apr – New cultural centre opens in Beirut
		Nov – Trade protocol	Nov – Delegation in Beirut for international political science conference
1964	Nov – Opposition leader in USSR		
1965	Sept – First parliamentary delegation in USSR		Sept – Journalists in USSR
			Oct – Writers' delegation in Lebanon
		Dec – Trade protocol	
1966	Mar – Deputy foreign minister Kuznetsov in Lebanon – CP delegation in USSR for XXIII congress		
			June – Religious delegation in Lebanon
		July – Aviation delegation in USSR for air service talks	
	Sept – Deputy foreign minister Semenov in Lebanon		
	Nov – Municipal delegation in Beirut		
1967		Mar – Trade protocol	Mar – Writers' delegation in Lebanon for Afro-Asian conference
	May – Parliamentary delegation in Lebanon		
	Oct – Government delegation in USSR for anniversary	Oct – Economic delegation in Lebanon for talks on co-operation	Oct – Agreement on cultural exchange
	Nov – CP delegation in USSR		Nov – Muslim delegation in USSR
		Dec – Technical assistance agreement on granary, subway and mineral survey	
1968		Apr – Trade protocol	
	June – Foreign minister in USSR	? – Air service agreement	
	Oct – CP delegation in USSR		
	Dec – Israeli retaliatory raid on Beirut airport		Dec – Education official in Armenia
1969		Feb – Trade protocol	

Political	Economic	Cultural
1969 (cont.)		
		Apr – Radio officials in Lebanon
	May – Moscow–Beirut air service inaugurated	
June – CP delegation in USSR for world conference		June – TU delegation in USSR – Journalists in USSR
		Aug – Gift of polio vaccine – Journalists in Lebanon
Sept – Lebanon expels Soviet officials after plot to steal plane		Sept – Publishers in USSR
Oct – CP secretary Shawi in USSR – Clashes between Lebanese and Palestinian guerrillas		
1970		
Mar – Moscow city delegation in Beirut		Mar – TU delegation in USSR
May – Youth leader in USSR for Komsomol congress		
June – Parliamentary speaker in USSR		June – Minister of tourism in USSR: agreement – First Red Cross delegation in USSR
	July – Economic minister in USSR: trade agreement	July – Cultural protocol for 1970
Aug – CP legalized in Jordan		
		Oct – TU leader in Moscow for WFTU meeting
Nov – CP delegation in Armenia for anniversary		

References

(1)   During the years 1965–67 Russia ranked ninth among foreign importers of Lebanese goods, but was insignificant as an exporter of goods to Lebanon; The Middle East and North Africa, 1969–70, p. 443.

(2)   See Korneyev, Nauchnyye svyazi Akademii nauk SSSR so stranami Azii i Afriki, pp. 225–29.

(3)   U.S. Department of State, RSES-35, 12 August, 1970, p. 65.

(4)   For a review of Soviet commentaries during this Karame government (he was Premier seven times between 1955 and 1969), see Mizan, May 1960, pp. 7–9.

(5)   See V. Viktorov and I. Sashko, in Mirovaya ekonomika i mezhdunarodnyye otnosheniya, No. 1 (January), 1960 (noted in Mizan, May 1960, p. 7).

(6)   E.g. L.N. Chernov, in Narody Azii i Afriki, No. 5 (September–October), 1961, p. 30; Pravda, 31 March and 8 September, 1963.

(7)   LCP views on the Sino-Soviet dispute were reported, inter alia, in Pravda, 17 August and 4 September, 1963, and 12 April, 1964.

(8)   In partial support of this hypothesis, it is interesting to note the relative formality of Soviet reporting of Shawi's visits to Moscow – for instance, the TASS communiqué of 10 October, 1969, which reads like an official protocol.

(9)   TASS statement in Pravda, 26 October, 1969.

(10)   The Russians of course denied the Lebanese charge – e.g. Radio Moscow, 1 October, 1969 – but it was widely believed.

(11)   Kudryavtsev's view was given in an article in New Times, No. 41 (11 October), 1967, p. 25; the more hopeful appraisal appeared in Izvestiya, 25 September, 1970.

Diplomatic ties between the USSR and Libya were agreed upon in September 1955, embassies being exchanged a few months later, and it may be argued that this marked the high point in Soviet-Libyan relations until after September 1969. Exchanges of all sorts were minimal. Trade was virtually non-existent until an agreement was negotiated in 1963 and thereafter was insignificant; along with Jordan and Saudi Arabia, Libya ranked at the bottom of Russia's list of trading partners in the Middle East and North Africa throughout the 1960s. Aid was offered in 1958 but was refused - according to Soviet accounts, because of American objections. (1) A gift of two hospitals was accepted and their completion was announced in December 1964.

Despite this meagre record of co-operation, Soviet comment on Libya was not necessarily harsh. Professor Potekhin, for instance, considered in 1956 that Libya was more a victim than an accomplice of Western imperialism and observed that while British and American bases "enormously impair the independence of Libya . . . nonetheless Libya is no longer a colony, but a sovereign state". (2) Articles marking the 10th anniversary of Libya's independence in 1961 took favourable notice of the current Five-Year Plan and emphasized Libya's neutrality; Libyan foreign policy, it was said, "is based on the principles of non-participation in aggressive military blocs, peaceful coexistence and international co-operation". (3) Commentaries during the 1960s continued in this vein, emphasizing in particular the liability of the foreign bases and the growing "popular" demand for their evacuation.

In the absence of significant economic contacts, the Russians had few instruments with which to fashion an active policy in Libya. No Communist organization existed, and while there were radical elements, especially among the youth, these elements were more drawn to Cairo than Moscow; the Russians apparently felt that any effort to cultivate "progressive" circles in Libya would arouse suspicions in Egypt and therefore serve no good purpose. Meanwhile, the steady development of new oil fields, which made Libya by 1968 the fourth largest oil exporter in the world, had the effect of bringing King Idris's

regime into even closer relationship with Europe and isolating it from Arab politics; this tendency was particularly pronounced after the closing of the Suez Canal in 1967, which accelerated sales of Libyan oil in the crucial European market. The Soviet Union under these circumstances could merely keep existing ties open and await developments.

The overthrow of the monarchy and establishment of a republic in September 1969 opened a new era in Soviet-Libyan relations. The Russians immediately recognized the new regime and praised it. Igor' Belyayev, Pravda's chief commentator on Arab affairs, compared the Libyan "revolution" with the recent upheaval in the Sudan as marking the trend of the times: "The process of active political transformation has spread to a country traditionally among the most backward states in the Middle East." (4) Comment continued to be favourable as the young Libyan officers consolidated their grip on the nation and implemented their radical programme: British and American bases were evacuated in the spring of 1970; foreign oil companies were partially nationalized by mid-summer and foreign banks by the end of the year. (5) The Russians meanwhile began talks with Libya in March 1970 on the surveying and exploitation of new oil fields in the Libyan Sahara. There were also negotiations on expanded trade, on an air service between the two countries and on other matters.

If evidence of Soviet influence with the new regime, given its "progressive" character, was less dramatic during 1970 than some foreign observers had anticipated, this was again due to the reliance of the Libyan leaders on Cairo. Nasser's death a year after the Libyan revolution doubtless affected this relationship, since it was Nasser above all who had inspired the Libyan officers. The Libyan regime, however, joined with Egypt and the Sudan six weeks after Nasser's death in establishing the Federation of Arab States, a move which the Russians strongly applauded as a step towards unity. (6) Whether the new union would have the effect of bringing the Libyans into a closer relationship with Cairo, and so continue to circumscribe bi-lateral Soviet-Libyan ties, time alone would tell.

Chronology

	Political	Economic	Cultural
1951 Dec	– Independence		
1955 Sept	– Agreement on diplomatic relations		
1958		Feb – Economic aid offered	
1959		July – Gift of 2 hospitals, medical training centre	
1960		Oct – Contract for hospitals	
1961 Mar	– Parliamentary delegation in USSR	Mar – Central Asian commercial delegation in Libya	Apr – Muslim delegation in Libya
1962			Jan – Bolshoy dancers in Libya Apr – Muslims in Libya
1963		Apr – Aid to earthquake victims May – Trade delegation in Libya: first agreement Sept – Air service agreement	Mar – Writers in Libya Sept – Journalists call in Libya during conference cruise
1964		Dec – Hospitals completed	Aug – Muslim delegation in USSR
1966 May	– Supreme Soviet delegation in Libya		
1968			Sept – Delegation in Tashkent for writers' conference
Oct	– Parliamentary delegation in USSR		
?	– Municipal delegation in USSR for city planning conference		
1969 May	– Naval vessels call at Tripoli		
July	– Foreign minister in USSR		
Sept	– Military coup ends monarchy; republic proclaimed; foreign bases to close; USSR recognizes new regime		

Political	Economic	Cultural
1970		
	Mar - Oil minister in USSR for aid, trade talks	
	May - Oil experts in Libya to estimate deposits	
	- Transport delegation in Libya for talks on air service	
June - Wheelus field evacuated by USA	June - Sales agreement on Moskvich cars	
	July - Air service inaugurated	
	Sept - Contract for oil surveys	Sept - Journalists in Libya
	Dec - Libyan banks nationalized	
	- Air transport delegation in USSR: agreement	

References

(1)   New Times, No. 39 (September), 1959, p. 19.

(2)   Sovetskoye Vostokovedeniye, January 1956 (reviewed in Mizan, January 1962, p. 2).

(3)   V.M. Fedorenko, in Aziya i Afrika segodnya, No. 12 (December), 1961 (excerpts in Mizan, May 1962, p. 22); see also Pravda and Izvestiya, 24 December, 1961.

(4)   Pravda, 6 September, 1969, p. 5.

(5)   For enthusiastic Soviet coverage of these developments, see, inter alia, V. Kudryavtsev in Pravda, 3 February, 1970; P. Demchenko in Izvestiya, 7 July, 1970; and an unsigned article in Pravda, 24 December, 1970.

(6)   E.g. Pravda, 11 November, 1970.

Morocco, at the outermost fringe of the Arab world and with ties closer to Europe than the Middle East, would seem at first glance an unlikely object of Russian attention. Moroccan good will was at no time critical to Soviet interests; nor was this a potentially "progressive" state by Moscow's standards. Morocco was described as "an absolute monarchy" in a standard Soviet reference work in 1962, inasmuch as all legislative and executive authority was concentrated in the person of King Hassan II. (1) The Soviet Arabist G.I. Mirskiy, generally considered a "revisionist" where social changes in Arab states were concerned, compared Morocco in 1964 to the Ivory Coast, Nigeria and certain Latin American dictatorships - countries where local élites were said to have "close relations with feudalists" and to have "joined forces with foreign monopolies". (2) These judgments of Morocco's domestic, political and economic structure did not alter appreciably over the years. Yet Soviet relations with Morocco were cordial during most of the period under review, no less so in fact than with some Third World nations more highly praised in Russian commentaries.

Fluctuations in the temperature of Soviet-Moroccan relations usually reflected the uneven course of Morocco's relations with other Great Powers or with its neighbours. The Sultan's lingering irritation with the French, for instance, because of their kidnapping of Algerian rebels under his protection in 1956, was partly responsible for the establishment of diplomatic relations with Moscow 18 months later. Russian support for the Sultan's claim to Mauritania (expressed in a veto of Mauritania's application for membership in the United Nations in December 1960 and in Brezhnev's personal assurances during his state visit to Rabat a month later (3)) opened the way for more intimate ties early in the 1960s; by the same token, Russia's gradual desertion of Morocco on the Mauritanian issue was in part the cause of more restrained ties by 1963. A more direct cause of coolness in 1963 was Rabat's rivalry with its other immediate neighbour, Algeria, by this time a close ally of the USSR. The Russians could not take Morocco's part, or even express a very convincing neutrality, in this struggle, and in consequence relations with Rabat grew strained, especially during the border war between Morocco and Algeria which broke out in the autumn; this conflict, a Soviet authority on Morocco wrote in 1964, "was provoked by Moroccan reactionaries, at the instigation of American and French imperialists". (4) The impasse in Soviet-Moroccan relations lasted until a new Moroccan crisis with France, over the Ben Barka episode of October 1965, made possible another era of improved relations. (5)

The Six Day War in June 1967 brought greater stability to Russian-Moroccan relations. Although Morocco was too distant from the Eastern Mediterranean to play a significant role in Arab councils, Hassan did identify with the Arab cause. The Russians sought to strengthen this identity. From 1967 on, the pace of Soviet activity in Morocco increased in all areas, including at least two courtesy calls at Moroccan ports by units of the Mediterranean squadron (see Chronology and below). At the end of 1967, acknowledging that the accumulation of Soviet arms in Algeria posed a new threat to Morocco, the Russians arranged further arms transfers to Rabat via Czechoslovakia. The Russians' intense interest in the Arab "summit" conference held in Rabat in December 1969 suggests that the Russians urged this location for the

conference on their Arab allies in the vain hope of strengthening the moderates on the Palestinian issue (Morocco, Jordan, Tunisia and the UAR) against the extremists (Syria, Iraq, Southern Yemen and Al-Fatah).(6)

The Moroccan Communists played a small role in Soviet strategies in Morocco, as in most Arab countries when diplomatic relations were satisfactory. When the PCM was banned in 1959, Soviet commentators made the expected protests and argued that now an extra burden was placed on the Leftist trade unions. (7) In 1963, large numbers of Communists (including the Secretary-General, Ali Yata) were arrested during the border war with Algeria and protests were again sounded in the Soviet press; they persisted after the crisis was resolved. (8) When he was not under arrest, Ali Yata made frequent visits to Moscow and was accorded a reception there not unlike that given other Arab Communist leaders. In 1968 the PCM was renamed the Liberation and Socialist Party and legalized under this name; an LSP delegation under Ali Yata took part openly in the World Communist Conference held in Moscow in June 1969. However, the arrest of Ali Yata on his return to Morocco left the status of the new party in doubt; Soviet protests on this occasion were less severe than in 1963 and 1964 but called for Ali Yata's early release. (9)

Economic, Military and Cultural Relations

Soviet economic aid to Morocco to the end of 1970 was extended in a single credit of approximately $44 million, negotiated during King Hassan's visit to Moscow in 1966. The credit was to cover a dam and power plant on the Dra River, a metallurgical plant and vocational training centre at Casablanca, and various projects for mineral exploitation. (10) Progress on all of these undertakings was reported during the following years. A further credit of approximately $18 million was said to be under negotiation at the end of 1970. (11)

Trade developed rapidly after the initial trade agreement of April 1958: a fourfold increase, for instance, was reported during the years 1959-62. (12) Further expansion was recorded during the latter half of the 1960s, especially after the Six Day War. For the period 1965-68, Morocco ranked seventh among Russia's trading partners in the Middle East and North Africa (see Table C); Russia, meanwhile, ranked fourth among Morocco's trading partners in 1966-67, accounting for about four per cent of total Moroccan trade. (13)

Arms deliveries, following the initial agreement of December 1960, included aircraft and tanks valued at an estimated $10 million; most of this equipment, however, was soon obsolete. (14) Transfers were suspended during the Moroccan-Algerian crisis in 1963 and 1964 but were apparently resumed after the crisis ended. An additional $10 million in arms was reportedly delivered up to the end of June 1967. (15) Military exchanges in 1968 and 1969 suggest that further arms transfers were contemplated. Meanwhile, arms valued at $16 million were reportedly made available by Czechoslovakia, presumably to spare the Russians the embarrassment of contributing to an arms race between Morocco and Algeria. (16)

Cultural relations between Russia and Morocco also improved after the June war. A Soviet consulate was opened in Casablanca at the end of 1967 and a new cultural centre was inaugurated in Rabat in 1968. The number of athletic, trade union, arts and other such exchanges increased several times over during these years. (17)

* * *

Soviet motives in Morocco, to judge from this record, were flexible and policies took shape as opportunities arose. It is accordingly difficult to judge the success or failure of Russian behaviour in this conservative Arab nation. Morocco's adherence to the so-called Casablanca group in 1961 (18), the evacuation of Moroccan bases by the Americans and French, and the closer ties between Morocco and Russia's moderate Arab allies like Egypt after the Six Day War represented distinct gains for Moscow (though it is not clear that these developments owed anything to Russian strategies). On the other hand, the Russians made no perceptible impact on the social and economic policies of the Hassan regime; nor was their influence on Morocco's foreign policies significant. So far as influence was concerned, the French, despite their periodic difficulties with Rabat, continued to dominate Moroccan politics through their economic and military ties. France, in the latter part of the 1960s, regularly consumed about 40 per cent of Moroccan exports, provided 40 per cent of Moroccan imports, extended nearly 40 per cent of all foreign aid, and still maintained a powerful leverage in the Moroccan Army through earlier association and arms transfers. (19) The American record was less formidable, yet American economic aid in 1966 and 1967 nearly matched French, and Morocco's arsenal of modern arms by the end of the decade was predominantly American. The Soviet Union could challenge the French and American advantage in Morocco represented by these outlays only by an effort it was unprepared to make. The Russians were respondents in Morocco, ready to turn to their advantage the errors of other powers; they were never themselves architects of a forward policy.

MOROCCO

Chronology

	Political	Economic	Cultural
Pre-1958			
Mar 1956	Independence		
Oct 1956	France kidnaps FLN leaders under Moroccan protection; riots in Rabat		
1958			
Apr	– Government delegation in USSR for political, economic talks	Apr – First trade agreement	
Aug	– Embassies exchanged		
1959			
Jan	– CP delegation in USSR for XXI congress		
Apr	– Diplomatic relations with CPR		
Oct	– CP banned in Morocco		
1960			
		Feb – Aid for flood victims	
			Aug – Education delegation in USSR
Nov	– Military delegation in USSR: arms agreement		Nov – TU delegation in Morocco
		Dec – Trade protocol for 1961	
1961			
Feb	– BREZHNEV IN MOROCCO for 2-day visit		
Mar	– Sultan Mohammed dies; succeeded by Hassan II		
	– Government delegation in Morocco to meet Hassan		
July	– CP secretary Ali Yata in USSR		
			Sept – Muslim delegation in USSR
Oct	– Ali Yata in USSR for XXII congress		Oct – Education delegation in USSR
Nov	– Military delegation in USSR for anniversary		
	– Marshal Sokolovskiy leads military delegation to Morocco		
Dec	– Military delegation in USSR for aid talks		
1962			
Jan	– Mikoyan in Morocco on 3-day visit	Jan – Trade protocol for 1962	
		Mar – Air service agreement	
May	– Defence minister Malinovskiy in Morocco		
			July – TU delegation in USSR
Sept	– Reported arms deliveries to Morocco (20)		

	Political	Economic	Cultural
1963			
		Jan – Trade protocol for 1963	
Mar	– Hassan in USA for talks on evacuation of US bases in Morocco		
May	– Government delegation in CPR – Elections in Morocco show right swing		
June	– Hassan in France: aid agreement extended	June – Gift of polio vaccine	
			Sept – Cultural delegation in Morocco
Oct	– Algerian-Moroccan border war; CP leaders arrested		Oct – TU delegation in USSR
Dec	– Chou En-lai in Morocco – US bases evacuated	Dec – Trade protocol for 1964	
1964			
Mar	– Border war with Algeria ends		
			Apr – Textile workers in Morocco
1965			
			Feb – TU delegation in Morocco
May	– CPR foreign office official in Morocco		
		Sept – Radiology centre promised	
Oct	– Crisis with France over Ben Barka episode: aid suspended, ambassadors withdrawn		
		Dec – Long-term trade agreement	
1966			
Mar	– Parliamentary delegation in Morocco for anniversary – Ali Yata leads CP delegation to Moscow for XXIII congress		
			Apr – TU delegation in Morocco – Writers in Morocco
July	– Foreign minister in USSR		
		Aug – Economic delegation in Morocco for aid talks	
Oct	– HASSAN IN USSR for 5-day visit	Oct – CREDIT AGREEMENT for metal plant, power station, mining ($44m)	Oct – First cultural, scientific agreement
Nov	– Military delegation in USSR for anniversary		
1967			
Feb	– Hassan in USA for arms talk: reported agreement ($14m) (21)		
			Apr – Scientists in Morocco
		May – Economic delegation in Morocco: protocol on dam, industrial projects	

	Political	Economic	Cultural
1967 (cont.)			
June	– Public works minister in USSR		
		July – Trade delegation in USSR	July – Cultural protocol – Minister of tourism in USSR
Oct	– CP delegation in USSR for anniversary	Oct – Aid agreement with USA ($34m)	
		Nov – Trade, economic delegation in Morocco	
Dec	– Czech-Moroccan arms agreement (estim. $16m)	Dec – Radiology centre completed in Casablanca	
1968			
		Jan – Contract for power station	
		Apr – Trade delegation in Morocco	
May	– Foreign office official in Morocco		
			June – Minister of Islamic affairs in USSR
July	– CP becomes Liberation and Socialist Party: legalized	July – Foreign trade minister in Morocco: agreement for 1969–73	
			Sept – Cultural protocol
Oct	– First Soviet naval vessels visit Morocco		Oct – Cultural centre opens in Rabat
Nov	– Military delegation in Morocco		
		Dec – Protocol on mineral prospecting	
1969			
		Feb – Contract for dam	
Mar	– Liberation and Socialist party delegation in Moscow for preparatory committee and world Communist conference		
Apr	– PODGORNY IN MOROCCO for 6-day visit	Apr – Trade protocol	
			May – TU leaders in USSR
June	– Chief of Staff in USSR		
Aug	– Ali Yata arrested		Aug – Cultural protocol
Sept	– Warships call at Tangier		
			Nov – Muslim delegation in Morocco
Dec	– Arab "summit" in Rabat		
1970			
		Feb – Economic delegation in USSR: trade protocol and agreement on joint commission	Feb – TU delegation in USSR
			Sept – Cultural protocol
		Oct – Contract for thermal power station at Jerada	
		Nov – Trade protocol on oil products	

Political	Economic	Cultural

<u>1970</u> (cont.)

Dec - Trade delegation in USSR:
agreement on orange sales

References

(1)   Afrika segodnya, 1962 (quoted in Mizan, May 1962, p. 26).

(2)   Mirovaya ekonomika i mezhdunarodnyye otnosheniya, No. 6 (June), 1964, pp. 63-64.

(3)   See Pravda, 11 February, 1961, reviewing Brezhnev's visit; Brezhnev was then Chairman of the Praesidium of the Supreme Soviet - that is, Soviet chief of state.

(4)   Yu. M. Golvin, Morokko, 1964 (reviewed in Mizan, March 1965, p. 14); also V. Mayevskiy in Pravda, 17 October, 1963.

(5)   Ben Barka, a Leftist Moroccan leader sought for complicity in a plot against King Hassan, was abducted in Paris in October 1965; the French claimed that the Moroccan Minister of the Interior arranged the abduction, thereby violating France's sovereignty.

(6)   For Soviet coverage of the Rabat conference, see Mizan, November-December 1969, Supplement A, pp. 2-3.

(7)   E.g. G. Ye. Kanayev, Profsoyuznoye dvizheniye v Morokko (1962), reviewed in Mizan, March 1964, pp. 22-24.

(8)   During a three-week period in November and December 1963, Pravda carried no fewer than five articles protesting against the Moroccan arrests; see Mizan, December 1963, p. 31.   For subsequent protests, see Pravda, 2 June, 1964 and 17 July, 1964.

(9)   E.g. Pravda, 8 August, 9 October and 2 December, 1969.

(10) U.S. Department of State, RSB-80, 21 July, 1967, p. 5.

(11) Radio Rabat, 24 December, 1970.

(12) Vneshnyaya torgovlya Soyuza SSR za 1962 god, see Mizan, October 1963, Appendix, p. xviii.

(13) The Middle East and North Africa, 1969-70, pp. 533-34.   An unofficial Moroccan statement in 1968 that trade with the USSR represented 10 per cent of total Moroccan trade was undoubtedly exaggerated; see Radio Rabat, 5 and 6 July, 1968.

(14) See Stuart H. Schaar, "The Arms Race and Defense Strategy in North Africa", American Universities Field Staff, XIII, 9 (December 1967), p. 4; also Adelphi Papers, No. 15 (December 1964), p. 15 and Stephen P. Gibert, "Wars of Liberation and Soviet Military Aid Policy", Orbis, Fall 1966, p. 840.

(15) Joshua and Gibert, Arms for the Third World, p. 23. According to a French source, MIG fighter aircraft were delivered to Morocco at the end of 1967 after Hassan protested against the sale of missiles to Algeria earlier in the year; see "Les Relations entre l'Algérie et l'Union soviétique", Est et Ouest, 1-15 June, 1969, p. 16.

(16) See Stuart H. Schaar, loc. cit., p. 4; also the New York Times, 16 July, 1968 (cited in Joshua and Gibert, op.cit., p. 22).

(17) See U.S. Department of State, RSE-25, 7 May, 1969, p. 26.

(18) Russia's interest in the Casablanca group, consisting mainly of "progressive" African states south of the Sahara, is discussed in my parallel volume, Soviet-African Relations.

(19) See The Middle East and North Africa, 1969-70, pp. 533-34.

(20) Adelphi Papers, No. 15 (December 1964), p. 15.

(21) Stuart H. Schaar, loc.cit., p. 4.

Saudi Arabia is the only sovereign nation in the Middle East with which the USSR maintained no diplomatic relations during the period covered by this study. Relations between the two states were accordingly non-existent, apart from a trickle of trade, the visits to Mecca of occasional Soviet Muslim delegations, and the rare visits of Russian correspondents to Riyadh.

Moscow's attitude towards Saudi Arabia, however, was not necessarily hostile. In the latter half of the 1950s, for instance, as Russians were feeling their way into the Arab world, it was occasionally recalled by Soviet commentators that Russia had been the first foreign power to recognize Ibn Saud's assumption of rule over the Hijaz in 1926 and that a Soviet Legation had existed in Riyadh for the next dozen years. Saudi opposition to the Baghdad Pact was of course approved and King Sa'ud's expressions of non-alignment respected. The author of a 1957 volume on Saudi Arabia wrote that the efforts of both Ibn Sa'ud and of his son King Sa'ud (1953-64) to create a centralized state "accorded with the aspirations to unity and independence shared by the disunited population of the amirates and tribes of Arabia". As David Morison wrote in Mizan in 1959, in a review of this book and other recent Soviet writing on Saudi Arabia, Moscow appeared to view the Saudi government "rather as a victim of American designs than an executant of them". (1) As late as the spring of 1962, Soviet specialists on the Middle East continued to view Saudi Arabia as non-aligned: G. Mirskiy and R. Avakov, for instance, in an important article on class structure in developing countries, bracketed Saudi Arabia with Ethiopia, Afghanistan, Nepal, and Yemen (nations which enjoyed good relations with Moscow at this juncture) as countries which were essentially feudal, yet for historical reasons neutralist in their foreign policies. (2) The Russians, to judge from these commentaries, would have been prepared at any time up to 1962 to establish diplomatic relations with Saudi Arabia but were kept from it by the kingdom's traditional isolationism. (3)

King Sa'ud's support for the Imam of Yemen, following the latter's overthrow in September 1962, marked a turning point in Russia's attitude toward Saudi Arabia. In October an Izvestiya correspondent wrote of the "complete bankruptcy of King Sa'ud" and implied that even Crown Prince Faisal was dissatisfied with the nation's course. (4) Khrushchev told the Supreme Soviet in December that King Sa'ud's regime was "hanging by a thread" and cited as evidence of the depraved conditions within Saudi Arabia the persistence of slavery there. (5) Slavery then became for a time a central focus in Soviet commentaries on the kingdom - an issue on which it was always possible, needless to say, to arouse high passions. An item in Pravda in the following September, reporting the emancipation of 1,500 slaves, pointed out that there were "tens of thousands" left in bondage; "if emanci-

pation proceeds at the present pace, the process will take a hundred years." (6)

There was some let-up in Soviet criticism of Saudi Arabia after Prince Faisal assumed power from King Sa'ud in 1964 (he took on full executive power in May and succeeded to the throne in November). Pavel' Demchenko wrote in Pravda immediately after the succession that Faisal was "regarded as a supporter of reforms" and noted that he had signed a resolution at the recent Cairo conference of non-aligned nations calling for the liquidation of foreign bases. (7) An Izvestiya correspondent, admitted to Riyadh soon after the accession, reported favourably on the changes already taking place in Saudi life; he also quoted Faisal as saying: "We have no differences with the Soviet Union and nothing to prevent developing our relations and co-operation." (8)

This milder attitude towards Saudi Arabia was undoubtedly prompted as much by the cautious approach of Khrushchev's successors (only a month in power) as by rash expectations of Faisal; the new regime in Moscow presumably wished to review Soviet relations with different Arab states - with neglected ones, like Kuwait and Saudi Arabia, no less than with long-established allies, like the UAR and Algeria. The mood, however, did not last. As cease-fire agreements in Yemen repeatedly broke down and persistent Saudi support of the Yemeni Royalists led to increasing estrangement with Cairo, the Russians reverted to their harsher judgments of Saudi Arabia. All that had changed was that a younger monarch now ruled in Riyadh, able to pursue with greater vigour traditional Saudi goals of hegemony based on conservatism and reaction. (9) By the end of the 1960s, despite a significant improvement in relations between Cairo and Riyadh, Soviet-Saudi relations remained parlous.

References

(1) Mizan April 1959, p. 5; the 1957 volume by the Pravda commentator I.P. Belyayev was entitled Amerikanskiy imperializm v Saudovskoy Aravii.

(2) Mirovaya ekonomika i mezhdunarodnyye otnosheniya, No. 4 (April), 1962 (translated in Thornton, Third World in Soviet Perspective, p. 295).

(3) A Saudi Foreign Office official visited Moscow in September 1962, possibly to discuss the establishment of diplomatic relations, but events in Yemen (see below) over-shadowed his visit and nothing came of it.

(4) Izvestiya, 13 October, 1962.

(5) Pravda, 13 December, 1962.

(6) Pravda, 7 September, 1963.

(7) Pravda, 13 November, 1964.

(8) Izvestiya, 29 November, 1964.

(9) See Mizan, March-April 1968, pp. 55-57.

The guiding principle of Soviet policies in Aden, during the turbulent years before its independence in 1967, was to avoid a firm commitment to any of the factions struggling for power in the protectorates and to focus attention instead on the evils of British imperialism. Thus British-inspired projects for federation in South Arabia were regularly denounced, while the various nationalist movements were pictured as united in their search for independence. (1) Negotiations in London in 1964, looking towards the inclusion of Aden in the South Arabian Federation and the independence of all of South Arabia by 1968, were the subject of particularly acid criticism by Russian spokesmen. Khrushchev, speaking in Cairo in April, said that any agreement with the British over Aden was "like an agreement between a hanged man and the rope on which he dangles"; (2) scholarly commentaries, though less colourful, were in the same vein. (3) The Russians meanwhile grew cautious on the question of eventual union between Aden and Yemen. In the 1950s, when there had not appeared to be controversy in the matter among nationalists in Aden, Moscow supported Yemen's claim to the British protectorate (see under Yemen); in 1964 the Soviet-Egyptian communiqué issued at the end of Khrushchev's visit to the UAR pointedly ignored the question of merger, despite Nasser's warm support of it, because the matter was now at issue among rival factions in Aden.

As independence drew closer and the internecine struggle in the protectorate grew more fierce - especially between the Cairo-backed Front for the Liberation of Southern Yemen (FLOSY) and the Marxist-oriented National Liberation Front (NLF) - the Russians persisted in their neutrality. It was the NLF which finally prevailed in 1967 and it was this leadership which Moscow recognized when the People's Republic of Southern Yemen was proclaimed. (4)

During the three years following Aden's independence, relations between the new republic and Russia developed rapidly, military relations in particular. No announcement was made of the value of Soviet arms and services made available to Southern Yemen, but to judge from the frequency of high military exchanges co-operation was extensive. (5) Rumours circulated in 1970 that the Russians were constructing a base on one of the islands off the Southern Yemeni coast, but they were promptly denied in Aden. (6) A technical assistance agreement was meanwhile concluded, along with various other agreements, during President Ash-Sha'bi's visit to Moscow in January 1969; the amount of the credit was not announced at the time, but subsequent reports indicated loans and gifts totalling $13,200,000 (see Chronology). By mid-1970 the Russians were engaged in the construction of eight dams, three maintenance shops, and many wells in Southern

Yemen, in addition to extensive co-operation in the fields of medicine and fishing. (7) More than 300 Southern Yemeni students were in East European countries during 1970, the majority of them in the USSR. (8)

The Russians appear to have maintained their neutral posture with respect to persistent domestic upheavals, caused by rivalry not only between the NLF and other parties, such as FLOSY, but within the NLF itself, where a bitter struggle was waged between radicals and moderates. In June 1969 Ash-Sha'bi was forced to resign in what the Russians described as a "purely internal" affair. (9) Moscow immediately recognized the new government (which was in fact regarded as more pro-Soviet than its predecessor), and by early 1970 Soviet commentators were praising its leaders as "patriots who aim to build a new life on the principles of scientific socialism"; Southern Yemen, it was said, had entered the "national democratic stage" of its revolution. (10) These favourable judgments persisted throughout 1970. In July a Pravda correspondent, noted that where many other Arab countries had to experience "both religious-feudal and bourgeois-liberal stages" before the emergence of a "socialist-oriented regime", Southern Yemen had "bypassed these stages"; thanks to "radical revolutionary elements" in the NLF, Southern Yemen was already on the "course of socialist development". (11) It was therefore fitting, another Pravda correspondent observed in October, that the former British protectorate should assume the name of "people's democracy" - the Yemen People's Democratic Republic. (12)

*   *   *

The Chinese rivalled the Russians in Southern Yemen, as in Yemen, and one would be hard put to say which had the upper hand by 1970. The Chinese credit extended in September 1968 was the first from a socialist country, and progress on a number of Chinese-supported projects was subsequently reported. Meanwhile, Peking found many supporters among the wide spectrum of radicals in Southern Yemen, both in and out of the NLF; certainly there were more "Maoists" in Southern Yemen, relative to its size, than in any other Arab state. One might imagine that Peking's close relationship with the Ash-Sha'bi government would damage relations with the post-June 1969 regime, believed to incline towards Moscow. The Russians, for their part, encouraged estrangement by occasionally calling attention to Chinese subversive activity among radical elements in the Eastern province, where, it was alleged, Peking sought to form a "small Biafra" for its own purposes. (13) Sino-Southern Yemeni relations, however, did not deteriorate. To judge from persistent and even growing ties between China and Southern Yemen during 1970, the Russians had met their match in this strategic South Arabian nation.

SOUTHERN YEMEN

Chronology

	Political	Economic	Cultural
Pre-1967			
June 1964	London conference on independence (in 1968)		
1967			
Aug	– British begin withdrawal from Aden		
Nov	– Delegation in USSR for anniversary – Republic proclaimed; recognized by USSR and CPR		
1968			
Feb	– Defence minister in USSR		
Apr	– Military delegation in South Yemen		
June	– Soviet naval squadron calls at Aden		
Aug	– Military assistance agreement		
Sept	– Military mission in South Yemen – Foreign minister in CPR: agreement on diplomatic relations	Sept – CPR credit for economic development ($12m) (14)	Sept – Cultural minister in USSR
		Oct – Gift of anti-locust chemicals	Oct – TU officials in USSR
Nov	– Defence minister again in USSR		
		Dec – Economic delegation in South Yemen for aid talks – Fisheries delegation in South Yemen	
1969			
Jan	– PRESIDENT ASH-SHA'BI IN USSR for 11-day visit: reported arms agreement (15) – Naval vessels call at Aden	Jan – Agreements on technical co-operation, trade, fisheries, air communications (reported credit of $13.2m) (16)	Jan – Cultural agreement
			Feb – TU delegation in South Yemen
			Mar – Film festival in Aden
		Apr – Aeroflot office opens in Aden	
May	– Ash-Sha'bi again in USSR en route to North Korea – Military delegation in South Yemen		
June	– Ash-Sha'bi overthrown in military coup		
			Oct – Medical mission in South Yemen
Nov	– Naval vessels call at Aden	Nov – Trade and aid protocols	
1970			
		Jan – Gift of 2 seiners from Far East fleet	
		Feb – Chinese aid delegation in South Yemen	
Apr	– National front delegation in Moscow for Lenin centenary	Apr – Protocol on irrigation canals	
			May – Education delegation in South Yemen: cultural protocol and agreement on scholarships

Political	Economic	Cultural

<u>1970</u> (cont.)

July – Aden municipal delegation in Moscow
     – National front delegation in USSR to study CPSU training

Aug – <u>High government delegation in CPR</u>

Sept – Defence minister in USSR on holiday

Nov – Supreme Soviet official in South Yemen for third anniversary

July – Fishing delegation in USSR to discuss co-operation

Aug – <u>Aid agreement with CPR</u>

Sept – Education delegation in USSR to study teacher training

Oct – TU delegation in Moscow for WFTU meeting

Dec – Education delegation in South Yemen

References

(1) E.g. L.N. Kotlov and Z.I. Levin, writing in <u>Poslednyye kolonii v Azii</u> (1958), and A. Nil'skiy, in <u>Sovremennyy Vostok</u>, No. 9 (September), 1959 (reviewed in <u>Mizan</u>, October 1959, pp. 4-6).

(2) <u>Mizan</u>, May 1964, p. 62, quoting impromptu remarks at a trade union meeting.

(3) E.g. <u>Mirovaya ekonomika i mezhdunarodnyye otnosheniya</u>, No. 1 (January), 1964, pp. 102-6 and No. 5 (May), 1964, pp. 74-76; also a chapter by L.V. Vol'kova in <u>Kolonializm vchera i segodnya</u> (1964).

(4) For a discussion of events in Aden leading to independence, see <u>The Middle East and North Africa, 1969-70</u>, pp. 619-27; also, for Soviet views on these developments, Laqueur, <u>The Struggle for the Middle East</u>, pp. 108-9.

(5) According to an article by Joy Gerville-Réache in <u>The Christian Science Monitor</u> (3 April, 1970), Russia provided Southern Yemen with artillery, tanks, and at least a dozen MIG-17s, with Soviet pilots to fly them; the latter claim must of course be questioned, though Soviet instructors were quite probably sent to Southern Yemen.

(6) See the denial of the Southern Yemeni Premier on Radio Kuwait, 24 September, 1970; also Nicholas Ashford in <u>The Times</u>, 11 January, 1971.

(7) Radio <u>Aden</u>, 23 August, 1970.

(8) U.S. Department of State, RSES-35, 12 August, 1970, p. 63.

(9) Radio Moscow in Arabic, 26 June, 1969.

(10) O. Gerasimov in <u>International Affairs</u>, No. 2-3 (February-March), 1970, pp. 107-8.

(11) A. Vasil'yev, <u>Pravda</u>, 13 July, 1970; see also a TASS statement on 13 October, 1970 marking the seventh anniversary of the beginning of the Southern Yemeni revolution.

(12) O. Orestov, <u>Pravda</u>, 26 December, 1970.

(13) Radio Peace and Progress, 13 August, 1969.

(14) U.S. Department of State, RSE-65, 5 September, 1969, p. 2.

(15) <u>The Military Balance</u>, 1969-1970, p. 60.

(16) Radio Moscow, 2 April, 1970.

As the Russians intensified their interest in the Middle East in the mid-1950s, they were helped in Syria by the overthrow of the Shishakli regime in early 1954 and the restoration of a quasi-democratic system. New political forces in Syria emerged as a result of this change, notably the Ba'th Party, a loose grouping of Arab nationalists with varying ideologies but united by a common antipathy to Western domination in the Middle East. In the period 1954-58, the general posture of the Syrian Ba'thists was Leftist, which facilitated collaboration with the USSR as well as with local Communists.

The Syrian Communist Party (CPS) was a powerful instrument for the Russians during these years, not only because of its organization and size (an estimated 10,000 in 1955, which made it the largest Communist party in the Middle East) (1) but also because of the prestige of its First Secretary, Khalid Bakdash. Bakdash, a wealthy and articulate Syrian of Kurdish descent, was by 1955 a widely respected figure in the international movement, having spent many years in exile abroad and having been a frequent visitor in the USSR. He was also widely known and respected at home; returning to Damascus after the overthrow of Shishakli, Bakdash was elected to Parliament in the general elections of 1954 and in the next few years played an important part in Syrian politics. From this new vantage point he continued to interpret Syrian developments to the Russians.

This combination of circumstances, unmatched elsewhere in the Middle East, made Syria a special object of Russian interest from 1954 to the end of 1957. Soviet arms were delivered to Syria in early 1956 (and may have reached Damascus as early as the autumn of 1954). (2) Foreign Minister Shepilov included Damascus in his Middle East itinerary in June 1956. President Quwatli made a state visit to Moscow in October, the first Arab leader to do so; his visit preceded Nasser's maiden visit by a year and a half. The $98 million credit extended to Syria in 1957 was the largest to an Arab country up to that time and preceded the first Soviet credit to Cairo by more than six months. Meanwhile, the Russians on two occasions - in 1955 and 1957 - came to the defence of the Syrians when they appeared to be threatened by Turkish-Iranian troop concentration on their northern border. (3)

The pace of this relationship, however, was too much for the fragile Left Ba'thist-Communist alliance in Damascus. In a series of intricate and rapid political manoeuvres at the end of 1957 and in early 1958, conservative Syrian leaders joined forces with pan-Arabists in Cairo to effect a merger of the two nations as the United Arab Republic - a merger Nasser had long desired. The Russians greeted the formation of the UAR evasively. For some weeks after the announcement no comment at all appeared in the major dailies; when it did, it was non-committal on the virtues of merger per se. Konstantin Ivanov made derisory reference in March to the "fetish of Arab unity", (4) reflecting long-held Soviet antipathy towards pan-Islamic movements, but the existence of the UAR was accepted without demur. Nasser was not less cordially received in Moscow during his first state visit in April and May because Syria had ceased to exist as an independent state.

However good a face the Russians chose to put upon the merger, it was clearly a setback to their strategies in the Middle East. The Syrian Communists were again obliged to go underground; Khalid Bakdash returned to exile in Eastern Europe. Meanwhile, the Russians had lost direct contact with their most promising ally in the Arab world, since all relations with Damascus now had to be channelled through Cairo. These considerations not only contributed to the impasse in Soviet-Egyptian relations during 1959 and 1960 but also made the Russians alert to the hazards of further mergers in the Arab world: Khrushchev, for instance, warned an Iraqi delegation in 1959 that in the light of Syrian experience Baghdad should proceed very carefully in contemplating any union with another Arab state (see under Iraq).

As time passed, criticism of Syria's submergence in the UAR became more outspoken, if not in the Soviet press itself, at least in international journals usually reflecting Moscow's views. Bakdash, for instance, wrote in World Marxist Review in early 1961 that in Syria there was need for "a struggle for liberation from Egyptian colonialism". (5) A Russian author, writing in the same journal later in the year on the dangers of pan-Africanism, cited the "deplorable example" of the UAR, which he said amounted to "the subordination of Syria by Egypt". (6) After Syria left the UAR in September 1961 Soviet comments were more outspoken on mergers of this sort in the hope of discouraging them in the future. (7)

In retrospect, the check to Soviet strategies in Syria in 1958 was perhaps a blessing in disguise for Russia's Middle East policies. The Russians had proceeded too rapidly in Damascus; the gains made by local Communists between 1954 and 1958, largely a reflection of Soviet influence, were unacceptable to Arab leaders accustomed to a more deliberate pace of social and economic changes. Had tensions not been released in 1958, in the merger of Syria with Egypt, they might have grown to more dangerous levels a year or so later. Conservative Arabs in Syria and elsewhere might well have turned to the Western powers to seek intervention against this new threat to their independence; or the Western powers might have intervened without waiting to be asked. The temporary loss of influence in Damascus was a small price for the Russians to pay for avoiding these alternative "solutions" of the Communist problem in the Middle East. Syria's merger with Egypt, in short, was the Russians' escape valve, although they probably did not appreciate this at the time.

Soviet-Syrian ties were re-established after Syria's withdrawal from the UAR in 1961 but were not for some years as close as before the merger. The period 1961-66 was one of exceptional political instability in Syria. There were eight coups in Damascus before the "revolution" of February 1966 which finally established a relatively stable regime. The Russians reacted differently to these coups, depending on whether the forces brought to power were judged to be more progressive or more conservative, but Moscow officially recognized each new regime and managed to move slowly ahead in the programmes previously agreed upon (see below). The general judgment of Syria's political climate, however, was negative, especially where the Ba'thists were concerned. "Chaos prevails in any country which the Ba'thists rule", a Radio Moscow broadcaster asserted after a Right Ba'th coup in March 1963. (8) The Soviet Arabist Georgiy Mirskiy, writing of the same coup later in the year, considered Ba'thist politics in Damascus to be a "merry-go-round . . . [where] no one is trusted, everyone is out to cheat someone else, superiors suspect their subordinates and vice versa, and alliances and coalitions are formed only to fall apart the next day". (9)   The adoption of Leftist slogans by Right Ba'thists, an article in Pravda proclaimed, "cannot save them from the hatred of the Arabs or remove the vast gulf which separates them from their own people". (10) In a book published in early 1965, Mirskiy compared the Syrian Ba'th to a "medieval order, rigidly centralized and unable to co-operate sincerely with anyone"; the central idea of Ba'thist leaders, Mirskiy wrote, was "to 'Ba'thize' the whole Arab world". (11)

By the time Mirskiy's book appeared, however, Left Ba'thist elements had come to the fore in Damascus and the political outlook had changed.   The Rightist leader, Al-Bitar, had been replaced as Premier in October 1964; nationalization was extended to oil and mineral resources in December; conversations between Ba'th leaders and the Communists, looking towards a normalization of relations after eight years, were opened in January. (12)   Under these circumstances Moscow's attitude towards the Ba'th moderated.   First Bakdash (writing as a rule in World Marxist Review, but occasionally in Pravda), then Soviet observers, took note of the fact that Syria had "moved to the Left" and that "young and energetic" leaders were emerging; though still described as a "petty bourgeois party", the Ba'th was now said to be drawing considerable support from workers and peasants. (13)   These more favourable appraisals of Syrian developments continued to the end of 1965, as further economic and military talks between the two nations were carried on in Moscow and Damascus.   Even the return of Al-Bitar in December, in consequence of a short-lived Rightist swing in the Ba'th party, did not wholly dampen the Russians' confidence. "Bitar", one Soviet correspondent wrote (hopefully) in February 1966, "has of late adopted a more flexible line and this has enabled him to ally himself with the 'moderates'". (14)   The correspondent would have done better to reserve judgment, for within a fortnight Al-Bitar had been overthrown and arrested and a new regime established under the pro-Soviet Ba'thists, Yusuf Zu'ayyin and Nur ad-Din Atasi (respectively Premier and President in the new regime).

The Russians' sharply fluctuating views on the Syrian Ba'th between 1961 and 1966, it may be said, do little credit to their perception of politics in Damascus.   The Ba'th party, despite its small size (an estimated 2,000 during this period), was after all the Syrian revolution itself in microcosm.   Like single parties in most developing nations, it was the only vehicle for social change and political modernization.   Later the Ba'th would become less critical in Syrian politics, but in the early 1960s it included all elements which played a significant role in these processes; whether it appeared to be Rightist or Leftist at a given juncture was no more than a reflection of how the centre of political gravity was shifting in a complex revolution.   The Russians, then, in reviling the Ba'th as they did until 1964 (because its leadership seemed to them too Rightist, or too anti-Communist), were in effect reviling the Syrian revolution itself.   Given the temperament of Syrian revolutionaries, the Russians' intransigence in this matter might well have affected the future course of Soviet-Syrian relations; however, they moderated their views in time - quite possibly on the sound counsel of Khalid Bakdash.

The "revolution" of February 1966 accelerated the tempo of Soviet-Syrian relations.   Aid and trade programmes were expanded, cultural exchanges increased

and political ties intensified - including ties with the Syrian Ba'th, now recognized as a "progressive" Arab party comparable to Nasser's Arab Socialist Union (ASU) and the Algerian National Liberation Front (FLN).   These trends in the relationship were well established before the Six Day War.   After the war, since Syria was a principal victim of "Israeli aggression", relations became even closer, at least to all outward appearances.   By 1968 Syria was heavily dependent on the USSR in many areas of its development (see below).   The Soviet press, meanwhile, was generally favourable towards trends in Syria.   Where Soviet and Syrian objectives coincided, Russian commentators were enthusiastic; where there were differences in policy, they were restrained; and where complex domestic rivalries were at issue, the Russians preserved a discreet official silence.   Economic and cultural development lagged, it was sometimes noted, because of defence expenditures that ran as high as 60 per cent of the total budget, but the Israelis not the Syrians were to blame for this. (15)

The official Soviet attitude towards Syria, then, is not difficult to chronicle during the years after the 1966 revolution.   Syria was becoming, by all relevant measurement, one of the two or three most critical countries in Soviet calculations in the Middle East and ranked with the most critical half a dozen in the entire Third World.   What is more difficult, but no less essential, to grasp are the unpublicized differences of outlook in Moscow and Damascus which, despite the closeness of the relationship, made the two nations increasingly wary of each other. The central issue dividing Russians and Syrians was how best to proceed with regard to Israel.   Before the Six Day War their views on the Palestinian question had been more or less similar and their probable complicity in bringing on the crisis has been noted.   After the war their attitudes diverged.   The Soviet Union sought a political solution. Most leaders in Syria - possibly because of embarrassment over the Syrian performance during the fighting (16) - pressed for early reprisals and eventually a total defeat of Israel.   This posture led Syria to boycott the Arab conference at Khartoum in August, which it was felt would adopt too mild a policy, and to deny recognition of the United Nations resolution of 22 November calling for a non-military settlement.   It also led the Syrians to provide full support to the fedayeen: Palestinian commandos were trained in Syria, arms (presumably Russian arms) were made available to them, and Syrian sanctuaries were always available for guerrilla formations returning from raids on Israel through Lebanon or Jordan.   The Russians by contrast sought a limited role for the fedayeen and accordingly resented Syria's unlimited support of them; from Moscow's viewpoint, this led to a weakening of the Arab alliance because of understandable irritation in Jordan and Lebanon, the chief targets of Israeli reprisals following fedayeen attacks.

These fundamental differences in foreign policy placed a heavy burden on Soviet-Syrian friendship.   Yet the differences were concealed for the simple reason that neither nation could tolerate a serious impasse in the relationship - the Syrians because of their reliance on Soviet arms, the Russians because a Syrian defection from the Arab bloc would provide a nucleus for precisely those radical forces in the Middle East that Moscow most wished to hold in check.   Both parties accordingly maintained the fiction of agreement in matters of foreign policy.   The Russians, for instance, conveniently ignored Syrian opposition to the cease-fire proposal of July 1970 (though similar opposition in Baghdad drew a sharp rebuke). They also ignored Syria's intervention in the Jordanian civil war in September, at least officially, though Soviet diplomats undoubtedly worked behind the scenes to restrain their allies in Damascus. (17)

The Russians were no less circumspect in dealing with internal politics in Syria. Official attention was devoted as a rule to the activities of visible Syrian leaders such as President Atasi and, until his removal in the autumn of 1968, Premier Zu'ayyin. Real power, however, the Russians knew, lay with the military, with the Chief of Staff Salah Jadid until early 1969, then increasingly with the Defence Minister and Air Force Commander Hafiz Asad. The Russians faced an awkward choice during the extended confrontation of these two generals. Jadid was known to be sympathetic towards Moscow, along with Atasi and Zu'ayyin, but he was also an ardent supporter of the fedayeen; Asad, on the other hand, was resentful of Soviet influence in Syria yet comparatively moderate, like the Russians, in his approach to the Israeli and Palestinian questions. (18) The Russians probably favoured Jadid, but when Asad finally assumed full powers in a coup in November 1970, they promptly accepted his leadership. A new scientific and technical protocol was signed in Damascus on the day following the coup. Changes in the state apparatus, a Russian radio commentator remarked, were an internal matter "exclusively concerning the Syrians". (19) The important thing, a seasoned Soviet observer noted a fortnight after the crisis, was that the new regime had pledged to preserve the "socialist-oriented reforms" of the previous government and to co-operate with "progressive Arab countries", especially the UAR; Syria's decision to join the Federation of Arab States (Libya, Sudan, and the UAR) was applauded. Under these circumstances "the continuity of Syria's basic anti-imperialist policy" was assured. (20) In February 1971 the Russians received Asad cordially on his first visit to the USSR as the new Syrian leader.

Relations between Moscow and the Syrian Communists appear to have grown more distant during the latter part of the 1960s. For a time after the February 1966 revolution their policies towards the Ba'thists were similar. When Bakdash returned from exile in the spring of 1966, with the permission of the new leaders, the CPS pledged co-operation with the neo-Ba'thists. (21) At least one known Communist was included in the neo-Ba'thist cabinet, though the party itself was still officially illegal. (22) But Russian and Syrian Communists viewed co-operation differently: the Russians urged an intimate relationship, in hopes that the new Ba'th leadership would follow the course of the FLN in Algeria or the ASU in Egypt, leading eventually to a merger of the two parties; Bakdash, always outspoken in matters of Syrian Communist policy, argued that the CPS must continue to be "an independent revolutionary force", since the changes in Syria after the February revolution did not mean a shift towards socialism or even a serious step in that direction. (23) Any "co-operation" offered by the Communists, however, lost significance as the centre of political gravity shifted to the military and the prestige of the Syrian Ba'th declined. By 1970 Communist influence in Damascus was negligible and nothing in Soviet commentaries suggested the Russians expected this situation to change. The CPS loyally supported the cease-fire proposals of July when the Syrian government opposed them - but to what avail? In

December, presumably as an expression of confidence in the new regime, a Soviet journalist explicitly denied rumours of mass Communist arrests in Damascus. (24)

Economic, Military and Cultural Relations

Although there was confusion for some years over the size of the initial 1957 credit, Soviet sources in subsequent years noted it as $98 million. (25) This was intended for assistance in 14 projects, including a 770-kilometre highway, a railway, a fertilizer plant, a factory for making railway wagons, dams, mapping, irrigation, and preliminary exploration of water use on the Euphrates. Work proceeded slowly during the years Syria was in the UAR and several of the projects were cancelled. A new aid agreement was negotiated in 1962, drawing on unused funds from the 1957 credit, and thereafter work proceeded more systematically. In 1966, after the ascendancy of the Left Ba'thists, a second credit was negotiated for the long-awaited Euphrates dam and power complex, an earlier West German offer having been withdrawn in 1965. Numerous protocols and contracts on this major undertaking - one of the largest in the Middle East and often compared (by Syrians) to the Aswan High Dam - were signed in the following years. Work began in the spring of 1968. The cost of the total project was estimated at $628 million and the first stage at $260 million; the Soviet credit of April 1966 ($133 million) was for the first stage. (26) In early 1969 250 Soviet engineers were said to be at work on the project. (27) From 1965 on the Russians were also extensively engaged in oil prospecting in Syria. It was estimated at the end of the 1960s that Soviet credits constituted half of all foreign aid received by Syria for its economic programmes. (28)

Trade, meanwhile, developed rapidly after 1965, more than doubling during the next few years (see Table C). By 1968 Syria ranked fourth among Russia's trading partners in the Middle East; Russia was Syria's principal partner by this date, absorbing about 10 per cent of all Syrian foreign trade. (29)

Soviet military aid to Syria exceeded economic aid even before the June 1967 war and, of course, greatly exceeded it in the following years. The initial agreement (with Czechoslovakia) was concluded in 1956 and thereafter, except during the years when Syria was a part of the UAR, agreements were negotiated periodically, regardless of what regime was in power. It is estimated that arms transfers before the June war totalled more than $300 million; deliveries during the years following the war appear to have totalled nearly twice this sum. The major items delivered were tanks and aircraft, but all types of lesser weapons were included. By 1970 Syria was almost totally dependent upon the USSR for its arms. An effort was made in 1969, at the insistence of General Asad, to alter this dependency by buying arms in Paris and Peking; the French, however, reportedly refused to sell arms to Syria, and Peking would consider sales only for use by the Palestinian commandos. (30) The Syrians' reliance on Soviet arms accordingly persisted; it was undoubtedly stimulated by the presence in Syria of an estimated 600 Soviet military advisers. (31)

Cultural exchange, compared to economic, military, and political activity, seemed inevitably more modest. It was not significantly lower, however, than Soviet co-operation with comparable Arab states. Student exchange grew noticeably after the June war. According to the Syrian Minister of Higher Education, there were 1,000

Syrians studying in the USSR in September 1969 - presumably both academic and technical; (32) if the report were accurate, Syria ranked first in this respect among all Afro-Asian nations.

*   *   *

When the record of Soviet-Syrian relations is fully reviewed there remains a nagging uncertainty as to why this nation, on which the Russians have lavished such attention over the years and for which they have at times had such an "inexplicable affection" (as one student of Arab affairs has put it), (33) has never been ranked in Soviet commentaries alongside the UAR, Algeria, Guinea, Burma, and other "progressive" states.   The obvious reason, perhaps, is that by the time Syria finally became eligible for such a rating - after breaking away from Egypt and after the ascendancy of the Left Ba'thists - its policies vis-à-vis Israel were too much at cross-purposes with Moscow's to encourage a favourable regard on other counts.   It is also true that in the latter half of the 1960s the Russians were less interested in making distinctions between "progressive" and other states in Africa and Asia than they had been when the concept of national democracy was more in vogue.   There is, however, another consideration.   That is the quality of the Ba'th itself, whether Right, Left, or "neo".   As Walter Laqueur has pointed out, (34) Syrian Ba'thists, preoccupied with a constant struggle for survival, not only amongst themselves but in later years against the Army, were incapable of ideology.   Their "socialism", in consequence, was transparent by Soviet standards, and their promises casual.   The Russians, in dealing with favoured nations in the Third World, learnt to tolerate diversity and even error in notions of progress, but they could not condone indifference.   Since the Ba'th appeared to Russian ideologues to be indifferent to the things that mattered most, the only relationship possible between the USSR and Syria was a political tie.   How close or how lasting this should be was a matter for diplomats, not ideologues, to determine.

SYRIA

Chronology

	Political	Economic	Cultural
Pre-1955			
1946	Independence		
Feb 1954	Military regime overthrown; presidential system restored		
Aug 1954		Delegation in Damascus for trade fair	
Nov 1954			Scientists in USSR
Dec 1954			Muslim delegation in USSR
1955			
Mar	- Turkish-Iraqi troops mass on border to pressure Syria into joining Baghdad Pact		
Nov		- First trade agreement	
1956			
Feb	- CP secretary Bakdash in USSR for XX congress - Soviet arms delivered to Syria (35)	- Economic delegation in Syria: promise of aid for granary, oil tanks, cement plant (36)	
June	- Foreign minister Shepilov in Syria		
Aug	- Diplomatic relations with CPR		- First cultural agreement
Sept	- Parliamentary delegation in Syria		
Oct	- PRESIDENT QUWATLI IN USSR for 4-day visit on eve of Suez crisis		
Nov	- Reported arms credit (37)		
1957			
May			- Cultural protocol
June			- Education delegation in USSR
July	- Defence minister Al-Azm in USSR for arms, aid talks		
Aug	- Diplomatic crisis between Syria and United States		
Sept	- Turkish troops again mass on Syrian border; USSR warns Turkey	- Economic delegation in Syria: CREDIT AGREEMENT on railway, fertilizer plant, dam, irrigation, surveys ($98m)	- Cultural delegation in USSR
Oct			- Journalists' delegation in USSR
Dec	- Government delegation in USSR	- Trade protocol - Protocol on fertilizer plant	
1958			
Jan	- Syria, Egypt merge to form UAR; USSR shifts embassy to Cairo; Bakdash goes into exile		

	Political		Economic		Cultural
1959					
Jan	– Bakdash in USSR for XXI congress	Jan	– Protocol on railway construction in Syria		
		Aug	– Protocol on irrigation		
		Dec	– Contracts for dams, power stations		
1960					
		Sept	– Further protocols on railway construction, fertilizer plant		
Oct	– Bakdash in USSR for anniversary and world CP conference				
1961					
Sept	– Syria withdraws from UAR; embassies re-opened in Damascus and Moscow				
Oct	– Bakdash in USSR for XXII congress				
1962					
Feb	– Defence minister heads government delegation to USSR	Feb	– Technical assistance agreement renewed	Feb	– New cultural agreement
Mar	– Military coup in Syria				
		June	– Contract for agricultural centres		
				Aug	– Cultural protocol for 1962-63
Sept	– Military delegation in USSR				
Nov	– Another military delegation in USSR	Nov	– Gift of polio vaccine		
		Dec	– Air service agreement		
1963					
		Feb	– Economic delegation in USSR and CPR: Chinese credit ($16m)	Feb	– Geophysicists in Syria
Mar	– Right Ba'thists seize power in Damascus				
		June	– Contract for cement plant		
1964					
		Mar	– Agreement on diesel fuel deliveries to Syria, petroleum deliveries to USSR		
		May	– CPR delegation in Syria for aid talks		
July	– Bakdash heads CP delegation to USSR for ideological talks				
		Aug	– Industries minister in USSR		
Oct	– Defence minister in USSR				
		Autumn	– Nationalization decrees in Syria		

SYRIA

	Political	Economic	Cultural
1965			
Feb	– Military delegation in USSR	Feb – Contract for oil prospecting	
Mar	– Foreign minister in CPR		
Apr	– Bakdash in USSR – Foreign minister in USSR		
June	– Chou En-lai in Syria		
Oct	– Military delegation in CPR	Oct – Trade delegation in Syria: new trade agreement	
		Nov – Protocol on railway tunnel construction	
Dec	– Right Ba'thists again in power		Dec – TU delegation in Syria
1966			
Jan	– Government delegation in Syria		
Feb	– Left Ba'th coup: Atasi becomes president, Zu'ayyin premier		
Mar	– CP delegation in USSR for XXIII congress – Government delegation in Syria		
Apr	– ZU'AYYIN IN USSR for 7-day visit – Military delegation in USSR – Bakdash returns to Syria from exile	Apr – CREDIT AGREEMENT on Euphrates dam, power station ($133m)	Apr – TU delegation in USSR
May	– Reported arms agreement (38)		May – Cultural protocol
		June – Protocol on oil tanks	June – Moscow patriarch in Syria – TU delegation in Syria
Sept	– Deputy foreign minister Semenov in Syria	Sept – Trade minister in Syria – Protocol on railway construction	Sept – Journalists in Syria
		Oct – Contract for oil survey – Trade delegation in USSR	
Nov	– Syria and UAR sign defence pact		
		Dec – Foreign aid chief Skachkov in Syria: protocol on Euphrates dam	
1967			
Jan	– First Ba'th delegation in USSR		
		Mar – Power minister in Syria – Trade protocol	
		Apr – Contract for oil equipment	
May	– ATASI IN USSR to discuss Middle East crisis		May – TU delegation in USSR
June	– Reported arms agreement (39)		
July	– PODGORNYY IN SYRIA for 3-day visit		July – New cultural, scientific agreement
Aug	– Defence minister in USSR – Good will delegation under Mukhitdinov in Syria	Aug – Deputy trade minister in Syria	
Sept	– Bakdash in USSR		
Oct	– Deputy defence minister in Syria	Oct – Deputy power minister in Syria	

	Political	Economic	Cultural

1967 (cont.)

| Nov | – Government delegation in USSR for anniversary
– CP delegation in Moscow for talks
– ZU'AYYIN IN USSR for 4–day visit | | Nov – Journalists' delegation in Syria: radio, TV agreements |
| Dec | | – Contract for Euphrates dam construction | |

1968

	Political	Economic	Cultural
Feb		– Aid for Palestinian refugees	
Mar	– Defence minister Grechko in Syria – Government delegation in Syria for start of work on Euphrates dam	– Trade minister Patolichev in Syria	– Teachers in Syria
Apr	– Bomber squadron visits Syria – Naval vessels call at Latakia		– News exchange agreement
May		– Electrical power delegation in USSR	– Cultural protocol
July	– CPSU delegation in Syria for talks with Ba'th – Chief of staff in USSR: arms agreement		– Education minister in USSR
Aug		– Patolichev heads trade delegation to Syria: protocol	– Cultural minister in USSR
Oct		– Contract for equipment in construction of Baghdad–Damascus highway – Railway delegation in Syria for economic talks	– Muslim delegation in USSR – TU delegation in USSR
?			– Minister of tourism in USSR
Nov		– Additional contracts for Euphrates dam	
Dec	– Azerbaydzhani delegation in Syria		– Teachers' delegation in USSR – Agricultural workers in Syria

1969

	Political	Economic	Cultural
Jan	– Ba'th delegation in USSR to study cadre training	– Oil minister in Syria for talks	
Feb	– New crisis in Damascus: Rightist coup checked	– Economic and trade minister in USSR for aid, trade talks	– TU delegation in Syria to give relief supplies to war victims
Mar		– Aid for flood victims	– Jurists in Syria
Apr			– Press delegation in Syria
May	– Military delegation in CPR	– Contract on railway	
June	– CPSU theoreticians in Syria – CP delegation in USSR for world conference		
July	– ATASI IN USSR for 8–day visit – Ba'th delegation in USSR	– Technical assistance agreement	– Teachers' delegations in USSR – Communications minister in USSR: agreement on tele-communications – Aviation workers in USSR

SYRIA

	Political	Economic	Cultural
1969 (cont.)			
			July (cont.) – Minister of Islamic affairs in USSR – Medical workers in USSR
		Aug – Deputy trade minister in Syria for Damascus fair – Industries minister in USSR	
Sept	– Bakdash on holiday in USSR		Sept – TU delegation in Syria – Scientists, teachers in Syria
Oct	– Atasi again in USSR en route to and from North Korea	Oct – Contract for Euphrates project	
		Nov – Agriculture minister leads delegation to USSR for conference on collective farms – Economic, trade minister again in USSR	
1970			
Jan	– Military delegation in Syria – Ba'th delegation in USSR	Jan – Deputy power minister in Syria for talks on Euphrates project	
			Feb – Muslim delegation in Syria
Mar	– Cruiser calls at Latakia – CP delegation in Syria		Mar – Communications protocol: direct telephone and radio links
Apr	– CPSU training delegation in Syria for talks on cadres – CP, Ba'th delegations in Moscow for Lenin centenary	Apr – Economic minister in USSR: 5-year agreement	Apr – Agricultural workers' spokesman in Syria for peasant congress – TU official in Moscow for Lenin centenary – Cultural protocol for 1970-71
		June – Power officials in Syria to visit Euphrates dam	
		July – Economic delegation in Syria: protocol on training centres for oil, power workers	July – Farmers in Syria
Sept	– Youth delegation in USSR for talks with Komsomol	Sept – Deputy foreign trade minister in Damascus for trade fair	
Oct	– Kosygin meets Atasi at Nasser's funeral		Oct – Teachers' delegation in Syria – TU delegation in Moscow for WFTU meeting
Nov	– Coup in Damascus: Asad heads new government	Nov – Deputy oil minister in Syria: agreement on co-operation	
		Dec – Protocol on power line – Railway delegation in USSR to purchase equipment	Dec – Armenian cultural delegation in Syria

References

(1) See Black and Thornton, Communism and Revolution, p. 313.

(2) This was reported, for instance, in an article by Howard Reese in the Washington Post, 14 September, 1969, p. 15; delivery was said to include Second World War tanks.

(3) More detailed analyses of Soviet-Syrian relations during this period may be found in Laqueur, The Soviet Union and the Middle East, pp. 247-61; Black and Thornton, op.cit., pp. 311-16; and Mizan, January-February 1966, pp. 23-28 (consisting mainly of a review of Patrick Seale's The Struggle for Syria, Oxford, 1965).

(4) Ivanov's article is in International Affairs, No. 3 (March), 1958, p. 57.

(5) World Marxist Review, No. 1 (January), 1961, p. 58.

(6) I. Plyshevskiy, in World Marxist Review, No. 7 (July), 1961, p. 31.

(7) See, for instance, the chapter by A.M. Goldobin in Noveyshaya istoriya stran zarubezhnoy Azii i Afriki, Leningrad, 1963, pp. 562-66 (reviewed in Mizan, October 1963, pp. 8-10).

(8) Radio Moscow, 11 April, 1963 (cited in Laqueur, The Struggle for the Middle East, p. 86).

(9) New Times, No. 34 (28 August), 1963, p. 13.

(10) Pravda, 5 March, 1964.

(11) G.I. Mirskiy, Arabskiye narody prodolzhayut bor'bu, 1965 (cited in Mizan, March-April 1966, p. 81).

(12) These events are described in more detail in Laqueur, The Struggle for the Middle East, pp. 87ff.

(13) Izvestiya, 20 February, 1965; for other Soviet commentaries on Syrian developments after the economic and political changes at the end of 1964, see Mizan, March-April 1966, pp. 80-82.

(14) Nikolay Shimmel, in New Times, No. 6 (9 February), 1966, p. 7.

(15) R. Petrov in Za rubezhom, No. 31, 1970, p. 8.

(16) The rapid withdrawal of army units from the Golan Heights and the holding of Syria's best troops near Damascus were much criticized in Arab capitals after the war and subsequently became an issue in the struggle for power in Damascus; the allegation of opponents of Syria's strong man at the time, General Salah Jadid, was that he had kept his best troops near Damascus to protect his regime. See New Middle East, No. 8 (May 1969), p. 47.

(17) The Soviet press made no mention of Syrian intervention but a communiqué from the Ministry of Foreign Affairs on 23 September noted that "contact" was being maintained with Damascus (and other Arab capitals) in order to hasten the end of the Jordanian fighting; Pravda, 24 September, 1970. The Chinese were more explicit about Moscow's role: the Russians, according to a New China News Agency dispatch on 25 September, deliberately "plotted" with the Americans to prevent the Syrians from coming to the aid of the beleaguered Palestinians. Most Western observers took it for granted that the Russians discouraged Syria's ventures and urged the withdrawal of Syrian forces.

(18) For accounts of this prolonged political crisis, see New Middle East, No. 8 (May 1969), pp. 47-49 and No. 14 (November 1969), pp. 48-49; the latter article emphasizes rivalries not only between Jadid and Asad but also between the Alawites, who were dominant in the military, and the Sunnis, who constituted a majority of the country.

(19) Radio Moscow, 18 November, 1970.

(20) A. Vasil'yev, Pravda, 30 November, 1970.

(21) See, for instance, the editorial of a CPS journal in Damascus in early April 1966, translated in World Marxist Review, 8 July, 1966 (cited in Laqueur, The Struggle for the Middle East, p. 302).

(22) A. Yodfat, "The USSR and Arab Communist Parties", New Middle East, No. 32 (May 1971), p. 29.

(23) Kommunist, No. 17 (November), 1967, p. 49.

(24) R. Petrov, New Times, No. 48 (2 December), 1970, p. 15, (cited in USSR and Third World, Vol. I, No. 1, p. 21). In July, before the coup, Soviet journals had reported the torturing of Communists in Syrian jails; e.g. Trud, 18 July, 1970.

(25) E.g. Soviet Union-Friend of the Arab Peoples, p. 45; The USSR and Developing Countries, p. 68. Western sources have estimated the credit as high as $150 million; see Goldman, Soviet Foreign Aid, p. 150.

(26) One Western source estimates the Soviet credit at $157 million; The Middle East and North Africa, 1969-70, p. 688.

(27) International Affairs, No. 1 (January), 1967, p. 115.

(28) The estimate was made by P.A. Belyayev, a member of the Soviet economic advisory group in Damascus, in an interview with Radio Moscow on 21 November, 1969.

(29) The Middle East and North Africa, 1969-70, pp. 691-92.

(30) See Howard Reese, writing in the Washington Star, 14 September, 1969, p. 15; also Aryeh Yodfat in Mizan, March-April 1969, p. 89 (citing Arab news sources).

(31) See Adelphi Papers, No. 59 (September 1969), p. 12.

(32) TASS, 11 September, 1969. The U.S. State Department estimate at the end of 1969 is somewhat less: 510 Syrians in academic programmes and 305 in technical; see RSES-35, 12 August, 1970, p. 59.

(33) Peter Mansfield, Nasser's Egypt (Harmondsworth Penguin Books, 1969), p. 79, cited by Robert E. Hunter in Adelphi Papers, No. 59 (September 1969), p. 5.

(34) Laqueur, The Struggle for the Middle East, p. 93.

(35) Joshua and Gibert, Arms for the Third World, p. 12, citing Arab and Western sources.

(36) Berliner, Soviet Economic Aid, p. 201, estimates a loan of $3 million for these projects; Soviet sources, however, do not confirm a credit at this time.

(37) Joshua and Gibert, op.cit., p. 13.

(38) The Military Balance, 1967-68, p. 53.

(39) Ibid.

Soviet relations with Tunisia, as with Morocco, were often an inverse reflection of Tunisia's with France. Thus the Bizerte crisis of 1961, like the French-Moroccan crises over the kidnapping of FLN leaders in 1956 and the Ben Barka episode of 1965 (see under Morocco), led to a significant improvement in Russian-Tunisian ties. Before this crisis relations had been nominal. Diplomatic relations had been established, more or less routinely, after Tunisian independence in 1956, but contacts had remained virtually non-existent and Soviet commentaries on Tunisia were critical. R.G. Landa, for instance, wrote in 1960 that the "national bourgeois" regime of Habib Bourguiba was powerless to cope with the nation's domestic problems and as a result its influence was "gradually declining". (1) A Russian Arabist wrote in early 1961 that Bourguiba's foreign policy was frustrated by "vacillations", which alienated Tunisia from its natural allies in the Arab world and in Africa. (2)

The Bizerte crisis, (3) during which more than 800 Tunisians were killed, abruptly altered Soviet views of Tunisia. Khrushchev expressed the Soviet Union's full sympathy for the Tunisians and condemned "the aggression of French colonialists". (4) In early August the Tunisian Foreign Minister went to Moscow to seek emergency supplies and to negotiate a loan, intended to replace extensive French aid which was of course suspended during the crisis. Meanwhile, the attitude towards internal developments in Tunisia softened. A 1962 volume on Tunisia considered the ruling Neo-Destour party, which had previously been regarded as an instrument of the national bourgeoisie and middle class, as representative also of "the nationalistically inclined section of the working class". (5) The Tunisian Communists, who had received considerable attention in Soviet commentaries when relations with Tunis were minimal, were now often ignored, despite the fact that 1961 and 1962 were years when Soviet commentators were as a rule more open in their praise of Third World Communists and severe towards nationalists who repressed them. The banning of the PCT and arrest of Communist leaders in early 1963 were accorded the expected treatment in the Soviet press (6) but did not affect the modest Russian-Tunisian détente. On the occasion of Tunisia's National Day in June 1963 cordial greetings were exchanged between the two nations and commentaries ignored the Communist issue; an article in Izvestiya said that Russia and Tunisia faced "no questions of dispute or unresolved problems". (7)

Soviet-Tunisian relations proceeded normally during the following years, but they did not develop beyond the 1963 level. Trade remained stationary after the mid-1960s. Work progressed slowly on projects covered by the 1961 loan and a smaller credit extended in 1964. These projects included five dams, three with power stations; an irrigation system; a technical institute, and the development of fisheries; (8) by the end of the decade, only the Qasset dam had been completed. Political exchanges, meanwhile, were meagre and included few of cabinet rank. Cultural exchange was more active, especially in the fields of medicine, sport and education; Tunisia at one point (1967) ranked third among all African and Middle East countries with technical trainees in the Soviet bloc. (9)

Soviet comment on Tunisia was relatively infrequent after 1963 and less uncritical than formerly. An article by Pravda's North African correspondent Yu. Potemkin in December 1967, for instance, noted some progress in economic development, thanks to modest planning and nationalization, but found the recent Destour programme a conglomeration of "social-reformist" and genuinely socialist slogans; (10) this balancing of small Tunisian gains against larger shortcomings was characteristic of Soviet appraisals during these years. Irritations on both sides inevitably cropped up from time to time - over Russia's invasion of Czechoslovakia, for instance, over the Russians' naval build-up in the Mediterranean and over Tunisia's adherence to the Common Market (11) - but none of these irritations created a decisive trend in the relationship. Soviet-Tunisian ties neither advanced nor deteriorated significantly in the latter half of the 1960s.

Little in this record should give surprise. As far as the Tunisians were concerned, given their uncertain relations with France early in the 1960s, it was useful to be able to turn to the Russians for help; and given their changeable relations with other Arab states in the latter part of the 1960s, especially with Algeria and the UAR over the Palestinian problem, it was prudent not to be too isolated from the Arabs' principal supplier of arms. The Russians, meanwhile, had no illusions about Tunisia's relative indifference to the Arab-Israeli conflict, yet hoped to bring the Tunisians in line with moderate Arab opinion regarding a settlement. This object - plus, as always, naval access to Tunisian ports should the opportunity ever arise - warranted Moscow's modest outlay in Tunisia. The Russians could not, at this rate, compete for influence with France and the United States, but there is no good evidence that this was their intent. (12)

Chronology

	Political	Economic	Cultural
1956			
Mar	– Independence		
June	– Embassies exchanged		
July			– Cultural delegation in USSR
Sept		– Aid agreement with France	
1957			
1958			
Oct			– Cultural delegation in USSR
1959			
Jan	– CP delegation in USSR for XXI congress		
Aug			– Education delegation in USSR
1960			
Jan		– Trade agreement	
Dec	– CP delegation in Moscow for world conference		
1961			
Jan		– Trade delegation in USSR: protocol	– TU delegation in USSR
Feb	– Bourguiba in France for talks with De Gaulle		
May	– Good will mission to CPR stops in USSR		– Women leaders in Tunisia (first Soviet delegation to visit Tunisia)
July	– French–Tunisian fighting over Bizerte base		
Aug	– Foreign minister in USSR	– CREDIT AGREEMENT for dams, power station, irrigation, technical institute ($28.5m) – Gift of food, medical supplies	
Oct	– CP Secretary in USSR for XXII congress		
1962			
Feb		– Protocols on 1961 credit – Aid to Algerian refugees	– Oceanographic research vessel calls in Tunisia
Mar		– Trade agreement for 1962–64	
May			– Cultural delegation in USSR
Sept		– Contract for dam construction	
1963			
Jan	– CP banned in Tunisia		
June	– Parliamentary delegation in USSR		
July			– Tashkent mufti in Tunisia
Aug		– French credit to Tunisia ($40m)	
Sept			– Journalists in Tunisia

TUNISIA

	Political	Economic	Cultural
1963 (cont.)			
Oct	– French quit Bizerte base	Oct – Protocol on technical institute	Oct – Health minister in USSR – Muslim leader in Tunisia
			Nov – Education delegation, dancers in Tunisia
Dec	– Government delegation in Tunisia	Dec – Rezala dam completed	Dec – Cultural relations chief Romanovskiy in Tunisia: first cultural agreement
1964			
Jan	– Chou En-lai in Tunisia: agreement on diplomatic relations		
Mar	– Foreign minister in USSR	Mar – Air service agreement – Agreement on aid for Tunisian fisheries	
		Apr – France reduces aid over nationalization issue	
Oct	– Delegation under Orientalist Gafurov in Tunis for Neo-Destour party congress		
		Nov – Trade delegation in USSR: agreement for 1965-68	
		Dec – CREDIT AGREEMENT for Qasset dam ($5.5m)	Dec – Medical aid agreement: Soviet specialists to work in Tunisia
1965			
Apr	– Tunisia breaks with UAR over Israeli policy		
		July – Aviation delegation in USSR – Housing minister in USSR	
1966			
Mar	– CP delegation in USSR for XXIII congress		
			May – Cultural delegation in USSR: protocol
			July – News service director in USSR
		Oct – Planning chief in USSR	
1967			
			Mar – Radio delegation in Tunisia: news service agreement
			June – Doctors in Tunisia – Cultural protocol for 1967-68
Sept	– Tunisia suspends relations with CPR after anti-Chinese demonstrations in Tunis		
Oct	– CP delegation in USSR for anniversary – Arms agreement with France		
1968			
		Jan – Aviation minister in Tunisia	Jan – Cultural minister Furtseva in Tunisia
Apr	– Parliamentary delegation in Tunisia		

Political	Economic	Cultural
1968 (cont.)		
May – Bourguiba in USA		May – Teachers in Tunisia to help organize technical schools
	July – Qasset dam completed	
		Aug – TU delegation in Tunisia
	Oct – Economic delegation in Tunisia for aid, trade talks: trade agreement for 1969–72	Oct – Cultural delegation in Tunisia
1969		
		Jan – Co-operative leaders in Tunisia
Mar – CP delegation in USSR for preparatory commission and world congress (June)		
	Apr – Tunisia adheres to Common Market	
		May – Cultural delegation in Tunisia: protocol for 1969–70
		Aug – TU delegation in Tunisia for labour congress
1970		
Apr – CP delegation in USSR for Lenin centenary		
Oct – Kosygin meets Tunisian ministers at Nasser's funeral		

References

(1) Voprosy istorii, No. 5 (May), 1960, p. 74.

(2) Afrika, 1956–61, pp. 46–50.

(3) The crisis developed in July 1961 when Bourguiba demanded evacuation of the naval base, the last important French stronghold in Tunisia; this ended a period of greatly improved French–Tunisian relations, especially since De Gaulle's coming to power in France in 1958. The heavy fighting, which lasted less than a week, left the French in firm control of the base.

(4) Pravda, 1 August, 1961; Khrushchev was addressing a group of Arab and African diplomats in Moscow.

(5) N.A. Ivanov, Gosudarstvenny stroy Tunizii, 1962 (reviewed in Mizan, February 1963, p. 4).

(6) See, for instance, the unofficial protests in Pravda, 20 and 22 January and 15 March, 1963.

(7) V. Radin, Izvestiya, 1 June, 1963; also V. Mayev-skiy in Pravda on the same date.

(8) The USSR and Developing Countries, pp. 71–72; also Goldman, Soviet Foreign Aid, pp. 151–52.

(9) U.S. Department of State, RSB–65, 31 May, 1968, p. 14; the leaders were the UAR and Iran.

(10) Pravda, 21 December, 1967.

(11) For sharp newspaper exchanges relating to Czecho-slovakia, see Mizan, September–October 1968, Supplement A, p. 15. Bourguiba's criticism of the Soviet naval build-up was voiced during his American tour earlier in the year; see The Middle East and North Africa, 1969–70, p. 711. Tunisia's decision to associate with the Common Market was criticized in a broadcast of Radio Peace and Liberty, 12 April, 1969.

(12) France was Tunisia's chief trading partner in the latter half of the 1960s, consuming about a quarter of Tunisian exports and providing about a third of total imports (as compared to Russia's three per cent share of both exports and imports). The United States, meanwhile, provided about half of Tunisia's foreign aid; during the decade 1957–67, American aid totalled an estimated $528 million. See The Middle East and North Africa, 1969–70, pp. 716–20 passim and New Middle East, No. 17 (February 1970), p. 28.

Soviet relations with Turkey during the years under review were burdened by two circumstances: traditional Turkish suspicions of Russia, heightened by Moscow's behaviour towards Turkey after the Second World War; (1) and, in consequence of these suspicions, Ankara's heavy reliance on the West. More than any other nation in the Middle East, and perhaps in the entire Third World, Turkey depended upon the Western powers, especially the United States, for its security and its prosperity. By 1955 Turkey had already received an estimated $500 million from the United States through the Marshall Plan and Truman Doctrine; during the next dozen years American military aid to Turkey totalled an estimated $1.7 billion - more than twice as much as U.S. aid to any other Third World nation (excluding South Korea and South Vietnam) - and total economic aid from 1947 to the end of 1967 is estimated at $1.9 billion. (2) Turkey had meanwhile joined NATO in 1951 and a Balkan alliance with Greece and Yugoslavia soon thereafter; the Turkish treaties of 1954 and 1955 with Pakistan and Iraq formed the nucleus of the Baghdad alliance. Détente with Ankara under these circumstances was not easy.

Early in the 1950s the Russians tried periodically to assure the Turks of Soviet good will - in renouncing claims to Kars and Ardahan, for instance (in 1953), and in occasional friendly references to the Turkish nationalist hero, Kemal Atatürk. However, the normal approach to Ankara was belligerent, not moderate. Turkey was Russia's scapegoat in the Middle East and Adnan Menderes the anti-hero. It was more profitable to picture Turkey as the agent of reaction and imperialism in order to accent Russia's new identity with the Arab world. Pravda's "Observer" accused Ankara, on the occasion of the visit of the West German Defence Minister in 1955, of embarking on a "neo-Nazi-Turkish alliance stimulated by Western militarists". (3) Official communications with Ankara were often warnings that Turkey's defence alignments jeopardized Soviet security or that threats against Arab nations, as in the massing of Turkish troops on the Syrian border in the autumn of 1957, would not be tolerated. (4) This attitude persisted throughout the 1950s.

In 1960 a scheduled visit to Moscow by Premier Menderes signalled, for the first time since the war, a détente in Soviet-Turkish relations - a détente the Russians presumably wished because of current difficulties with their Arab allies and mounting uneasiness over Iran's ties with the United States. The visit, however, did not take place; Menderes was overthrown in May and his successor, General Gürsel, reaffirmed Ankara's alignment with CENTO, NATO and the Western powers. The Turkish-Russian impasse continued as before. New warnings were periodically sent to Ankara charging the Turks with "full responsibility" for any activities on Turkish territory which threatened Soviet security - such as the construction of military or rocket bases and the holding of NATO manoeuvres in the Straits. (5) In February 1962 Admiral Gorshkov, Commander in Chief of the Soviet Navy, reminded Turkey that "our Black Sea Fleet alone is sufficient to raze to the ground the countries adjacent to the Black Sea which have become NATO military bridge-heads". (6) Threats like these tended to overshadow occasional expressions of good will, such as Khrushchev's in December 1962 when he recalled the close relations of

Lenin and Kemal Atatürk and hoped better Russian-Turkish relations would "ensure that the Black Sea will not divide but unite us". (7) The end of 1962 was a favourable moment for Soviet overtures, since the Turkish regime was at this time uneasy about American defence policies following the removal of missiles from Turkey in the aftermath of the Cuban crisis. (8) No détente occurred, however, and relations continued to be strained for nearly two more years.

The long-awaited rapprochement between Turkey and the Soviet Union came, curiously enough, as a result of the Cypriot crisis of 1964 - not because the Russians supported Ankara's policies in Cyprus, but because they objected to them less than Turkey's Western allies. Turkey was particularly isolated and friendless in 1964 as a result of the Cyprus issue and accordingly sought understanding where it could. Moscow's did not come immediately. Russia strongly supported the Greek Cypriots as the crisis matured and pledged arms when Turkey attacked the island in August (see under Cyprus). Khrushchev called the attack "barbarous" and saw it as a NATO manoeuvre with Turkey playing the role of broker to the imperialists. (9) In October, however, the Turkish Foreign Minister, Erkin, visiting Moscow a fortnight after Khrushchev's fall, was apparently able to persuade the new Soviet leadership to see the Cypriot question in a different light and to adopt at least a neutral position in the matter. The joint communiqué at the end of his visit, while formally neutral on the Cypriot issue, gave the impression - without being very specific as to detail - of a certain identity between Moscow's views and Ankara's; (10) the same impression was given in communiqués which climaxed other important political exchanges during the following years. (11) Khrushchev's successors, weighing all considerations, had obviously decided that Turkey's good will was more important than the cause of the Greek Cypriots, whatever support the latter may have had from Arab nationalists and Cypriot Communists.

Although Moscow's rapprochement with Ankara came during and over the Cypriot crisis, one should not lose sight of the wider considerations that prompted the Russians' new attitude towards Turkey. As in Iran, the most important of these considerations was the desire to neutralize Turkey as a potential base for activity directed against the USSR. To this end Kosygin reportedly offered Turkey a non-aggression pact in June 1965; (12) although it was not accepted, the offering of it marked a significant shift in Russian strategies.

Another motive for improved relations with Ankara was to guarantee unrestricted passage of Russian naval vessels through the Dardanelles. Although peacetime passage had not been seriously in question since the Montreux Convention of 1936, the matter took on a particular significance to the Russians after 1964 as they developed their Mediterranean squadron; indeed, the effectiveness of this squadron, both as a naval weapon and as a political instrument, depended largely on mobility through the Turkish straits.

It is also possible that intensified Soviet interest in Turkey was related to expectations of social and political upheaval there, the symptoms of which grew more evident in the latter half of the 1960s and especially after the elections of October 1969. Soviet commentators devoted considerable attention to these symptoms and grew increasingly critical of the Demirel government's inability to restore order. Land reform was considered inadequate, unemployment was growing, the value of the lira was falling on the world market, labour and student unrest was spreading (especially after the declaration of martial law in June 1970), and opposition to Turkey's continued membership in NATO was said to be rising in all segments of Turkish society. (13) The Russians could not, of course, have known how matters would eventually be resolved in Turkey, but any resolution of the domestic crisis could affect their interests: a military or other coup (like the one which toppled Demirel's regime in March 1971) might reaffirm and strengthen Turkey's ties with NATO; if, on the other hand, a Leftist regime were to come to power in Ankara, Moscow would wish to be in a position to come into early rapport with it. Soviet policies, in short, had to be flexible enough in Turkey to meet all contingencies.

The growing candour in Soviet appraisals of Turkey's domestic problems did not prevent the gradual expansion of Soviet-Turkish ties during the latter half of the 1960s. Economic co-operation increased and political exchanges multiplied (see below). Periodic joint communiqués specified agreement on a variety of international problems, including procedures for settling the Palestinian as well as the Cypriot problem; Turkey persistently supported the Arabs against Israel after the Six Day War. (14) As Brezhnev observed in early October 1970, Russo-Turkish relations, all things considered, were developing "not too badly" although there had been "some difficult moments" in the past. (15) The "difficult moments" were not over, it soon developed. Ten days after Brezhnev's remarks a Soviet passenger aircraft was hijacked in flight by two defecting Lithuanians, the Russian stewardess killed, and the hijackers given sanctuary in Turkey; less than a week later an American military aircraft, with American and Turkish officers aboard, was forced down inside the USSR after flying over Soviet territory. The Russians behaved with a certain restraint in both episodes. Though Soviet journalists wrote with understandable feeling about the hijacking incident and scolded both Turkish reactionaries for making a "shameful farce" of the case and Turkish courts for not extraditing the criminals, official pressure on the Demirel government appears to have been kept at a minimum. (16) The border violation was more serious, Moscow seems to have felt. This was not an "accidental" occurrence, an official Note to Turkey asserted; nor was it "the first time American aircraft based in Turkey have made flights along the Turkish-Soviet border for provocative and reconnaissance purposes". Turkey was warned of the "dangerous consequences" if it continued to tolerate this activity. The Soviet government, the Note concluded, "anticipates that the Turkish government will take the necessary steps to prevent similar violations". (17)

What seems particularly noteworthy in Soviet reaction to the two incidents, probably the most troublesome in Russo-Turkish relations since 1964, was Moscow's desire to avoid a diplomatic crisis which could lead to a prolonged impasse in the relationship. It was one thing for Soviet correspondents to criticize the Demirel regime for its inability to cope with domestic problems, but quite another for the Russian government to humiliate Ankara in a direct confrontation. Turkey was proving to be a thornier ally than Iran or Pakistan, among the states of the Northern tier, but the reasons for détente with Ankara did not lose their force because of random hijackings and overflights across the Soviet-Turkish border.

Economic and Cultural Relations

Some Russian aid was extended to Turkey in the 1930s, which makes Turkey the first underdeveloped nation to receive Soviet credits so far as is known. (18) Credit was also reportedly extended in 1957 for a glass works (see Chronology). The first credit of consequence, however, was a $200 million loan in 1965. (19) This was intended for a steel mill, oil refinery, aluminium plant, distillery and expansion of the glass works which had been completed in 1961. Utilization of the 1965 credit appears to have been reasonably prompt, to judge from the number of protocols and exchange of technical delegations that followed the agreement (see Chronology). By 1969 as many as 1,000 Russian technicians were said to be in Turkey supervising the aid programmes. (20) An additional loan was reported in October 1969 for Turkey's third iron and steel complex at Iskenderun; the credit was apparently the largest extended to a Third World state by the USSR during 1969, but estimates of the amount vary widely. (21)

Trade, meanwhile, which had remained modest though constant through the 1950s, grew rapidly after 1964; during the period 1964-69, Turkey ranked fourth among Russia's trading partners in the Middle East and eighth in the Middle East, Africa and Asia combined.

Cultural co-operation between Turkey and the Soviet Union was slight. The cultural agreement negotiated during Foreign Minister Erkin's visit in November 1964 was never ratified, because of opposition by Rightist elements in the Demirel government; this prevented any regular exchange, though several groups of Soviet artistes performed in Turkey during 1967 and 1968. Student exchange was virtually non-existent because of Ankara's continuing ban on study by Turkish students in Communist states. (22) Academic exchanges, arranged through the Soviet Academy of Sciences and its counterpart in Turkey, were somewhat more numerous, but still few when compared to similar programmes in other countries. (23)

TURKEY

	Political		Economic		Cultural
Pre-1959					
June 1920	Embassies exchanged				
Nov 1951	Turkey enters NATO				
July 1953	USSR renounces claims on Kars, Ardahan				
		Sept 1953	Agreement on joint use of Sadarabad dam		
		Dec 1953	Trade agreement		
Apr 1954	Turko-Pakistani pact				
Feb 1955	Turko-Iraqi treaty (Baghdad pact)				
		Summer 1957	Reported credits for glass and calcium plants ($17m) (24)		
1959					
Jan	- CP delegation in Moscow for XXI congress				
Feb	- US-Turkey talks on defence pact with bases				
				Dec	- Health minister in USSR
1960					
		Mar	- Trade protocol		
May	- Menderes overthrown; Gen. Gürsel becomes premier; USSR recognizes new regime				
		July	- Agricultural delegation in USSR		
		Oct	- Commercial delegation in USSR for trade talks	Oct	- Education delegation in USSR
Nov	- CP delegation in USSR for world conference				
1961					
		Feb	- Trade protocol		
		Apr	- Rail service agreement		
Oct	- CP delegation in Moscow for XXII congress - Inönü becomes premier	Oct	- Transit agreement - Glass works completed	Oct	- Historians in Turkey
1962					
		Jan	- Trade protocol		
				May	- Academic delegation in USSR
Oct	- Deputy foreign minister in USSR				
1963					
		Mar	- Trade protocol		

TURKEY

Political	Economic	Cultural
<u>1963 (cont.)</u> May – First parliamentary delegation in USSR		
	July – Agreement on reservoir	July – Armenian patriarch in Turkey visits Soviet Armenia
	Oct – Communications agreement	
<u>1964</u>		
	Mar – Trade protocol	
Aug – <u>Turkey attacks Cyprus</u>		
Oct – Foreign minister Erkin in USSR		
		Nov – First cultural agreement (not ratified)
	Dec – Economic delegation in USSR	
<u>1965</u> Jan – Podgornyy heads Supreme Soviet delegation to Turkey (first in 30 years)		
Feb – <u>Ürgüplü replaces Inönü as Premier</u>	Feb – Trade delegation	
May – Foreign minister Gromyko in Turkey		
June – Ankara delegation in Moscow		
Aug – ÜRGÜPLÜ IN USSR for 8-day visit	Aug – Expanded trade agreement	
	Sept – Economic delegation in Turkey to study aid projects	
Oct – <u>Demirel becomes premier after elections</u>		Oct – Scientists in USSR
Nov – Moscow delegation in Ankara	Nov – Agreement on joint construction of Arpacoy dam	
	Dec – CREDIT AGREEMENT for steel mill, refinery, distillery, etc. (estim. $200m)	
<u>1966</u>		
	Feb – Trade protocol	
Mar – CP delegation in USSR for XXIII congress	Mar – Gift of medical supplies	
	Apr – Technical delegation in USSR for talks on oil, steel projects	
July – Parliamentary delegation in USSR	July – Technical delegation in USSR	
	Aug – Trade minister Patolichev in Turkey: new agreement	
Sept – Deputy foreign minister Semenov in Turkey		
Dec – KOSYGIN IN TURKEY for 7-day visit		

	Political	Economic	Cultural
1967			
		Jan – **Aid** to earthquake victims – Economic delegation in Turkey to discuss bauxite deposits – Trade delegation in USSR	Jan – Academic delegation in Turkey
	Feb – Border agreement	Feb – Economic delegation in USSR: protocol on aid projects	
	Mar – Government delegation in USSR		
		May – Contract for aluminium plant	
		June – Further protocol on 1965 credit	
		Aug – Air service agreement – Additional aid to earthquake victims	
	Sept – DEMIREL IN USSR for 10-day visit	Sept – Protocol on refinery – Trade delegation in Turkey	
	Oct – Government delegation in USSR for anniversary		
1968			
		Jan – Protocol on 3rd metallurgical plant	
		Feb – Trade delegation in Turkey: protocol	Feb – Academicians in Turkey to lecture on Oriental studies
	Apr – Supreme Soviet delegation in Turkey	Apr – Railway agreement	
		May – Aviation minister in Turkey – Protocol on iron, steel mill	
		June – Foreign aid chief Skachkov in Turkey to inspect Soviet projects – Protocol on Arpacoy dam	June – Red Cross delegation in Turkey
	July – Foreign minister in USSR		July – Journalists in Turkey
		Aug – Shipping delegation in USSR – USSR represented in Ismir fair (pavilion closed after pro-Czech demonstration)	
1969			
	Jan – Frontier demarcation committee in USSR: agreement on procedures (Mar)	Jan – Economic delegation in USSR: protocol on aluminium works	
		Feb – Trade delegation in USSR: protocol for 1969	Feb – Geologists in Turkey
		Apr – Commercial delegation in USSR	
	June – CP secretary in USSR for world conference	June – Protocol on metal works at Iskenderun	
		July – Contract on oil storage units	
		Aug – Agreement on power line	Aug – Journalists in USSR
			Sept – Red Cross delegation in Turkey

	Political		Economic		Cultural

1969 (cont.)

	Political		Economic
		Oct	– CREDIT AFREEMENT for steel works (reported $166m)
Nov	– PRESIDENT SUNAY IN USSR for 8-day visit		
Dec	– Ankara municipal delegation in Moscow		

1970

	Political		Economic
		Jan	– Delegation in USSR for talks on sulphuric acid plant
		Mar	– Steel delegation in USSR for talks on training – Railway transit agreement – Trade protocol for 1970-71
Apr	– CP secretary in Moscow for Lenin centenary	Apr	– New Aeroflot route opens
May	– Deputy foreign minister Vinogradov in Turkey	May	– Subway experts in Istanbul to survey projected line
June	– Martial law imposed in Istanbul following riots		
		Aug	– Soviet trade organizations take part in Izmir fair – Protocol on 1969 credit for Iskenderun works
Sept	– Foreign office official in USSR – Istanbul municipal delegation in Leningrad – Ankara municipal delegation in Moscow	Sept	– Specialists on measures, standards in Ankara for international congress
Oct	– Soviet plane hijacked to Turkey – Turkish, American officers held in USSR after airspace violation	Oct	– Skachkov in Turkey for aid talks – Transportation agreement

References

(1)   Notably, claims on the Turkish cities of Kars and Ardahan and demands for joint Soviet-Turkish defence of the Dardanelles; see Laqueur, The Soviet Union and the Middle East, pp. 129-30.

(2)   For the estimate of arms transfers, see Joshua and Gibert, Arms for the Third World, p. 130 (citing U.S. Department of Defense sources); for American economic aid see Laqueur, The Struggle for the Middle East, p. 27.

(3)   Pravda, 12 November, 1955.

(4)   For a review of Soviet commentaries on Turkey during this period, see Laqueur, The Soviet Union and the Middle East, pp. 205-7 and 258-59; also William B. Ballis, "Soviet-Turkish Relations During the Decade 1953-1963", Bulletin, Institute for the Study of the USSR, September 1964, pp. 5ff.

(5)   See, for instance, Pravda, 14 May, 1960, 7 February and 26 September, 1961.

(6)   Pravda, 2 February, 1962.

(7)   Pravda, 13 December, 1962, in a report to the Supreme Soviet.

(8)   Laqueur, The Struggle for the Middle East, p. 16.

(9)   Sovetskaya Kirgiziya, 18 August, 1964 (quoted in Mizan, September 1964, pp. 21-22).

(10) Pravda, 7 November, 1964.

(11) E.g. after Kosygin's visit to Turkey in December 1966 (Pravda, 28 December, 1966); Premier Demirel's to Moscow in September 1967 (Pravda, 30 September, 1967); and President Sunay's to Moscow in November 1969 (Pravda, 22 November, 1969).

(12) Laqueur, The Struggle for the Middle East, p. 22 (citing Akis, June 1965).

(13) The sharpest criticism appears to have been prompted by a particularly acid report by the veteran correspondent Vladimir Rogov following a visit to Turkey in early 1970; Trud, 17 and 20 February, 1970.   See also articles in Izvestiya, 3 June, 1970, and in Pravda, 21 June, 1970 and 24 December, 1970.

(14) Demirel first made clear the Turkish position on the Palestinian question in a statement to TASS on 20 September, 1967.

(15) Pravda, 6 October, 1970.

(16) Soviet press commentaries on the incident are reviewed in Current Digest of the Soviet Press, Volume XXII, No. 42, pp. 6-7 and 13; see especially Kudryavtsev's article in Izvestiya, 21 October, 1970.

(17) Pravda, 27 October, 1970.

(18) According to Russian sources, a credit of $8 million was granted in 1932 for the purchase of industrial equipment and additional credit was extended in 1934 for a textile mill; International Affairs, No. 6 (June), 1969, pp. 124-25.

(19) This is the estimate given in the U.S. State Department's tally for 1965 (RSB-50, 17 June, 1966, p. 4). Marshall Goldman dates the credit a year earlier and estimates it at $168 million; Soviet Foreign Aid, p. 153.

(20) See Klieman, Soviet Russia and the Middle East, p. 49.

(21) The U.S. Department of State estimate - shown in the Chronology - is $166 million; RECS-5, 9 July, 1970, p. 6.   Radio Ankara, however, reported on 20 October, 1969 that this credit amounted to $263 million; see Mizan, November-December 1969, Supplement A, p. 12.

(22) U.S. Department of State, RSE-25, 7 May, 1969, pp. 83-85.   Eighty Turkish engineers, however, were reported in 1970 to have attended courses in the USSR, in connexion with Soviet projects in Turkey, and 1,250 Turks were to be trained on location; Radio Moscow, 27 December, 1970.

(23) Korneyev, Nauchnyye svyazi Akademii nauk SSSR so stranami Azii i Afriki, pp. 177-83.

(24) Berliner, Soviet Economic Aid, p. 201, citing American news sources.

Yemen, for so small and backward a country, received a disproportionately large amount of Moscow's attention between 1955 and 1970. Soviet credits to Yemen, for instance, were greater than to any African nation south of the Sahara, except Nigeria and Ethiopia; by the end of the 1960s Yemen ranked high among Third World recipients of Russian arms (see below).

If Soviet interest had been concentrated in the years after 1962, when a republic of relatively Leftist outlook was established, the interest would be more easily understood. But Russia's attention to Yemen was no less active during the years when Yemen was ruled by a monarchy as absolute as Ibn Sa'ud's. The Soviet Orientalist A. Sultanov, who visited Yemen in early 1958, wrote of the "industrious" Yemenis beginning to exploit their rich resources of oil and uranium, the "modesty" of the royal family, the "progressive" attitude of students returning from Cairo University, and the staunch resistance of the nation to British imperialism. (1) Meanwhile, there were numerous exchanges between Russia and Yemen, including two visits to Moscow by the Crown Prince; in 1960 there were said to be more Soviet bloc technicians in Yemen than in any other Afro-Asian nation except Afghanistan. (2)

In seeking reasons for Moscow's attention to Yemen after 1955, it should be recalled that Yemen, along with Saudi Arabia and Egypt, had been an early object of Soviet interest in the Middle East before the Second World War; a Treaty of Friendship (the first recorded with an Arab nation) was concluded in 1928 and Soviet-Yemeni trade in the 1930s was of some consequence. This made a resumption of relations in the 1950s easier - the more so, perhaps, since Ibn Sa'ud proved resistant to Moscow's overtures. Yemen, meanwhile, despite its feudalist social structure, was more anti-Western in its foreign policy than other Arab monarchies - and even than some more liberal nations (like Lebanon) - because of its designs on Aden, a British protectorate. The Russians nurtured this "anti-imperialist" sentiment by supporting the Yemeni claim during the 1950s and referring to the Aden territories as "the occupied parts of Yemen". (3) In addition to these considerations, Soviet interest in Yemen was probably stimulated by oil and other natural resources (described in glowing terms in most Russian accounts of the country), not to mention harbours for the future; it is not without significance that the first Soviet project completed in Yemen was the improvement of the port at Hodeida (see below).

None of these considerations, of course, wedded the Russians to royalist rule in Yemen and the overthrow of the monarchy in September 1962 was immediately supported. Leading Soviet correspondents, such as Vladimir Kudryavtsev of Izvestiya and Pavel Demchenko of Pravda, hastened to San'a for interviews with the revolutionary leaders. In their reports they praised the new regime warmly, complimented it for seeking to place the nation on the "non-capitalist path of development", and cautioned foreign nations, especially Saudi Arabia, Jordan and Britain, against intervention. (4) Khrushchev, with characteristic imagery, greeted the Yemeni revolution in an address before the Supreme Soviet in December: "People are thrusting their way through the thick layers of medievalism to a new life, as a shoot in the desert, when it receives a drop of moisture, thrusts its way up through

the soil." (5)

The Soviet Union, in short, gave unambiguous support to Yemen after the 1962 revolution and this support grew as civil war between Royalists and the Cairo-supported government in San'a intensified. After Khrushchev's fall Soviet policies in Yemen were for a time more circumspect, as the new Russian leaders sought better relations with Saudi Arabia. Saudi-Egyptian rivalry over Yemen, it was argued, was not in the best interests of the Arab world. (6) The agreement in August 1965 between Nasser and King Faisal, in which the latter promised to relinquish support of the Imam on condition that Egyptian troops be withdrawn from Yemen, was accordingly applauded in the Soviet press. (7) However, when this agreement proved no more durable than its predecessors, the Russians reverted to their earlier posture in Yemen: that is, full support of the republic, whatever its shortcomings, (8) and unrelenting hostility towards its internal and external enemies.

The Arab-Israeli war of June 1967 brought affairs in Yemen, as in many other parts of the Arab world, to a new climax. Egyptian troops, said to number about 80,000 in Yemen by this time, (9) now had to be withdrawn and Egyptian equipment removed. Nasser was able, during the Arab summit meeting in Khartoum in August, to revive the 1965 agreement with King Faisal concerning a mutual withdrawal from Yemen and for a brief period the civil war appeared to be checked. The position of President Sallal, however, who had long been dependent on Cairo, was now undermined, and he was toppled in a coup in November (while en route, coincidentally, to the 50th anniversary celebrations in Moscow). Meanwhile, the declaration of a people's republic in Aden at the end of November under a regime sympathetic to union with Yemen but not particularly congenial with Cairo, gave a new dimension to the already complex political situation in San'a (see under Southern Yemen).

The Russians apparently took no direct part in these developments, but they approved the way things turned out. Soviet commentators welcomed the Nasser-Faisal agreement at Khartoum, for instance, since it brought two traditional Arab rivals together and strengthened Arab unity at a critical time; they also praised the new regime in San'a for its "positive neutrality" and cited Sallal's coolness towards the Khartoum agreement as a reason for his fall. (10) Meanwhile, Moscow replaced the Egyptian equipment withdrawn in August and increased the size of its military mission in Yemen (see below).

The Soviet Union continued to maintain outwardly cordial relations with Yemen after 1967 and to provide arms for the renewed struggle with the Royalists. The latter were again aided by Saudi Arabia, despite the Khartoum agreement, but the Egyptians, preoccupied with other matters, did not regain the influence in San'a they had had during the Sallal era. If Russian influence inevitably replaced Egyptian, this should not be understood as a significant Soviet objective. The Russians sought in the South Arabian Peninsula, beyond ports - as usual - where their naval and commercial vessels could refuel, "progressive" regimes which could serve as a counterpoise to the dominant conservative influence of Saudi Arabia. After 1967 the new republic of Southern Yemen replaced Yemen as an instrument for this purpose and Soviet attention accordingly shifted to Aden.

Commentary on Yemeni developments grew increasingly infrequent, especially after the end of the civil war in mid-1969. Although the Soviet press remained circumspect throughout 1970, it is likely that Soviet officials grew more and more irritated with Yemeni policies as the San'a government divorced itself from "progressive" Arab regimes and causes.

*　　　*　　　*

Yemen was one of the few states in the Middle East where Chinese activity posed a persistent problem to the Russians in the 1960s. Peking had cultivated friendly relations with the pre-republican regime as the Russians had; aid and political exchanges had often paralleled Russia's. Meanwhile, the radical outlook of many Yemeni revolutionaries after 1962 found a sympathetic response in Peking, especially as China's relations with the UAR and other major Arab states deteriorated. If Peking sought its "Albania" in the Arab world, Yemen for some years was a leading candidate. The magnitude of the Chinese threat to Soviet policies, however, should not be exaggerated. Chinese aid and technical assistance were small compared to Russian and trade remained negligible; meanwhile, arms, the principal commodity of interest to San'a during the long struggle with the Royalists, were provided by Moscow, not Peking.

Economic, Military and Cultural Relations

The two reported Soviet credits to Yemen, in 1956 and 1964, total $97 million, but if a portion of the earlier credit was absorbed into the latter, the total is of course less. (11) The initial projects included the deep-sea port at Hodeida (completed in 1961 and directed during the 1960s by Russian personnel), an airport near San'a (completed in 1963), and a number of minor enterprises. The 1964 loan covered a road from Hodeida to Ta'izz, a cement factory, fisheries, a hospital, several schools and a stadium. (12) Work proceeded slowly on all these projects, because of the civil war, but a few were completed by 1970.

Military assistance was greater than economic aid in cash value, amounting to an estimated $100 million by the time of the Arab-Israeli war in June 1967 and augmented by subsequent deliveries. (13) It is probable that Yemen ranked seventh or eighth among Afro-Asian recipients of Russian arms during the 1960s and was certainly one of the major recipients on a per capita calculation. Early deliveries, following an agreement (with Czechoslovakia) in 1956, included artillery, tanks and aircraft, all, presumably, of obsolete design since Yemen's need of arms before 1962 was slight; the value of arms delivered to the Imam, however, was said to be about $30 million. (14) Arms delivered to San'a after 1962, for use against the Royalists, were more modern in design but still relatively unsophisticated compared with weapons being received at this time by other Arab countries; a Soviet military mission was established in Yemen during this period to help the Egyptians train Yemeni troops. Following the Egyptian withdrawal in June 1967, Russian military activity in Yemen intensified. More advanced aircraft were delivered and Russians trained Yemeni pilots to use them; according to Royalist reports, Soviet pilots even flew combat missions. (15) Arms transfers continued as long as the civil war lasted. (16)

Cultural relations between Yemen and the Soviet Union were minimal during the years under review. The most significant activity was in education and technical training. Five hundred Yemenis were reported in Soviet educational institutions at the end of 1968, a higher number than from any other Arab nation except Iraq; (17) from 1965 to the end of 1967 Yemen sent more technical trainees to the Soviet bloc than any Arab nation except the UAR. (18)

Chronology

Political	Economic	Cultural
Pre-1955		
1928 Friendship treaty		
1955		
Oct – Friendship treaty renewed; agreement on diplomatic relations		
1956	Jan – Trade delegation in Yemen	
Feb – Arms agreement (with Czechoslovakia)	Mar – Trade agreement	
June – Crown Prince in USSR for 2-week visit	July – CREDIT AGREEMENT for air field, port construction, irrigation (estim. $25m) (19)	
1957		
1958		
Jan – Crown Prince in USSR and CPR	Jan – CPR credit ($16.3m)	Jan – Orientalist scholars in Yemen
	? – Geologists in Yemen to study mineral resources	
1959	Feb – Gift of wheat	
Nov – Deputy foreign minister leads delegation to Yemen	Dec – Protocol on 1956 credit	
1960	Mar – Protocol on canal construction	
	June – Protocol on port construction	
1961	Feb – Aid to fire victims	
Apr – Government delegation in Yemen for opening of port at Hodeida		
Dec – Yemen breaks relations with UAR		
1962		
Sept – Imam Ahmad dies; son overthrown by coup led by Col. Sallal with Cairo support; republic proclaimed; recognized by USSR and CPR		
Nov – Government delegation in USSR		
1963	Mar – Trade delegation in Yemen: agreement	
Note: Civil war between royalists and republicans grows during year		June – Cultural agreement
	Sept – San'a airport completed	

YEMEN

	Political	Economic	Cultural
1964			
			Jan – TU delegation in Yemen
		Feb – Gift of vehicles	
	Mar – PRESIDENT SALLAL IN USSR for 15-day visit; 1955 friendship treaty signed	Mar – CREDIT AGREEMENT for agricultural development, cement works, fishing industry (reported $72m); (20) gift of hospitals, schools	Mar – Cultural protocol for 1964
	June – Sallal stops in USSR en route to Peking	June – CPR credit (reported $28m) (21)	
		Aug – Protocol on road construction	
	Nov – Tentative agreement on cease-fire, but fighting resumes		
1965			
		Feb – Aid promised for stadium, urban construction	
	June – Supreme Soviet official in Yemen	June – Protocol on fisheries	
		July – Experts in Yemen to work on land reclamation	
	Aug – Saudi Arabia, Egypt agree on terms of Yemeni cease-fire		
		Sept – Hospital, school completed	
1966			
		Feb – Protocol on highway	
			Mar – Cultural protocol
		June – Protocol on 1964 credit	
		Sept – More schools completed	
1967			
		Jan – Gift of medicine	
	Feb – Military delegation in USSR – Government delegation under Mukhitdinov in Yemen		
			Mar – Cultural delegation in Yemen
		Apr – Air service agreement	
	Aug – Military delegation in Yemen for arms talks following Egyptian withdrawal	Aug – Contract for cement factory	
		Sept – Clinic completed	
	Nov – Sallal overthrown in military coup; USSR recognizes new regime – Foreign minister in USSR – Soviet MIGs delivered to Yemen with technicians		
	Dec – New republic of South Yemen (formerly Aden) associates with Yemen		
1968			
		Jan – Gift of additional medicines	

Political	Economic	Cultural
1968 (cont.)		
	Spring – Reconstruction bank chairman in CPR	
		June – Cultural protocol for 1968-69
Aug – Arms agreement		
Oct – PREMIER AL-AMRI IN USSR for 5-day visit		
	Dec – Deputy economic minister in Yemen for aid talks	
1969		
Jan – Naval squadron calls at Hodeida	Jan – Trade delegation in Yemen	
? – Another arms agreement reported (22)		
May – Tadzhik municipal delegation in San'a		
		June – Agreement on scholarships
	July – Agreement with CPR on technical school	
Sept – Deputy foreign minister Vinogradov in Yemen for opening of Hodeida-Ta'izz highway	Sept – Gift of wheat	
Oct – Deputy premier in USSR		
1970		
Jan – Destroyer calls at Hodeida		
	Mar – Chinese-built textile mill completed	
June – Youth leader in Moscow for Komsomol congress		
	July – Gift of wheat in drought	
		Aug – Muslim delegation in USSR
	Sept – Chinese-built technical school completed	
		Oct – Yemeni TUs join WFTU
Nov – San'a municipal delegation in Dushanbe		
Dec – CPR government delegation in Yemen for anniversary		

References

(1)   Sovremennyy Vostok, No. 6 (June), 1958 (reviewed in Mizan, October 1959, pp. 2-3).

(2)   U.S. Department of State, IR No. 8426, 21 March, 1961, p. 14.

(3)   See Mizan, October 1959, pp. 4-5.

(4)   E.g. Izvestiya, 26 October, 1962 and Pravda 6 and 10 November, 1962; other early commentaries on the new regime are reviewed in Mizan, November 1962, pp. 15-16 and December 1962, pp. 17-18.

(5)   Pravda, 13 December, 1962.

(6)   Y. Bochkaryov, New Times, No. 8 (24 February), 1965, p. 29.

(7)   E.g. Izvestiya, 26 September, 1965.

(8)   The "shortcomings" occasionally complained of in Soviet commentaries included, for instance, government officials being "more interested in building villas, night clubs and swimming pools than schools and hospitals" and excessive adventurism on the part of young San'a radicals; e.g. Pravda, 2 February, 1966 and 19 January 1967 (cited in Laqueur, The Struggle for the Middle East, pp. 106-7).

(9)   See The Middle East and North Africa, 1969-70, p. 845.

(10) See, for instance, K. Vishnevetskiy in Pravda, 14 November, 1967 and a Radio Moscow broadcast on 10 November, 1967.

(11) Two Soviet sources show $78 million to the end of 1964: USSR and Developing Countries, p. 70 and USSR - Friend of the Arab Peoples, p. 48.

(12) See Goldman, Soviet Foreign Aid, pp. 152-53.

(13) Joshua and Gibert, Arms for the Third World, p. 23.

(14) Ibid., p. 12; Goldman (op.cit., p. 152) reports that aircraft delivered in 1959 soon became unserviceable and were melted into scrap for licence plates.

(15) E.g. New York Times, 13 December, 1967, reporting a claim that a Russian pilot was found in a MIG fighter brought down by Royalist gunfire.   The report, which the Russians promptly denied, must be considered suspect but is credited by some Western students of Soviet military aid policies; see Joshua and Gibert, op.cit., p. 27.

(16) Two shiploads of Soviet arms were reportedly delivered in April 1968 and tanks were flown to San'a in November; Herald-Tribune (International edition), 24 April, 1968 and The Daily Telegraph (London), 8 November, 1968.

(17) U.S. Department of State, RSE-25, 7 May, 1969, p. 78.

(18) Compare figures in U.S. Department of State, RSB-10, 25 January, 1967; RSB-40, 12 May, 1967; and RSB-65, 31 May, 1968.

(19) U.S. Department of State, RSB-145, 18 September, 1962, p. 30.

(20) Goldman, op.cit., p. 152.

(21) China Quarterly, October 1964, p. 182.

(22) The Military Balance, 1969-1970, p. 60.

TABLES

A. Soviet political relations with Middle East states*

COUNTRY	(a) POPULATION	(b) INDEPENDENCE	(c) Diplomatic Relations USSR	(c) Diplomatic Relations CPR	55	56	57	58	59	60	61	62	63	64	65	66	67	68	69	70	(e) STATE	(e) OTHER
Algeria (S)	12.8	7/62	3/62(a)	9/58										1/	1/		2/				4/	
Algeria (O)											1/	/1	3/5	4/4	6/4	7/8	9/10	2/8	9/11	2/4		44/55
Cyprus (O)	.6	8/60	8/60							1/						1/1	/1	/1	1/	1/1		8/8
Egypt (S)	30.0	1922	3/54(b) 4/56					2/					1/	1/	1/		1/	1/		1/	7/4	
Egypt (O)					2/1	1/2	3/3	8/2	4/2	4/2	1/3		5/8	4/6	4/5	8/9	8/13	6/5	18/14	15/16		93/94
Iran (S)	28.0	—	1921										1/			1/	1/	1/	1/		5/4	
Iran (O)						3/	/1	2/	/1			1/1	1/2	3/		6/2	6/2	9/4	6/2	7/6		45/21
Iraq (S)	8.5	1932	7/58(c) 7/58													1/	1/				2/2	
Iraq (O)								2/		5/3 6/	2/1		1/2		2/	2/5	4/5	5/2	9/5	15/6		54/27
Jordan (S)	2.0	1946	8/63														1/				1/	
Jordan (O)													1/	1/			1/	2/1	7/3	2/3		13/10
Kuwait (O)	.5	6/61	3/63											1/1	1/	2/	1/3	1/	/1	1/		6/6
Lebanon (O)	2.4	1941	6/56(d)		/1	2/2	2/		1/	/1		/1			2/1	1/3	1/2	2/	1/1	2/1		14/13
Libya (O)	1.7	1951	9/55								1/1					/1		2/	/1	2/2		6/6
Morocco (S)	14.6	3/56	8/58	4/59							1/										1/3	
Morocco (O)								/1		2/	3/2	/1	/1	/1		2/3	3/2	1/4	/1	2/		14/15
Saudi Arabia	6.0	1926(e)																				
South Yemen (S)	1.5	11/67	11/67	12/67															1/		1/	
South Yemen (O)																	1/	3/4	1/1	6/3		11/8
Syria (S)	5.7	1946	?(f)	8/56												1/	2/1				5/1	
Syria (O)						1/3	5/1					3/	1/1	2/	2/1	2/5	3/6	6/7	10/6	5/10		39/40
Tunisia (O)	4.5	3/56	6/56	1/64(g)		1/		1/	1/		2/1	1/	2/4	2/1		3/1	/2	/6	/2	/		15/16
Turkey (S)	33.8	1920	1920							3/						1/		3/1			3/1	
Turkey (O)										3/			2/	2/4	2/4	3/2	4/3	2/5	5/2	4/4		30/21
Yemen (S)	5.0	1918	10/55	9/56				1/						1/							4/	
Yemen (O)					/1	1/ /1		/1	1/ /1	/1		/1	1/1	3/1		2/3		/1	1/3	2/		7/13
Total: STATE						3/		3/							4/	3/2	8/3	3/1	4/1	1/3	33/15	
OTHER					2/2	7/8	10/5	13/4	12/7	16/3	11/10	11/7	16/25	23/14	21/19	37/40	43/53	41/48	70/52	66/56		399/353

(d) EXCHANGES

118

Footnotes to Table A

*The columns include the following information:

    Column (a) – Estimated population in 1969 (in millions); this is to facilitate comparison of activity in nations of different size – in this and following tables.

    Column (b) – Date of independence or statehood (month/year).

    Columns (c) – Date of diplomatic relations with the USSR and China (not necessarily the date of exchange of embassies).

    Columns (d) – The upper figures refer to heads of state exchanges by year – that is, Presidents, Premiers, Kings etc.; Mikoyan's visits are also counted here because of his unique position in the USSR (though he was Chief of State for only a portion of the 16 years covered).   Unofficial visits by heads of state – for instance, in transit – are not counted unless they have particular political significance.   The lower figures refer to other major exchanges, including important parliamentary, ministerial, governmental and military missions, as well as major economic and cultural delegations and delegations of ruling parties; each delegation is counted as one, even though it may include representatives of several of these categories.   Exchanges of lesser missions, such as trade union delegations and minor economic and cultural dele- gations (including many listed in the chronologies) are not counted. [Note: Figures to the left of the stroke represent visits to the USSR; figures to the right of the stroke represent Soviet visits to the given Middle East country: to USSR/ to Middle East country.]

    Columns (e) – Total important exchanges with the USSR – that is, the sum of heads of state and other major exchanges shown in columns (d).

The data in Table A are drawn from the chronologies above; for an estimate of the reliability of these data, see Preface.

a De jure recognition; de facto recognition was extended to the Algerian provisional government in September 1960.

b Embassies were exchanged with Cairo in March 1954, but diplomatic ties had existed with Egypt for some years before this date.

c Diplomatic relations with Iraq were broken off after the signing of the Baghdad Pact in January 1955; they were resumed following the coup by Colonel Qasim in August 1958.

d Exchange of embassies; legations were exchanged after Soviet recognition of Lebanon in 1944.

e Russia recognized Ibn Sa'ud's assumption of rule over the Hijaz in 1926 and a Soviet legation existed in Riyadh until the eve of the Second World War; diplomatic ties were not resumed after the war.

f Diplomatic ties were established with Syria before 1955 but the exact date is uncertain; from January 1958 to September 1961 while Syria was in the UAR, relations with Damascus were channelled through Cairo.

g Tunisia suspended relations with China in September 1967.

B. Soviet economic aid to Middle East states*

	'55	'56	'57	'58	'59	'60	'61	'62	'63	'64	'65	'66	'67	'68	'69	'70	Total: USSR	Total: CPR
Algeria									100	127							227	50
Egypt			175 100		225				44	277	21						842	106
Iran									39		290			178		54	561	
Iraq				138	45										121	22	326	
Morocco												44					44	88
South Yemen															13		13	55
Syria		98										133					231	16
Tunisia						29				5							34	
Turkey		17									200				166		383[a]	
Yemen	25									72							97	44
TOTAL	25	115	275	138	270	29			183	481	511	177		178	300	120	2820	271

* The sums shown are in U.S. dollars and rounded to the nearest million. They represent the author's best estimate of Soviet credits extended to Middle East nations to the end of 1970, based on both Russian and Western sources; credits to separate countries are discussed above, normally towards the end of the section dealing with the country concerned.

a This total does not include credits to Turkey in the 1970s.

C. Soviet trade with Middle East states*

Country	First Trade Agr.	1955 Im	1955 Ex	1960 Im	1960 Ex	1965 Im	1965 Ex	1966 Im	1966 Ex	1967 Im	1967 Ex	1968 Im	1968 Ex	1969 Im	1969 Ex
Algeria	11/63		.8	0	2.3	3.7	15.3	5.8	18.6	16.1	31.2	27.4	31.6	61.6	57.7
Cyprus	12/61			.5	.5	3.4	3.4	4.3	3.3	4.4	2.9	4.3	3.4	5.8	5.1
Egypt	3/54	15.1	10.8	120.1	68.9	161.8	206.4	148.5	196.7	143.7	278.5	169.0	196.0	228.1	238.2
Iran	6/53	18.9	22.2	18.8	17.8	17.9	15.1	19.3	30.7	30.3	62.4	39.7	87.2	56.4	161.6
Iraq	10/58	.3	0	3.4	20.0	3.6	29.2	3.2	35.5	5.1	36.3	4.1	50.3	4.7	67.7
Jordan	1/69					0	2.8		3.6		3.1		3.4		4.3
Kuwait	8/66			0	.8	0	6.6		7.7		10.7		14.9		15.3
Lebanon	4/54	4.0	5.6	3.9	4.3	2.4	5.4	3.7	5.6	3.9	8.9	3.4	13.4	3.0	11.6
Libya	5/63			.4	1.0	5.0	5.4	.2	3.9	0	3.1	0	6.1	0	10.8
Morocco	4/58	2.3	1.4	3.9	5.7	10.9	8.4	9.4	10.7	20.1	19.8	18.2	19.0	17.9	37.1
Saudi Arabia				0	.4	0	3.5				1.8		3.9	.2	4.6
South Yemen	1/69												1.4	1.0	6.9
Syria	11/55		.3	7.7	10.8	18.4	12.5	20.1	22.4	18.0	33.9	20.7	41.7	37.3	47.8
Tunisia	1/60			1.5	3.2	3.5	6.3	3.7	8.6	4.3	6.1	5.4	3.3	3.4	4.2
Turkey	12/53	5.0	7.3	5.2	8.1	18.7	16.5	18.6	27.2	27.6	27.8	29.7	30.5	29.9	57.9
Yemen	3/56			1.3	3.5	1.0	7.9	1.5	11.7	.7	10.0	1.5	6.4	1.4	9.7
TOTAL		45.6	48.4	166.7	147.3	250.3	344.7	238.3	386.2	274.2	536.5	323.4	511.1	450.7	770.5

* All sums, expressed in millions of U.S. dollars, are taken from official Soviet trade statistics. The Soviet totals do not always correspond exactly to sums shown in official summaries prepared by Russia's trading partners in the Middle East but they are never far from them. The intent of Table C is to indicate the general volume and direction of trade with Middle East nations over the years reviewed, especially from 1965 to 1969 (final figures for 1970 were not available at the time of publishing); students of Soviet trade requiring more detailed figures should consult the annual Soviet

compilations and breakdowns in Vneshnyaya torgovlya SSSR za - god, articles in the Soviet journal Vneshnyaya torgovlya which discuss Soviet-Third World trade, and the official trade statistics of the Middle East nations concerned.

Where no figure is shown, there was no trade reported in Soviet compilations. Zero (0) indicates trade totalling less than $50,000. Imports (Im) are to the USSR; Exports (Ex) are from the USSR.

D. Soviet military relations with Middle East states*

	(a) First Agreement	(b) Total Value	(c) Types	(d) Military Exchanges			(e) Naval Visits
				'55-'59	'60-'64	'65-'70	
Algeria	10/63	400	Bombers and fighter aircraft including advanced models (MIG-21s); tanks; missiles; patrol craft; artillery; small arms		1/2	3/10	5
Cyprus	9/64	30	Anti-aircraft guns				
Egypt	9/55	4500	Bombers and fighter aircraft, chiefly advanced models (SU-7s, MIG-21s, and MIG-21J); helicopters; tanks; missiles (both SAM-2s and SAM-3s); submarines, destroyers and other naval craft; artillery and rockets; various small arms and other equipment	2/	2/3	8/7	3[(a)]
Iran	1/67	110	Anti-aircraft guns; trucks; armoured vehicles			1/2	1
Iraq	11/58	800	Bombers and fighter aircraft, including advanced models (SU-7s, MIG-21s); tanks; missiles; artillery; small arms		4/	7/3	2
Jordan						1/	
Libya							1
Morocco	11/60	20	Fighter aircraft (not in use in 1970)		3/2	2/1	2
South Yemen	1/69	5	Fighter aircraft; tanks; artillery			3/2	3
Syria	2/56	900	Bombers and fighter planes, including advanced models (SU-7s, MIG-21s); helicopters; tanks; missiles; patrol craft; artillery; small arms	1/	4/	4/2	2
Yemen	?/56	100	Bombers; fighter aircraft (including MIG-19s); tanks; artillery				1
TOTAL		6865		3/	14/7	29/27	20

* Data on Soviet military relations with Middle East nations are meagre and often unauthenticated; they must therefore be treated with care. However, it is useful to summarize what is known of Soviet activity in this area, bearing in mind the gaps in our knowledge. The data available are organized as follows:

Column (a) - Date of initial arms agreement or, if no agreement is reported, the date of earliest known arms deliveries.

Column (b) - The estimated value of Soviet military credits or sales in millions of U.S. dollars, to the end of 1970. [Note: It is not usually clear whether reported sums of Soviet military aid represent cash transactions or credits extending over several years; the figure shown, then, is the estimated total commitment, whether actual or projected. The estimates are mine, drawn from a variety of sources. Among them are the following (see Bibliography for full listings): Joshua and Gibert, Arms for the Third World (covering Soviet military aid to 1967 and bringing up to date an earlier study by Stephen Gibert published in Orbis, Autumn 1966, pp. 839-58); Uri Ra'anan The USSR Arms the Third World (especially for early shipments to Egypt); the annual Military Balance published by the Institute of Strategic Studies in London; the same Institute's periodic Adelphi Papers (especially Nos. 26, 28, 52 and 59); also periodic summaries by military correspondents, e.g. New York Times, 5 September, 1967; Washington Star, 14 September, 1969; The Christian Science Monitor, 3 April, 1970; and New Middle East, No. 20 (May 1970), pp. 11-14 and No. 33 (June 1971), p. 25.]

Column (c) - The major types of arms transferred. [Note: These data came principally from the annual publication of the Institute of Strategic Studies, The Military Balance (see Bibliography); the quantity of different Soviet arms reported on hand in 1970 is indicated in the country studies.]

Column (d) - Exchanges of major military delegations not including Soviet military missions assigned to a given Middle East nation for a period of time or groups of Middle East military personnel going to the USSR for specialized training. [Note: Figures to the left of the stroke represent Middle East delegations visiting the USSR; figures to the right of the stroke are Soviet delegations visiting the country concerned. These exchanges are included in Table A under the category of "other major exchanges".]

Column (e) – Reported courtesy visits to Middle East nations by Soviet naval units. [Note: Nearly all these visits took place after 1965.]

a Although only three official naval visits to the UAR were reported, units of the Mediterranean fleet were often stationed in Port Said and Alexandria for prolonged periods.

E.   Soviet cultural relations with Middle East states*

Country	(a) First Cultural Agreement	(b) Volume	(c) Cultural Centre	(d) News Agency	(e) Friendship Society	(f) Student Exchange '65–'66	(f) Student Exchange '69–'70
Algeria	2/61	ext	x	x	x	230	260
Cyprus		occ	x		x	130	330
Egypt	11/59	ext	x	x	x	210	450
Iran	8/66	mod			x		
Iraq	5/59	mod	x	x	x(a)	900	50
Jordan	10/67	occ	x(b)	x		50	120
Kuwait	3/67	occ					10
Lebanon	10/67	mod	x	x		270	230
Libya		occ		x			
Morocco	10/66	mod	x	x		60	100
South Yemen	1/69	occ					240
Syria	8/56	ext		x		300	600
Tunisia	12/63	mod		x	x	50	160
Turkey	10/64(c)	occ				30	
Yemen	6/63	occ				420	300
TOTAL	13		7	9	6	2650	3300

* The following data are included in this table:
    Column (a) – Date of initial cultural agreement (month/year).
    Column (b) – Volume of cultural activity in the latter half of the 1960s, measured by exchanges of various types: extensive (ext), moderate (mod), or occasional (occ); if activity is negligible, no entry is made.
    Column (c) – Existence of a Soviet cultural or information centre. [Note: In several countries more than one Soviet cultural centre operated during the years under review.]
    Column (d) – Existence of a TASS news agency, including one attached to a Soviet embassy.
    Column (e) – Existence of a Friendship Society to promote cultural relations with the USSR. [Note: The absence of a Friendship Society may mean of course that cultural relations are satisfactorily promoted by other agencies – for instance, a local unit of the Afro-Asian People's Solidarity Organization (AAPSO) or the Soviet Information Centre.]
    Column (f) – Estimated number of students enrolled in courses in the USSR during the school years 1965–66 and 1969–70, rounded to the nearest 10. [Note: Where no figure is available for the USSR, 75 per cent of the total reported in the East European bloc is used to approximate the number in Russia; estimates of the number of students in the bloc appear in the summary of cultural relations between Communist and non-Communist countries prepared annually by the U.S. Department of State (see Bibliography).]

a The Iraqi-Soviet Friendship Society was ruled illegal by Iraqi courts in 1966 but was re-established in December 1968.

b Agreement was reached in July 1969 on the establishment of a Soviet cultural centre in Jordan.

c Not ratified by Turkey.

BIBLIOGRAPHY

Note: This Bibliography lists selected monographs, journal articles, yearbooks and other material relevant to a study of Soviet policies in the Middle East, plus a few studies that relate to Moscow's Third World policies more generally. Russian sources listed in the Bibliography are restricted to those which shed direct light on Soviet relations with Middle Eastern states; a wider listing of Soviet commentary on these nations during the years under review would quickly run to many hundreds – even thousands – of items. Unless otherwise indicated, all Russian volumes listed were published in Moscow.

Adelphi Papers. See Institute of Strategic Studies, below.

Armstrong, John A. "Soviet Policy in the Middle East", chapter in Kurt London, ed. The Soviet Union: A Half Century of Communism, Johns Hopkins, 1968, pp. 423-54.

Becker, Abraham S. and A.L. Horelick. Soviet Policy in the Middle East, Rand, 1970.

Bolton, A. Soviet Middle East Studies (annotated bibliography published irregularly by the Central Asian Research Centre, London).

Chertkov, D.G., R.N. Andreasyan, I.I. Mozhayev. SSSR i razvivayushchiyesya strany (sotrudnichestvo v razvitii ekonomiki i kul'tury), 1966, 106 pp.

Duncan, W. Raymond, ed. Soviet Policies in Developing Countries, Ginn-Blaisdell, 1970 (views of Soviet policies by 13 Western scholars).

Ekonomicheskoye sotrudnichestvo Sovetskogo Soyuza s ekonomicheski slaborazvitymi stranami, 1962.

Fouad, Mahmoud Hassan. "The Economics of Foreign Aid: the UAR Experience with the US and USSR Programs, 1952-1965", University of Southern California doctoral thesis, 1968.

Fredericks, Edgar Jesse. "Soviet-Egyptian Relations, 1955-1965, and their Effect on Communism in the Middle East and the International Position of the Soviet Union", American University doctoral thesis, 1968.

Gibert, Stephen P. "Wars of Liberation and Soviet Military Aid Policy", Orbis, Fall 1966, pp. 839-58 (estimates of Soviet aid are based on the findings of a research project conducted at Georgetown University, entitled "Soviet Military Programs as a Reflection of Soviet Objectives", June 1965).

Goldman, Marshall I. Soviet Foreign Aid, New York: Praeger, 1967.

Grigor'yev, A. Sovetskiy soyuz – drug arabskikh narodov, 1967 (a brief but detailed summary of Soviet aid projects; the English edition is entitled Soviet Union – Friend of the Arab Peoples).

Guseynov, K.A. Internatsional'nyye svyazi profsoyuzov SSSR c profsoyuzami stran Azii i Afriki, 1965, 180 pp. (also in English, entitled Trade Union Association: USSR, Asia and Africa, 1967).

Halpern, Manfred. "The Middle East and North Africa", chapter in Cyril E. Black and Thomas Perry Thornton, Communism and Revolution, Princeton, 1964.

Holbik, Karel. The United States, the Soviet Union and the Third World, Hamburg, 1968.

Hurewitz, J.C., ed. Soviet-American Rivalry in the Middle East. Proceedings of the Academy of Political Science, Columbia University, Vol. XXIX, No. 3, 1969 (papers prepared for a conference on Middle Eastern affairs, December 1968).

Institute of Strategic Studies (London).
    Adelphi Papers (published irregularly). The following were of use in the present volume:
        No. 26 (March 1966). "Source of Conflict in the Middle East".
        No. 28 (October 1966). John L. Sutton and Geoffrey Kemp, "Arms to Developing Countries, 1945-1965".
        No. 41 (September 1967). Michael Howard and Robert E. Hunter, "Israel and the Arab World: The Crisis of 1967".
        No. 52 (October 1968). Geoffrey Kemp, "Arms and Security: the Egypt-Israeli Case".
        Nos. 59-60 (September, October 1969). Robert E. Hunter, "The Soviet Dilemma in the Middle East. Part I: Problems of Commitment. Part II: Oil and the Persian Gulf".

Joshua, Wynfred and Stephen P. Gibert. Arms for the Third World: Soviet Military Aid Diplomacy, Johns Hopkins, 1969 (this updates Mr. Gibert's earlier estimate of Soviet military aid; see above).

Klieman, Aaron S.   Soviet Russia and the Middle East, Johns Hopkins, 1970.

Knigi glavnoy redaktsii vostochnoy literatury izdatel'stva "Nauka", 1957-1966: annotirovannyy katalog, 1968, 304 pp. (lists about 1,400 major Orientalist works, with brief notes on contents).

Korneyev, S.G.   Nauchnyye svyazi Akademii nauk SSSR so stranami Azii i Afriki, 1969, 315 pp. (detailed summary of cultural ties between Russian and Afro-Asian scholars).

Kovner, Milton.   The Challenge of Coexistence; A Study of Soviet Economic Diplomacy, Public Affairs Press, 1961.

Laqueur, Walter Z.   Communism and Nationalism in the Middle East, London: Routledge and Kegan Paul, 1956.
————.   The Soviet Union and the Middle East, Praeger, 1959.
————.   The Road to War, 1967, London: Weidenfeld and Nicolson, 1968.
————.   The Struggle for the Middle East: the Soviet Union and the Middle East, 1958-68, London: Routledge and Kegan Paul, 1969.

Lavrichenko, M.V.   Ekonomicheskoye sotrudnichestvo SSSR so stranami Azii, Afriki i Latinskoy Ameriki, 1961, 144 pp.

Literatura o stranakh Azii i Afriki; yezhegodnik 1963, 1967 (although intended as an annual, published irregularly; this volume - listed as the third - was the only one consulted).

London, Kurt, ed.   Unity and Contradiction: Major Aspects of Sino-Soviet Relations, Praeger, 1962.
————. ed.   New Nations in a Divided World, Praeger, 1963 (the above two volumes include papers read at international conferences, respectively, at Lake Kawaguchi, Japan, in 1960 and in Athens in 1962; a number of the papers deal with Sino-Soviet strategies in Asia and Africa).

The Middle East and North Africa, 1969-70: A Survey and Directory, 16th ed. London: Europa Publications, 1970 (includes data on aid and trade from official local sources).

The Military Balance.   See Institute of Strategic Studies, above.

Na novom puti, 1968, 491 pp. (3rd and last volume of a series entitled Natsional'no-osvoboditel'noye dvizheniye v Azii i Afriki, prepared by the Institute of the Peoples of Asia under the general editorship of B.G. Gafurov; the "new course" is the path of non-capitalist development).

Nollau, Günther and Hans Jürgen Wieke.   Russia's South Flank: Soviet Operations in Iran, Turkey and Afghanistan, Praeger, 1963 (translated from German).

Noveyshaya istoriya stran Azii i Afriki, 1965, 593 pp (a reference work prepared by Moscow University; includes brief accounts of Soviet relations with Afro-Asian nations).

Page, Stephen.   The USSR and Arabia: the development of Soviet policies and attitudes towards the countries of the Arabian Peninsula.   London: Central Asian Research Centre (in association with Canadian Institute of International Affairs), 1971.

Pajak, Roger Frank.   "Soviet Military Aid: An Instrument of Soviet Foreign Policy toward the Developing Countries", American University doctoral thesis, 1966.

Prokhorov, G.M., ed.   Problemy sotrudnichestva sotsialisticheskikh i razvivayushchikhsya stran, 1966.

Ra'anan, Uri.   "Moscow and the 'Third World'", Problems of Communism, January-February 1965, pp. 22-31.
————.   "Tactics in the Third World: Contradictions and Dangers", Survey, No. 57 (October 1965), pp. 26-37.
————.   The USSR Arms the Third World: Case Studies in Soviet Foreign Policy, Massachusetts Institute of Technology, 1969 (early Soviet military policies in Egypt and Indonesia).

Rashidi, Ramezan Ali.   "Iran's Economic Relations with the Soviet Union, 1917-1968", University of Pennsylvania doctoral thesis, 1968.

SSSR i arabskiye strany, 1917-1960 gg; dokumenty i materialy, 1961, 855 pp. (prepared by the Ministry of Foreign Affairs; texts of all major agreements).

SSSR i strany vostoka; ekonomicheskoye i kul'turnoye sotrudnichestvo, 1961, 140 pp.

Samylovskiy, I.V.   Nauchnyye i kul'turnyye svyazi SSSR so stranami Azii i Afriki, 1963, 68 pp (a summary prepared by the Institute of the Peoples of Asia).

Sawyer, Carole A. Communist Trade with Developing Countries, 1955-65, New York: Praeger, 1966.

Shaffer, Harry G. and Jan S. Prybyla, eds. From Underdevelopment to Affluence: Western, Soviet and Chinese Views, New York: Appleton-Century-Crofts, 1968 (collection of articles on different Third World problems; mainly by Western scholars but including some Russians).

Shepilov, D.T. Suetskiy vopros. 1956, 159 pp (Soviet statements and other documentation on the Suez crisis, August-November 1956; prepared by the Russian Foreign Minister at that time).

Smolansky, Oles M. "The Soviet Union and the Arab East, 1947-1957: A study in diplomatic relations", Columbia University doctoral thesis, 1959.
————. "Moscow and the Persian Gulf: An Analysis of Soviet Ambition and Potential". Orbis, Spring 1970, pp. 92-108.

Soviet Union – Friend of the Arab Peoples, Moscow, 1968. See A. Grigor'yev, above.

Sultanov, A.F., ed. Sovetsko-arabskiye druzhestvennyye otnosheniya: sbornik statey, 1961, 144 pp. (reviews Soviet-Arab relations from the First World War to 1960).

Swanson, John Robert. "Soviet and Local Communist Perception of Syrian and Lebanese Politics, 1944-1964", University of Wisconsin doctoral thesis, 1969.

Tansky, Leo. U.S. and U.S.S.R. Aid to Developing Countries: A Comparative Study of India, Turkey and the UAR, Praeger, 1967.

Thornton, Thomas Perry, ed. The Third World in Soviet Perspective: Studies by Soviet Writers on the Developing Areas, Princeton, 1964 (an Introduction by Mr. Thornton reviews Soviet scholarship on the Third World to the end of 1962).

The USSR and Developing Countries (economic co-operation), Moscow, 1965, 88 pp. (though insignificant in appearance, this pamphlet gives considerable detail on Soviet economic activity in 25 Afro-Asian nations).

United States Department of State, Bureau of Intelligence and Research. Research Memorandum (called Research Study after 1969). The following in particular were relevant to the present study:
  "Soviet Diplomatic Relations and Representation".
        RSE-70, 9 September, 1969.
  "The Sino-Soviet Economic Offensive" (title varies: "Communist Governments and Developing Nations: Aid and Trade").
        No. 8426, 21 March, 1961.
        RSB-182, 12 December, 1962.
        RSB-43, 18 June, 1964.
        RSB-50, 17 June, 1966.
        RSB-80, 21 July, 1967.
        RSE-120, 14 August, 1968.
        RSE-65, 5 September, 1969.
        RECS-5, 9 July, 1970.
  "Educational and Cultural Exchanges between Communist and non-Communist Countries" (title varies slightly).
        RSB-46, 29 March, 1963.
        RSB-85, 4 November, 1964.
        RSB-49, 1 June, 1965.
        RSB-10, 25 January, 1967.
        RSB-40, 12 May, 1967.
        RSB-65, 31 May, 1968.
        RSE-25, 7 May, 1969.
        RSES-35, 12 August, 1970.

————. World Strength of the Communist Party Organizations, annual from 1948 (indicates activity as well as legal status and strength of all Communist parties).

Vneshnyaya torgovlya SSSR: statisticheskiy sbornik, 1918-66, 1967 (in addition to the periodic trade summaries such as this volume, the Ministry of Foreign Trade publishes an annual summary, Vneshnyaya torgovlya za - god, which includes a detailed breakdown of trade with some 60 Afro-Asian nations).

Walters, Robert S. American and Soviet Aid: A Comparative Analysis, University of Pittsburg, 1970.

Yearbook on International Communist Affairs, Stanford, 1966; 2nd edition, 1968 (includes extensive detail on the world Communist movement as well as on individual parties; prepared by the Hoover Institute on War, Revolution and Peace).

Zabih, Sepehr. The Communist Movement in Iran, Berkeley: University of California Press, 1966.

Periodicals

Aziya i Afrika segodnya (journal of the Institut Afriki and Institut narodov Azii, Akademiya nauk SSSR, March 1961 to present; monthly; for popular consumption).

BBC Summary of World Broadcasts (comprehensive world monitoring service; issued daily in several regional series).

Current Digest of the Soviet Press (published by the American Association for the Advancement of Slavic Studies, 1949 to present; weekly, indexed quarterly; translations cover all major statements on Soviet foreign policy, but coverage of Afro-Asian affairs is irregular).

Foreign Broadcast Information Service (comprehensive world monitoring service of U.S. Government; issued daily in six regional volumes).

International Affairs (English edition of Mezhdunarodnaya zhizn'; principal Soviet journal on world affairs for foreign readers, 1955 to present; monthly).

Joint Publications Research Service (translations from world press prepared by U.S. Government; issued daily in several series; includes many items from Soviet publications).

Kommunist (organ of the Central Committee of the CPSU, 1924 to present; published 18 times a year).

Mirovaya ekonomika i mezhdunarodnyye otnosheniya (organ of Institut mirovoy ekonomiki i mezhdunarodnykh otnosheniy, Akademiya nauk SSSR, 1955 to present; monthly; next to Narody Azii i Afriki, provides most significant scholarly coverage of Afro-Asian affairs).

Mizan (Central Asian Research Centre, London, 1959-1971; articles on Soviet relations with (from 1969) Middle East, (from 1960) Africa, (from 1966) South-East Asia; Mizan Supplement A (1966-1970) Soviet and Chinese reports on Middle East and Africa; Supplement B, ditto on South and South-East Asia. USSR and Third World (from January 1971) surveys reports and comment from all sources on this subject.)

Moscow News (1956 to present; weekly; useful for information on cultural exchange with Afro-Asian nations, especially to mid-1960s).

Narody Azii i Afriki (principal journal of Institut Afriki and Institut narodov Azii, Akademiya nauk SSSR, 1961 to present; bi-monthly; replaced Problemy Vostokovedeniya).

New Middle East (an independent journal published in London from October 1968; monthly; includes many articles on Soviet activity in the Middle East).

New Times (English edition of Novoye vremya, 1945 to present; weekly; popular journal on international affairs, mainly for foreign readers).

Novaya sovetskaya inostrannaya literatura po stranam Azii i Afriki (an important bibliographic source, mid-1960s to present; monthly).

Problemy Vostokovedeniya (journal of Institut Vostokovedeniya, Akademiya nauk SSSR, 1956-61; bi-monthly; replaced by Narody Azii i Afriki).

Sovremennyy Vostok (journal of Institut Vostokovedeniya and later Institut Afriki, Akademiya nauk SSSR, July 1957-February 1961; monthly; replaced by Aziya i Afrika segodnya).

USSR and the Third World (see Mizan).

Vneshnyaya torgovlya (official organ of the Soviet Ministry of Foreign Trade; monthly).

World Marxist Review (English edition of Problemy mira i sotsialisma, unofficial organ of the international Communist movement; published in Prague, September 1958 to present; monthly; includes both Russian and divergent views on world Communist developments).